COMPARE PMP'S THEORIES
WITH REAL-LIFE PROJECT MANAGEMENT

IHAB ANTABLI

Ihab Antabli, MEng.

ISBNs

EBOOK: 978-1-7778051-2-8

HARDCOVER: 978-1-7778051-1-1

PAPERBACK: 978-1-7778051-0-4

Published in Canada

"To the love of my family who always supports me."

-IA

ABOUT THE AUTHOR

IHAB ANTABLI, MEng., is a Professional Engineer, Project Management Professional (PMP) Certified, Freelance Small Building Designer for the Ministry of Municipal Affairs and Housing, and Leed Green Associate. He received his B.S. (1993) in Civil Engineering from the Beirut Arab University and a Masters in Engineering from Concordia University in Montreal (2008). He has worked as a project manager and engineer in Canada as well as internationally.

DISCLAIMER

The explanations, comments, details, and opinions of the author expressed in this guide constitute his personal opinions and should not be taken as representing those mentioned in the reference section. For example, although many quotes and definitions have been taken from the PMBOK or CCDC, the explanations or examples express how the author matches the selections with experience.

Table of Contents

LIST OF SAMPLES

LIST OF FIGURES

LIST OF TABLES

Preface

In this book, I would like to take you on a journey of exploration of project management. Some theoretical definitions will be provided to make technical terms easier to understand. Still, more effort will be devoted to portraying the real-life involvement with graphics and figures when necessary for further illustration.

The book Real-Life Project Management is a Canadian real-world experience from a project management perspective. The book is intended to serve as a comprehensive resource for students and managers on basic and advanced topics that a project manager will face daily in any construction company, especially in the North American region.

The book focuses on the description of situations following the PMBOK structure. Compare theories to reality. Even though there is a section dedicated to case studies, the whole book implements case study methods to explain the ten knowledge areas of project management.

An owner can use the book as a manual to help build a business system according to commonly used Canadian standards and methodologies. If the methods presented are close to how a manager would like to implement, a manager could make some adjustments. The project manager would inspire how to achieve a complete and efficient system.

The ultimate benefit of this book is when researching medium to large-sized businesses. Private and public procedures are explained from the point of view of the client or the contractor.

A new graduate project manager can gain a significant amount of knowledge and experience on reading this book. A good understanding of the knowledge explained, will help the non-Canadian and non-American project managers to gain full confidence in the systems used inside North American companies. Once an interview is conducted, he or she can easily prove to have the necessary knowledge and tools to start the job with minimal training for the company's specific system.

This book is beneficial for the owner, builder, managers working in construction, civil engineering, home builder companies, and managers working for design-build companies and consultants.

SECTION 1
PROJECT & CONSTRUCTION MANAGEMENT REAL WORLD COMPARED TO THEORIES

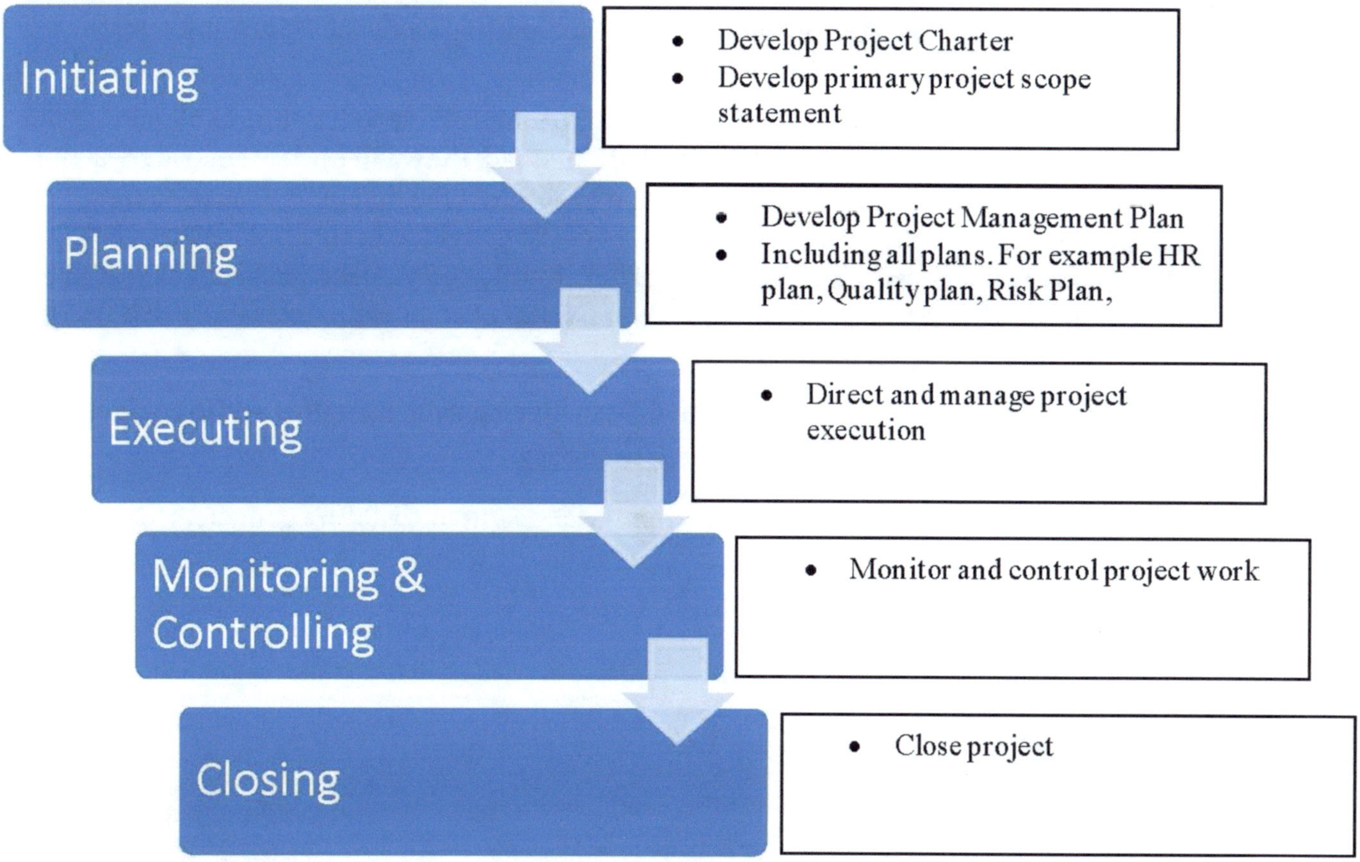

CHAPTER 1 - INTRODUCTION

Aim of This Book

In the Project Management Body of Knowledge book (PMBOK Guide) issued by PMI, the 10 project management knowledge areas are:

1 - Project Integration Management
2 - Project Scope Management
3 - Project Time Management
4 - Project Cost Management
5 - Project Quality Management
6 - Project Human Resources Management
7 - Project Communications Management
8 - Project Risk Management
9 - Project Procurement Management
10 - Project Stakeholder Management

This book or manual aims to compare project management practices in the real world rather than theory. This manual will focus on concrete examples of project management tools and techniques. A newly graduated project manager and an experienced dinosaur project manager can benefit from this manual.

The 10 project management knowledge areas mentioned above will not be explained in the same way and the same detail as in the PMBOK. Instead, they will be demonstrated as the most used tools in medium and large-size businesses. Instead of going through theory, graphics, documentation, and staff experience will be provided in this book. Start with the most critical area of knowledge. A project manager will need to start a new role. Please bear in mind that the 10 knowledge areas must be mastered at an appropriate level related to the position; power and responsibilities.

These 10 knowledge areas will be explained through concrete examples and introduce theory when necessary to match real-life with theory.

This book will start with Project Procurement Management to define contracts and purchasing methods.

5 Steps Project Management

In project management and during the application of the 10 knowledge areas, keep in mind the 5 steps you will need.

1 - Define
2 - Plan
3 - Organize
4 - Control
5 - Close

Short explanations for each as per below:

Define: State the problem; Identify Project Goals; List the Objectives; Determine Preliminary Resources and Identify Assumptions and Risks.

Plan: Identify Project activities; Estimate time and cost; Sequence Project Activities; Identify Critical Activities and Write Project Proposal.

Organize: Determine Personnel Needs; Recruit Project Manager; Recruit Project Team; Organize Project Team and Assign Work Packages.

Control: Establish Control Tools; Prepare Status Reports; Review Project Schedule; Issue Change Orders.

Close: Obtain Client Acceptance; Install Deliverables; Document the Project; Issue Final Reports; Conduct Post- Implementation Audit.

The 5 PMBOK®Guide Process Groups – 6th Edition

Every project needs the 5 Process Groups. These are the second large piece of the backbone of the PMBOK® Guide. The Process Groups are:

Initiating

These processes help you define a new piece of work – either a completely new project or the phase you are about to begin. They ensure that you have the authority to proceed.

Planning

These processes help you define objectives and scope out the work to be done. They also encompass all the workaround planning and scheduling tasks. Again, they can cover a complete project or just the phase you are working on right now. Or you might be closing one phase and planning the next in parallel.

Executing

You do these processes as you carry out your project tasks. This is the 'delivery' part of project management, where the main activity happens, and you create the products.

Monitoring and Controlling

These processes let you track the work that is being done, review, and report on it. They also cover what happens when you find out that the project isn't following the agreed plan, so change management falls into this Process Group. You'll run these processes alongside those in the Executing Group (mainly, but alongside the other Groups too), so you monitor as you go.

Closing

Finally, these processes let you finalize all the other groups' tasks when you get to the point to close the project or phase.

It would be nice if your project walked through each of these Groups in neat, linear order. That doesn't happen in real life. As you can see above, you'll spend time in each Process Group and then maybe go around again during the next phase. Monitoring and Controlling happens from Day 1 – it ramps while the project is in the delivery phases, but it goes on throughout. You can close a particular activity at any point, not just at the end of the project.

The Process Groups are not the same thing as a project life cycle. A life cycle shows how the project moves from start to finish in different phases. You might go through all the Process Groups or just some of them within one phrase, so don't confuse the two.

SECTION 2
PROJECT PROCUREMENT MANAGEMENT

Procurement is the act of obtaining goods, supplies, and/or services. Therefore, project procurement is acquiring all of the materials and services required for the project. Project procurement management encompasses the processes used for making sure project procurement is successful.

It is also important to determine how the project manager will handle changes once the contract is awarded during the planning phase. What happens when a supplier tells you they can no longer deliver on time? This book will provide more samples related to procurement in the Cost Management Section and explain cost management-related items during the procurement management process. Readers should simultaneously view the project's cost and procurement management.

Unless you're working in a small organization, you likely have a procurement team within your company. Therefore, it's natural to ask about their typical role with project procurement management and the project manager's responsibility. The details will depend on your organization. Some companies have procurement managers who work alongside the project manager and take care of most of these processes. In other cases, the procurement team may only be responsible for the transactional tasks.

CHAPTER 2 - TENDERING PHASE

Tender documents include Instruction to Bidders, Form of Tender, Articles of Agreement, General Conditions of Contract, Terms of Payment, Supplementary Conditions, Specifications, Working Drawings and Schedules, Construction Schedule Requirements, Addenda, and Definitions.

This book can be used as a manual to demonstrate the tendering process in two main parts. Consultant tender documents and contractor tender documents. It also illustrates with actual examples, the tender documents mainly used for private and public projects for the tender of the Consultant and the Contractor.

Bidding documents include the Request for Proposal (RFP) or Request for Quotation (RFQ).

RFI, RFP, RFQ, Contract- What is the Difference?

RFI

An RFI (Request For Information) collects all necessary information regarding specifications, plans, contracts, or other documents in the construction industry. It is an official document that can have a considerable impact on the planning and budget of your project if not appropriately handled. RFIs can be used for many reasons; mainly for additional information or when clarification is needed before a task can be undertaken. It can be produced at all stages of a construction project (from design to completion).

Purpose: When you are looking for information or are unsure of the solution to your problem.

Ask: General questions designed to educate and inform. The project is not clearly defined.

Style: Casual, asking for help.

Advantage: They're fast and help in giving information on the following steps to meet business needs.

Company Logo & Complete Address REQUEST FOR INFORMATION (RFI)			
RFI No.:		RFI Date:	
Project Address		Contract No.:	
Submitted By:		Submitted To:	
RFI Reference:	Drawing #, RFP#, etc...		
RFI DESCRIPTION			
Example RFI implementation phase. Based on on-site conflicts, we are unable to locate the CU platforms as per DWG M2.8. As such, we propose positioning the CU platforms as per the attached drawings. We also noted that the roofing is an inverted roof with a minimum of 6 inches of insulation. The location, as shown on drawings S2, is located directly above the residential corridor. Please advise how to proceed. Example RFI Tendering phase. Could you provide details about the bonding and insurance requirement for this RFP? ATTACHMENTS:			

Figure 1. RFI Sample

RFP

A Request for Proposal is a document used to obtain comprehensive proposals from capable and interested companies to demonstrate their skills, experience, and knowledge to take on the described project, including budget details, the timing of work, and a thorough description of the project scope. All project requirements will be addressed, showing the specific steps or solutions you will follow from day one to completion. An RFP is a formalized and structured way of getting detailed vendor information (including pricing). It allows you to detail the problem you wish to solve and invites vendors to suggest solutions.

Purpose: When you're ready to shop around and evaluate many factors before making a choice. Several vendors (e.g., Contractors/ Consultants are involved), to create the best project.

Ask: Specific, detailed questions about the service, product, and vendor's business. The overview of the project is understood; details still to be determined.

Style: Formal and direct. Statement of Work for the Project.

Advantage: Provides a clear comparison of vendor offers and capabilities.

RFQ

Including the Statement of Work that the companies will use to describe what will happen during the project. For example, the SOW should indicate all items that will be delivered, the timeline or timelines involved, and when invoicing will occur. You are spelling out everything that will be done, and the terms may be done for a fixed cost or based on the materials and time expended, subject to negotiations. The Contractor will be legally obligated to deliver what you agreed to in the RFQ terms, when it is time to formalize the contract.

Purpose: When you know the project scope precisely, mainly for smaller projects. You need to explore all of the financial details. A few vendors or one contractor can get the project's best price.

Ask: Questions about what it will cost to meet the requirements. Project details are identified.

Style: Structured and prescriptive. Pricing details.

Advantage: Removes distractions and allows buyers to focus on price.

RFP and RFQ are used interchangeably within companies. Some companies require RFP for larger projects and RFQ for smaller, well-defined projects.

In conclusion, an RFI educates. RFI responses explore how a vendor might solve a problem or fill a need. An RFQ quantifies. RFQ responses provide the cost of meeting a specific need. RFP compares. RFP responses evaluate the merits of each vendor compared to others.

Contract

A contract is a final document that you've been working toward to begin efforts on the new project. The contract will consider the various details specified in the original request for information. It may very well be adjusted in many ways, based on the parameters you went through when developing the request for proposal. A contract serves as a legal agreement that your organization and the other party signs. The contract will specify payments and timing of work to be done, any reporting requirements, and the duties of the contracting parties.

In this book, I will use the terms RFQ and RFP for the same purposes of illustration.

The consultant and Contractor tendering processes are very similar; all the instructions for this book used for the Contractor can be used for the Consultant and vice versa.

RFQ Process Overview

1. Preparation:
    a. Create RFQ

   b. Prepare RFQ Documents
   c. Define vendor list (Open, Closed, Pre-qualified, etc...)
   d. Identify risk tolerance
2. Management:
   a. Distribute the RFQ
   b. Answer vendor questions
   c. Observe Confidentiality
   d. Review responses
   e. Compare bids
   f. Award Contract
   g. Document results
3. Closing:
   a. Negotiate and sign the contract
   b. Notify unsuccessful bidders

Consultant Tendering

The company, developer, or Owner (Client) has to hire a consultant to draft the plans and specifications. It can be an internal (in-house) consultant or an external one.

Consultant RFP in Private Sector

In Private Sector, a client creates high-level specifications and scope of work for the services forecasted to be needed and sends them out for tendering through various channels.
For Example:

1. Search for consultants who have the expertise,
2. Use the previous consultants that the company used,
3. Send individual e-mails explaining what services are required. Be specific in your Request for Proposal (RFP),
4. The Consultant sends you his detailed quote with the inclusions and exclusions,
5. Look at every detail; look for potential tips or tricks. Such as "Customer will not receive AutoCAD drawings," or "Any communication with the municipality will be charged according to time and material," or "The quotation provided covers 1 site visit" or others. Some of these things may be acceptable to you or your business, while others are not.

The bigger your pool, the bigger the fish. In other words, if you get many responses to your RFQ, you will be able to negotiate for better service. **See Case Study # 1**

Recommendations for PMs regarding RFQ in Private Companies

The RFQ can be much more elaborate or less depending on several factors. Some of these factors are the complexity of the job, the dollar value, and your previous experience with the Consultant.

It is a good practice, even with small businesses, to send your draft proposal to someone in the company that you can trust; in many cases, this can be the business owner.

After receiving the first quote, start creating an Excel sheet showing the inclusions and exclusions for this consultant contract.

Once a Project Manager has chosen the best proposal, steps can be taken as below:

- Discuss with the Consultant, the Proposal to carry out the final review, including all the services in the contract.
- Negotiate the price. Some areas can be improved, if you find that the price is overestimated compared to other consultants. Sometimes, negotiate the unit rates. Below, fig. shows an example of how you can comment on a quotation and send it back to the Consultant for final revision. It will help if you show the supplier that you are doing your homework and that you are proactive in finding the best-case scenario to save money for your employer.

Figure 2. COMMENTS ON A QUOTE

The proposed fee structure is exclusive of HST and any direct disbursements to the project. Revisions, meetings, inspections or other services will be billed at hourly rates as follows:

		Note E : Here are the fees we have from our previous contract
Landscape Architect (Principal):	$ 155.00 per hour	150 $
Senior Project Manager:	$ 125.00 per hour	110 $
Senior Landscape Technician:	$ 95.00 per hour	95 $ (OK)
Technical/Support Staff:	$ 85.00 per hour	75$

- Use the company's standard contract form and send it for signature. Or sign the proposal (after consultation with the Owner).
- Now we have a consultant on board; let's keep the ball rolling and push to have the plans and specifications ready and hire a general contractor.

Do we need to push a consultant?

The short answer to this is yes. This is one of the most important reasons why most clients prefer to hire a project manager from the same discipline to the department developed. For example, if the employer is a home builder, they may need to hire a project manager who has a background in civil engineering, planning, and development, or construction to ensure an effective follow-up with consultants according to their specialty (civil, landscaping, structure, architecture, mechanics, etc.). **See Case Study # 2.**

Conclusion and Recommendations when Creating a Consultant Contract for a Private Company

- Understand the scope of work
- Try to get all items in a lump sum (Flat rate) quote
- Obtain the unit rates from the Consultant in the event of an additional cost for the scope of the work. Example: rate of additional site visits, hourly rate for the project manager, etc.;
- Don't be too formal. Call the Consultant or meet him at your office and discuss the contract together. Make sure all the elements are clear and well defined; And
- When signing the contract, stay in contact with the Consultant by phone. E-mails seem too formal in many cases; a call can break a lot of ice. It might be silly to mention this but remind the Consultant that your company is the client; this, in my experience, would help a lot when the contract calls for a change order.

Consultant RFx in Public Sector

The acronym RFx is used for talking about requests in general, where x can be either I (information), Q (quotation), or P (proposal).

A platform for sending the tenders is generally used in the public sector, either for consultants or contractors. Examples of these platforms are Bidingo, Bonfire, Merx, Bids&Tenders, Bidscanada, Procore, ConstructConnect, and others.

High-level specifications for the services needed are prepared internally. In many cases, other consultants are used to determine the scope of work required for the new construction, addition, or repairs.

Each Respondent is requested to provide a profile of their previous experience and capacity, to perform the work in this RFP (Request For Proposal) or RFQ (Request For Quotation). The client sends this form to be filled up. **See Case Study # 2.**

The Consultant's request for proposal may include and look like the one explained in case study#3 found at the end of this book.

Consultant RFQ in Public Sector

The client sends an RFQ or RFP – **See case study # 3** and requests pricing in a separate document like the example below:

Table 1. PRICING FORM RFQ CONSULTANT

RFQ# -PRICING DATA					
Proponent Name:				**Date:**	
Description of the Service:					
Item	**Description**	**Unit of measurement**	**Quantity**	**Unit Cost**	**Subtotal**
1	Preparation of Tender Documents	Lumpsum			
2	Contract Administration	Monthly			
3	Site Visits	1 Visit			
TOTAL					

Average Previous Evaluation Form Score	**78% > 70% OK**	Ranking For Pricing	Second
Compare to Estimation	+5%	Variance with the first bidder	+7.5%

Contractor Tendering

Contractor RFQ in Private Sector

When the complete package of plans and specifications is ready, the Owner must enter into an agreement with a General Contractor (GC). In the public and private sector, the Owner may choose to delegate this task to the Consultant since part of the Consultant's job is the administration of the construction of the contract. In many other cases, the Owner prefers to run the Contractor's bidding process on their own for different reasons. In both cases, the process for selecting the best Contractor is the same.

Invitation to tender can be a simple e-mail containing the plans and specs pertaining to the service requested and a summary sheet indicating the price. This summary sheet can be produced in an Excel sheet presenting the item's description and the quantities if necessary (similar to the Datasheet shown in the consultant section). The Contractor will respond to this form and provide a quote for the service requested. The Contractor will include in the quote, the exclusions and inclusions, as necessary.

A detailed Invitation to Tender and RFQ must be prepared for larger projects and complex work scope, and more stringent requirements are necessary. Usually, for large businesses and all public works, this case will be next discussed in detail.

Figure 3. Proposal for a small job

COMPANY ADDRESS
COMPANY E-MAIL

TEL

Proposal Submitted To:

CLIENT NAME

PROPOSAL NO.
104

Job Location:
OSHAWA

We hereby submit specifications and estimates for:

Re: Lot 200

- Dig 2' wide by 1' deep around rear and sides of foundation including under deck
- Backfill., repair and replace damaged grass

Total Price: $4,200 + hst

G.S.T. NUMBER

We Propose hereby to furnish material and labour - complete in accordance with the above specifications.

All material is guaranteed to be as specified.All work to be completed in a manlike manner according to standard practices. Any alteration or devia from above specifications involving extra costs will be executed only u written orders, and will become an extra charge over and above the estin All agreements contingent upon strikes, accidents or delays beyond our c Owner to carry fire, windstorm and other necessary insurance. Our worker fully covered by Workmen's Compensation Insurance.

Signature_______________

CONTRACTOR REPRESENTATIVE NAME

Acceptance of Proposal

The above prices, specifications and conditions are satisfactory and are hereby accepted. You are authorized to do the work as specified.

Signature_______________

Date of Acceptance: _______________

Signature_______________

Figure 4. Unit Price Proposal

Item No.	Specs	Description	Unit	Est. Qty.	Unit Price $	Amount $
SECTION I - TOPSOIL STRIPPING AND SITE PRE-GRADING						
Part "A" - Site Preparation						
A1	OPSS SP-1	Provisional: Construct, maintain and removal of site access where shown on the drawings including mud mat (50.0m long, 6.0m wide 300mm depth of 50mm to 100mm clear stone)	m	50	140.00	7,000.00
		Total Part "A" - Site Preparation				7,000.00
Part "B" - Topsoil Requirement						
B1	OPSS SP-5	Strip topsoil in two (2) layers and:				
		(i) Stockpile top layer in locations as shown in the meeting/drawings	m^3	8,700	4.90	42,630.00
		(ii) Haul, place and compact bottom layer (to minimum 93% Standard Proctor density) in bury trenches - Double handle 1700m3	m^3	5,600	6.20	34,720.00
		Total Topsoil Requirement - cu.m.		14,300		
		Total Part "B" - Topsoil				77,350.00
Part "C" - Cut & Fill Requirement						
B2	OPSS SP-6	Excavate fill material in bury trenches and place and compact as engineered fill (98% Standard Proctor density) in roads, Lots and Blocks	m^3	5,600	5.60	31,360.00
B3	OPSS SP-6	Excavate earth in Roads, Lots and Blocks, haul, place and compact as engineered fill (98% Standard Proctor density) in roads, Lots and Blocks	m^3	14,400	5.30	76,320.00
B4	OPSS SP-6	Provisional: Import approved fill material to the site, place, grade and compact as engineered fill (98% Standard Proctor Density) in roads, Lots/Blocks	m^3	0	35.00	35.00
		Total Cut & Fill Requirement - cu.m.		20,000		
		Total Part "C" - Cut & Fill				107,715.00

Contractor RFQ in Public Sector

Invitation to Tender

Most general contractors are made aware of proposed construction projects by reviewing Invitation to Tenders, such as those presented below. An Invitation to Tender will generally have enough information to enable a prospective Vendor (a Consultant or a Contractor) to assess whether they can submit a bid for the project. As previously stated, the book outlines the components of an Invitation to Tender for consultants in detail. The case is very similar to that of the General Contractors.

Once an Invitation to Tender has been reviewed and the Contractor has decided to pursue this project, they can review the complete tender documents at a specified location (Bidingo, Bonfire, Merx, Bids&Tenders, Bidscanada, Procore, ConstructConnect, and others). The Instruction to Bidders outlines the requirements, which a contractor must comply with. Items such as:

- Scope of Work,
- Schedule,
- Pre-qualified Vendor requirements-if any,
- Bonding Requirements,
- Site Examination,
- Preparation of Proposal,
- Opening of Tenders,
- Award of Contract,
- Return of Bond, and
- Subcontractor Listing

(as well as other requirements) will be provided in the Instruction to Bidders.

SAMPLE 1. Invitation to Tender- Stipulated Sum

Stipulated Sum- Invitation to Tender Example

Sudbury Lake
Senior Citizens' Apartment

Project: Construction of ten (10) unit wood framed senior citizens' apartment building in Sudbury Ontario

Project No. 2266685F56

Tender documents may be obtained only by General Contractors from the office of Best Housing Corporation located at 1234 Front Street, Toronto, Ontario, upon deposit of $180.00 certified cheque payable to Best Housing Corporation. Deposited amount will be refunded when the plans and specifications are returned to the architect in good condition, not later than 14 days after the closing date.

Tender documents may be viewed at the Construction Association Offices in Toronto.

Sealed tenders will be received at the office of Best Housing Corporation up to Wednesday, April 2020, at 2:00 p.m.

A Bid Bond must accompany tenders at 10% of the total tender price.

Tenders will be opened in public.

The lowest tender will not necessarily be granted the job.

Best Housing Corporation.
Toronto

SAMPLE 2. Invitation To Tender - Design-Built

Design-Built Invitation to Tender Example

Sudbury Lake
Senior Citizens' Apartment- Parking Garage

Invitation For Proposals

Proposals are invited from parties interested in the financing, design, construction, and operation of an above-ground parking garage on property currently owned by Best Housing Corporation. The project will involve demolishing an existing structure providing 200-250 parking spaces and one floor of usable office space.

Deadline for demolishing: Summer 2022
Deadline for construction: Fall 2022

Requests for information (RFI's) concerning the present site conditions and/or an opportunity to review the site should be addressed to the Corporation's senior director by February 14th, 2022.

Proposals will not be accepted after March 28th, 2022.

Mr. John Smith
Senior Director
Best Housing Corporation.
1234 Front Street, Toronto
Johnsmithtest@BestHousingCorporation.ca

SAMPLE 3. Invitation To Tender-Unit Price

TOWN OF WASAGA

Unit Price TENDER

TENDERS FOR THE CONSTRUCTION OF SEWERS,
CONSTRUCTION OF WATERMAIN, RECONSTRUCTION OF PAVEMENTS

Sealed tender, addressed to the Chairman and Members of The Town of Wasaga, Tender Opening Committee, 1st Floor, Town Hall, Wasaga will be accepted no later than Wednesday, July 20th, 2021

For the construction of the following work:

SEWERS

1- Construction of Road Storm Sewer, in open cut and in tunnel, varying in diameter from 600mm to 750mm, approximate length of 500 meters on Keele Street.

WATERMAIN

2- Construction of Watermains 2300mm in diameter, approximate length 340 meters on Wellington Street West.

PAVEMENTS, SIDEWALKS, AND CURBS

3- Reconstruction of 300 meters of Pavements, Sidewalks, and Curbs on Melbourne Avenue.
4- Reconstruction of 200 meters of Pavements, Sidewalks, and Curbs on St. Claren Avenue.

Documents are available at the Department of Purchasing and Supply, 2nd Floor, Town Hall, Wasaga.

Tenders will be opened publicly by the Tender Opening Committee on August 05th, 2021, at 9:30 a.m.

The date of commencement of work is July 5, 2000. Lowest or *any* tender may not necessarily be accepted.

Pre-qualified Contractors for Public Agencies

Most public companies require that a contractor be qualified before or after submitting a quote.

The employer (Owner) or a consultant prepares the Prequalification Documents that the Contractor must answer, to prove that the GC can execute the project based on their previous experience. The Rated Criteria is established internally, and a committee of professionals is set up to assess each Respondent. This evaluation process can sometimes be done after the submission of the proposals.

Several detailed criteria have been developed for the evaluation. For consistency and ease of application, each Evaluator will score each criterion in the same manner. A point system will be created; weighted points for each item will be calculated. A minimum threshold for passing contractors will also be predetermined.

Rated Criteria

A sample **example** of points assigned to Rated Criteria is as below:

Table 2. Rated Criteria

Item No.	Rated Criteria	Weighted (Points)	Minimum Threshold
1	Qualifications	15 Points	
2	Relevant Project Experience	70 Points	
3	Scheduling	15 Points	
	TOTAL	**100 Points**	**70 Points overall Minimum Required**

To illustrate this table, we have the following real-life example. The below example will be sent to vendors to ensure that all contractors know the evaluation scoring methodology.

SAMPLE 4. Rated Criteria

Qualifications (15 Points)

Proponents shall attach resumes for (2) key site personnel proposed for the project. Provide resumes for the following key site personnel:

- Project/Construction Manager
- Site Superintendent

Proponents' submissions will be evaluated based on a combination of the following:

- Past and current roles and specific responsibilities (beyond a list of completed projects)
- Education and training
- Relevant project experience, minimum of five (5) years of related construction activities (Civil Works, Envelope Repairs, Windows, Foundation works, Etc.)
- Total years of industry experience

Evaluators give their points according to established internal regulations, which are examples of these scoring points below.

0 points - Resume not provided.

1 or 2 points - The submitted resume **does not** adequately demonstrate an appropriate level of skills, qualifications, and experience.

3 or 4 points – The submitted resume for either a Project or a Site Superintendent only addresses very few of the critical requirements listed in the question.

5 or 6 points – The submitted resume shows some experience relevant to specific work detailed in the RFP Scope of Work; however, the resume inadequately demonstrates the appropriate level of skills, qualifications, and knowledge of the proposed key site personnel question. The resume is lacking in some critical areas but has met some of the basic requirements.

7 or 8 points - The submitted resume **adequately** demonstrates the appropriate level of skills, qualifications, and experience relative to the question and RFP Scope of Work.

9 or 10 points - The submitted resume is **very good** or shows the ability to **exceed** the question's requirements.

Relevant Project Experience (70 Points)

Proponents shall provide three (3) projects undertaken within the last (10) years of work similar in type, scale, scope, and complexity to the project described within this RFP with a minimum project value of $500,000 at award per project.

As part of the response to this question, Proponent shall submit the following additional information for each project:

- Certificate of Substantial Performance of the Contract for all listed projects.
- Photos depicting the overall project and scope of work before and after completion. A brief description shall accompany each photo.
- Description of the role of the Contractor, including identifying any subcontractor work coordinated by the Proponent.
- Description of the Proponent's project approach, identifying any construction challenges, solutions, and determining the project's relevance relative to the RFP scope

0 points – This score is to be applied for the following scenarios:

- A project example is not submitted; and/or
- The Proponent has indicated the Contract Type as "Trade or Sub-Contractor."

1 or 2 points – This score is to be applied for the following scenarios:

- Through the photos and description, the Proponent's submitted project example **does not demonstrate** relevant previous experience acting as a Prime Contractor, communicating directly with owners, and leading/coordinating the work of multiple sub-trades at a single worksite.

3 or 4 points – This score is to be applied for the following scenarios:

- The Proponent has below average experience or **barely** demonstrates relevant previous experience acting as a Prime Contractor, communicating directly with owners, and leading/coordinating multiple sub-trades works at a single worksite.

5 or 6 points – This score is to be applied for the following scenarios:

- The Proponent has submitted a project example, but it has met **very few** of the question requirements and inadequately details experience, or ability to project plan; and/or
- The overall project example is lacking in some critical areas but has met a **few** of the fundamental question requirements; and/or
- The submitted project example is less than $500K at award; and/or
- The Proponent **has not** addressed more than one requirement listed in the question; and/or the submitted project example has not been completed within the last ten years
- The Proponent has provided either a) photos or b) descriptions and **has not** provided the other required point.

7 or 8 points – The Proponent's submitted project example demonstrates **good experience** relevant to the services described in the RFP Scope of Work.

9 or 10 points – The Proponent's submitted project example **exceeds** the question's requirements and includes a description of similar services.

Scheduling (15 Points)

The Gantt chart must include but must not be limited to:

1. Start date
2. End date
3. Critical Path
4. Milestones
5. Key Activities
6. Indicate items that have an extended lead time for delivery
7. Project phases and operation phases
8. Substantial completion
9. Submission of close-outs
10. Commissioning and any specific requirements within the RFP, if applicable

11. Mark any work to be carried out by sub-contractors
- **0** - No answer provided
- **1 or 2** - Unsatisfactory,
- **3 or 4** - Barely Meets minimum acceptable level,
- **5 or 6** - Almost Meets,
- **7 or 8** - Adequately or more than sufficiently meets the minimum requirements,
- **9 or 10** - Exceeds the requirements of the critical criteria.

Contractor RFP

Table 3. Table Of Contents RFP Public Sector
SAMPLE 5. Table Of Contents RFP

Table of Contents

ATTACHMENT # 1 – CONFLICT OF INTEREST FORM
DEFINITION OF TERMS

SEE- CASE STUDY # 5- RFP TO HIRE A CONTRACTOR IN THE PUBLIC SECTOR FOR AN EXAMPLE.

RFQ Timetable

SAMPLE 6. RFQ TimeTable

RFQ TIMETABLE	
RFQ NO.	23-011
RFQ Title	Building New 12 detached houses for seniors
Deadline for Questions	
Submission Deadline	
Rectification Period	
Estimated Commencement of Contract	

Procurement Formats Dashboard

Table 4. Procurement Formats Dashboard

Invitational RFQ	Open RFQ	Invitation to Tender	RFP
Traditional Contract Law	Traditional Contract Law	Contract A (1) Tendering Law	Contract A (1) Tendering Law
Screening Typically in Pre-Selection	Mandatory Requirements (Flexible)	Mandatory Requirements (Duty to Reject)	Mandatory Requirements (Duty to Reject)
Typically low Bid	Low Bid or High Score	Low Bid	High Score
Low Risk on Cancellation	Low Risk on Cancellation	Low Risk on Cancellation	High Risk on Cancellation
Price Binding on Award	Price Binding on Award	Price Binding on Bid Close	Price Binding on Bid Close
Negotiations Typically Not Required	Negotiations Typically Not Required	Negotiations Not Permitted	Negotiations Not Permitted

(1) Contract A explained below

Contract A and Contract B

When a purchaser issues a tender call, often called a "request for tenders," and a bidder submits a compliant bid in response to that tender call, a binding process contract (also called "Contract A") is formed between the purchaser and each compliant bidder. Contract A consists of the terms of the bid process. Contract B, the performance contract, is the contract awarded to the winning bidder.

In Canadian contract law, Contract A is formed when a "request for proposal" is responded to, in the form of a compliant bid, sometimes also known as the submission of price. Many Contracts A are formed between the owner (person, company, or organization tendering the project) and the bidders as their bids are received. The owner must now deal fairly and equally with all bidders and must not show any favoritism towards any bidder(s).

Purchasing

Project procurement management includes the processes to purchase or acquire necessary products, services, or outcomes outside of the project team.

- Project Procurement Management Processes
- Plan Procurements
- Conduct Procurements
- Administer Procurements
- Close Procurements

Employees in the field or the project management team are advanced cash for regular and emergency purposes. This includes gas money, trip expenditures, and project costs. Sometimes, the staff is reimbursed for fronted purchases like coffee or food. In most cases, the acquisition includes office supplies while out of the office. Other companies create a cash box kept in the office in a lockbox or with staff for instant and emergency purposes.

As a general rule, no purchase of goods and/or services shall be authorized unless it is in accordance with the procurement policies and procedures approved by the Company.

Purchasing methods and quotation requirements

The following table shows methods of purchasing goods and services and the competition required at various procurement levels.

SAMPLE 7. Purchasing Policy

Amount	Purchasing Procedure	Quotation
Up to $2,000	Petty Cash, Blanket Order, Systems Contract, Commercial Card, Purchase Order	No quotation
$2,000 - $25,000	Purchase Order/Capital Order through Informal Quotation	1 written quotation required, 3 quotes where possible
$25,000 - $100,000	Purchase Order/Capital Order through Formal Quotation	3 written quotes required, open competitive process preferred
Over $100,000	Open Competitive Procurement through Competitive Procurement process	A minimum of 3 quotes

Purchase Requisition

Project managers, superintendents, and other employees can initiate a material or equipment purchase requisition by filling out a form or entering the requisition into the company system and pushing it to the next level based on purchasing authorities and the workflow assigned to each project.

SAMPLE 8. Requisition for Purchasing Supplies

LOGO AND ADDRESS	Requested By:	Request #: Date:
Supplier: Address: Tel: E-mail: Contact Name:	Deliver to: Deliver When: ☐ By Plane ☐ By Truck	Comments:

Quantity	Unit Price	Description	Quote 1	Quote 2	Activity Code	Total $	Budget$

Work Orders

A work order is a document that provides all the information about a maintenance task and outlines a process for completing that task. Work orders can include details on who authorized the job, the scope, who it's assigned to, and what is expected.

Difference Between A Purchase Order and A Work Order

A purchase order is often referred to as a "PO." Purchase orders are essentially an offer to purchase items from a vendor or other source. In many cases, the PO begins as a purchase requisition. A requisition is provided to either a buyer (who directly creates a purchase order) or approvers who approve the items on the purchase requisition. Once approved, the approved requisition moves to the buyer for a purchase order number.

SAMPLE 9. Purchase Order

ABC Company 1234 Front Street Toronto Contract Name: Phone:	**P.O. Number: P-123** Print Date: 05/26/2021
Vendor: Mobile Equipment 458 Whitby Road Whitby (ON), *Postal Code* Contact Name: Phone:	**Ship To:** 2589 Kirland Palace Whitby (ON), *Postal Code* Contract Number: Job Number: Contact Name Phone: Comments:

Description	Unit	QTY	Unit Price	Sub-Total
BB-235 Brass Bushings 11 inch	Ea	3	$500	$1500
MXC- AC 1500BTU	Ea	1	$1500	$1500
BXD001- Security tape	M	100	$0.5	$50
			Sub-Total	$3,050.00
			Taxes	$396.50
			Total	**$3,446.50**

A work order describes a unit of work to be performed. A work order may also begin as a work requisition, sometimes referred to as a "repair ticket." Typically, a maintenance manager receives the work request via a system, then evaluates it, and finally converts it to a work order, if appropriate.

SAMPLE 10. Work Order W.O.

ABC Company 1234 Front Street Toronto Contract Name: Phone:	**W.O. Number: W-123** Print Date: 05/26/2021
Vendor: Mobile Equipment 458 Whitby Road Whitby (ON), *Postal Code* Contact Name: Phone:	**Requester Information :** John Smith Project Superintendent Contract Number: Job Number:
Date Requested: 05/26/2021 Date Due: 05/26/2021 Maximum limit: $2,000 Estimated hours: Whitby (ON), *Postal Code* Contact Name: Phone:	Reasons ☐ Emergency ☐ Maintenance ☐ Safety ☐ Others: Specify:.. ....

Description of the Work Order

While performing the drywall patching and repairs for unit # 256, the washroom faucet needed to be replaced to stop the running water. Job must be completed immediately to protect the newly installed flooring.

The investigation behind the reason for this deficiency is taking place. If the cause were not the existing contractor, the contractor would be eligible for a purchase order.

Recommendations for the Project Manager

Possible Scenario: If the cause of this faucet problem was the original plumbing contractor, the plumbing contractor needs to be back-charged ($ Value of the PO should be deducted from his initial contract value- See definition of Back-charge in the Glossary). Communicate the current situation to the plumbing contractor.

CHAPTER 3 - CONTRACT

What is a contract

A contract is a written or spoken agreement intended to be enforceable by law. It consists of an actionable promise or promises.

An agreement between the Owner and Contractor is a contract between a builder or Owner of a project and the vendor or Contractor. The deal is carried out to define the scope of the projects, the possible timelines, the monetary specifications, and the default guidelines.

The Project Management team creates the contract after receiving responses to the Call For Tender, and the client chooses the best bidder. Most of the time, tender documents are part of the final contract documents. Most companies use predefined contract templates and require the supplier to sign with the customer and a third party if necessary. In addition to this template, the client will add the tender documents for a specific project, including all plans, specifications, and annexes, to the contract template to form the final part of the executed contract documents.

Canadian Construction Documents Committee (CCDC) is Canada's only source for recognized Canadian standard construction industry documents, offering consensus-built documents and transparent, balanced, and standardized contracts. All parties feel confident using forms that recognize established legal precedents and provide a solid legal foundation.

Types Of Contracts

The different types of contracts are Competitive Bid Contracts (Lump Sum), Secured Cost Contracts (Cost Plus), Negotiated Contracts (Design-Build), Civil Contracts (Unit Price), and Management Contracts (Construction Management and Project Management). They will be discussed as well as the advantages and disadvantages of each contract will be presented.

The most common type of contracts used for contracting and development work in the construction industry is:

- COMPETITIVE BIDDING CONTRACTS:
    - Lump Sum
- SECURED-COST CONTRACTS:
    - Cost Plus a % Fee
    - Cost Plus a Fixed Fee
    - Guaranteed Maximum
    - Shared Savings
- NEGOTIATED CONTRACTS:
    - Design Built

- CIVIL CONTRACTS:
  - Unit Price
- MANAGEMENT CONTRACTS:
  - Construction Management
  - Project Management

Competitive Bidding Contract

Before commencing with this section, the words bid (bidding) and tender (tendering) are synonymous. Competitive Bidding Contracts are also known as Stipulated Price, Lump Sum Contracts, or Fixed Fee.

The majority of contractors in North America obtain their work in a bidding competition with other contractors. The competitive bidding of public projects is generally required by law and standard procedures for public agencies such as Public Works Canada.

When preparing a lump sum bid for a project, the Contractor estimates how much the Project will cost using a completed set of architectural drawings, engineering drawings, and specifications as a basis of their calculation. After the Project's total cost is determined, the Contractor will add an appropriate amount for profit and overhead. The Contractor will submit their bid and guarantee the entire Project for the lump sum or fixed price and usually within a specified period.

The successful tender is usually the Contractor with the lowest bid, although most bidding documents state that the "lowest tender is not necessarily accepted." This gives the Owner the right to reject a tender if they feel the Contractor could not complete the scope of work outlined in the contract for the tendered amount submitted.

If the Contractor exceeds the lump sum amount submitted to the Owner at the end of the project, the Contractor is liable for this addition. The main **advantage** of this type of contract to the Owner is that they know the Project's cost before the job commences.

The **disadvantages** with this type of contract are that:

The Owner's risk is that the agreement is only as good as the accuracy of the contract documents. If errors in the contract document occur, then the fixed price may have to be re-negotiated.

If the work scope changes from the contract documents, then the fixed price will also have to be re-negotiated.

- The Owner is interested in getting the best quality of workmanship, and the Contractor wants to deliver the Project within the most economical means.
- The Contractor tends to always look for extras to the scope of work outlined in the contract documents.
- Contract award is usually the result of the lowest tender, which may be a result of missed items or mistakes

Aproject built with this contract may take a longer time to complete than any other contract form. This is because the working drawings and the specifications must be completed before the Project can be tendered. In other forms of contracts, the work can commence before the completion of tender documents, reducing the overall length of the Project.

Secured-Cost Contract

Cost-plus contracts are sometimes referred to as time and material contracts. In a cost-plus contract, the Owner agrees to pay the Contractor:

- The cost of the construction.
- Afee for the Contractor's service.

The construction cost includes all labor, material, equipment, and sub-trades required to complete the Project.

The Contractor's fee for the service they provide can be a:

- % of the total cost of construction
- a predetermined fixed amount

This type of contract is best used when the scope of the Project is challenging to define. A renovation project is an excellent example because the work to be done in some instances cannot be determined until existing components of the structure are exposed. The Contractor is not delayed when unforeseen occurrences are discovered, as the Contractor will be reimbursed for any work done. Savings in time may occur as the Contractor can start the Project without defining the scope of work.

The main **advantage** of a cost-plus contract to an owner is possibly the cost. Due to the uncertainty of work or the lack of finished drawings, if the Owner requested a stipulated price sum, a contractor would have to price the Project very high to account for numerous uncertainties they may encounter.

Disadvantages with a cost-plus contract are that:

- There is no incentive for the Contractor to reduce waste and save cost in the construction process as they will be reimbursed for all expenditures made.
- At the end of a project, the Owner may feel that the Contractor has not done an adequate job keeping the project cost in line.

Guaranteed-Maximum Contract

If an owner is not comfortable with a Cost Plus contract, a Guaranteed Maximum contract may be used. A Guaranteed Maximum contract is also known as a ceiling or upset price contract. This type of contract implies that the Contractor agrees to complete the Project for a specified maximum amount, although the working drawings may not be complete or the scope of work fully known.

The main disadvantage of this contractual arrangement is that both workmanship and material quality may be sacrificed to achieve the Guaranteed Maximum cap amount.

Shared-Savings Contract

Like a Guaranteed Maximum style of contract, the Shared Savings is a fixed amount referred to as the Target Price. The Owner and the Contractor share the savings and the overruns from the Target Price. The Shared Savings can be any agreed amount such as a 50/50 split for savings or overruns, where each party shares evenly in the gain or loss.

The main **disadvantage** with this type of contractual arrangement is that the quality of both workmanship and material may be sacrificed at the expense of receiving additional savings.

Negotiated Contract

Design-Built Contract

The Design Built contract has become a modern approach in recent years. In a Design-Built contract arrangement, the Contractor agrees to design and build the entire project for a fixed amount. With this arrangement, the owner contracts with a single firm to have their Project completed. The contractors may have a design person or team on staff, but usually, they will form a joint venture with a design company for the Project's duration. If a contractor pursues Design Built projects regularly, they may decide to hire a design person on staff or have an ongoing arrangement with a design firm. If the total project costs exceed the agreed amount, the contractor is liable for all cost overruns.

A Design Built contract can be extended to include not just the design and the construction of the project. **Turnkey** is when the contract consists of the following additional responsibilities:

- selecting the site
- financing the project
- leasing when construction is finished
- operating the building (property managers)
- maintaining the builder for a specified time

Civil Contract

Unit Price contracts are synonymous with civil works. In Civil Works, the owner will usually hire an engineering firm to design their project. Most of the time, the civil engineering company provides the client/ owner/ developer with their cost estimate to compare with the price received from the contractors. With this type of contract, the quantities required to complete the project (called a bill of quantities) are prepared by the engineering firm.

Contractors will be asked to bid on the project by deriving the unit price for each quantity listed in the tender.

Below is an example of price comparison for a Unit Price Form of Tender.

Figure 5. Real-Life Unit Price Form of Tender

		PROJECT Phase 2: Cost Estimate									
1.0	Pearl Street (cont'd)							Original Estimate by the engineering company	Contractor 1	Contractor 2	Contractor 3
1.1.2	MH7A	MH8A	65.00	200	PVC	m	$200.00	$13,000.00	$12,025.00	$13,000.00	$10,725.00
1.1.3	MH8A	MH9A	91.00	200	PVC	m	$200.00	$18,200.00	$16,835.00	$18,200.00	$15,015.00
1.1.4	MH9A	MH10A	56.70	200	PVC	m	$200.00	$11,340.00	$10,489.50	$11,340.00	$9,355.50
1.1.5	MH10A	MH11A	12.30	200	PVC	m	$200.00	$2,460.00	$2,275.50	$2,460.00	$2,029.50
1.1.6	MH11A	MH12A	118.60	200	PVC	m	$200.00	$23,720.00	$21,941.00	$23,720.00	$23,127.00
1.1.7	MH12A	MH13A	53.00	200	PVC	m	$200.00	$10,600.00	$9,805.00	$10,600.00	$10,335.00
1.1.8	MH13A	STUB before MH14A	37.70	200	PVC	m	$200.00	$7,540.00	$6,974.50	$9,123.40	$7,351.50
	MH				Type	Unit	Unit Price	Cost			
1.1.9	MH5A				701.01	ea	$4,300.00	$4,300.00	$6,500.00	$6,500.00	$4,800.00
1.1.10	MH7A				701.01	ea	$4,300.00	$4,300.00	$6,500.00	$7,000.00	$5,000.00
1.1.11	MH8A				701.01	ea	$4,300.00	$4,300.00	$6,500.00	$7,000.00	$5,400.00
1.1.12	MH9A				701.01	ea	$4,300.00	$4,300.00	$6,500.00	$7,000.00	$5,400.00
1.1.13	MH10A				701.01	ea	$4,300.00	$4,300.00	$6,500.00	$7,000.00	$5,400.00
1.1.14	MH11A				701.01	ea	$4,300.00	$4,300.00	$6,500.00	$7,000.00	$6,200.00
1.1.15	MH12A				701.01	ea	$4,300.00	$4,300.00	$7,500.00	$7,500.00	$7,000.00
1.1.16	MH13A				701.01	ea	$4,300.00	$4,300.00	$8,000.00	$9,300.00	$7,800.00
	Services		Quantity			Unit	Unit Price	Cost			
1.1.17	Single Sanitary Service		48			ea	$1,794.40	$96,000.00	$96,000.00	$88,516.80	$43,200.00
	Sub-Total Sanitary							$236,800.00	$248,920.00	$255,000.20	$184,259.00

The Unit Price, "Unit Price" for each item, must include the Price for all Equipment (Dozer, Truck), Labour, Profit, and Overhead (Office, Site).

The main **disadvantage** of the Unit Price Contract to the owner is:

- If the quantities prepared for the owner are not accurate, the project could be highly over budget at its completion
- As the contractor is paid for the work put in place, the owner must have a representative on-site to verify these quantities.
- If the prepared quantities in the tender vary significantly from the actual contract, disputes can arise.

Management Contract

Suppose a project is complex and the owner wants to control the actual construction cost by a contractor. In that case, they may consider a Management Contract (Construction Management or Project Management).

Construction Management Contract

A client can use a construction manager contract to help the owner and the designer control the cost, schedule, and quality.

The Construction Manager Contract will provide the owner and the project designer with management methodologies and applied construction techniques throughout the design/construction stages to complete the job.

A construction management contract can be estimated for:

- a percentage of the cost of the construction
- a fee for the firm's service.

A construction management contract will be essential if the owner wishes to expedite the project.

Project Management Contract

A Project Management Contract will ensure a firm act as the owner's representative. The Project Management firm is appointed at the earliest stage of the project when the project is first under consideration.

From that point on, the project management firm will fully identify the owner's needs and act as the owner's agent for all matters relating to the project.

Time and Material Contracts

As is the case with unit-price contracts, which deal with invoicing the quantities of work actually performed, time and material contracts are what we generally call hourly rate contracts. This type of contract is a hybrid between a cost-reimbursable contract and a fixed-price contract. For example, if the seller spends 1,400 hours on a project at $100 per hour, the seller will be paid $140,000 by the buyer. This type of contract is common for freelancers, and the main **advantage** of this type of contract is that the seller earns money for every hour spent working on the project. The **downside** to this type of contract is that the client must ensure that the invoices received, represent the actual time spent on that work. A client may need to hire a specialized project manager to help control the cost of this type of contract. Example of a civil engineer P.M. following the major tasks of a civil engineering consulting firm.

See Case Study# 2-Pushing a Consultant.

Risks on Selected Contract Formats

The below table shows an example of how risks are distributed on selected CCDC Contract Formats:

- CM=Construction Manager
- DB=Design Builder
- GC=General Contractor

Table 5. Risks on Selected Construction Contract Formats

Selected Construction Contract Formats				
Key Factors	**Design-Bid-Build (CCDC-2)**	**Construction Management-Owner at Risk (CCDC-5A+17)**	**Construction Management-CM at Risk (CCDC-5B)**	**Design-Build (CCDC-14)**
Design Responsibility	Owner's Consultant	Owner's Consultant (Input from CM)	Owner's Consultant (Input from CM)	Design-Builder
Contract Management	GC Manages Trades. Owner Manages GC & Consultant	Owner Manages CM, Trades, and Consultants	CM Manages Trades. Owner Manages CM and Consultants	DB Manages Entire Project Team
Pricing Format	Stipulated Sum in advance of Project Start	Time and Materials for CM, Stipulated Sum for Trades on Progress Basis	Time and Materials Default, Stipulated Sum Option	Stipulated Sum (Based on General Statement of Work)
Time Incentive	Medium (No Default Incentives)	Low (Owner Carries Delay Risk)	Low(Work Starts Before Final Design)	Medium (Work Often Starts Before Final Design)
Cost Saving Incentive	Medium (No Built-In Incentives)	Low (Owner Carries Cost Risk)	Medium (Owner /CM Share Risk)	Medium (No Built-In Incentives)

Figure 6. Contract Risks

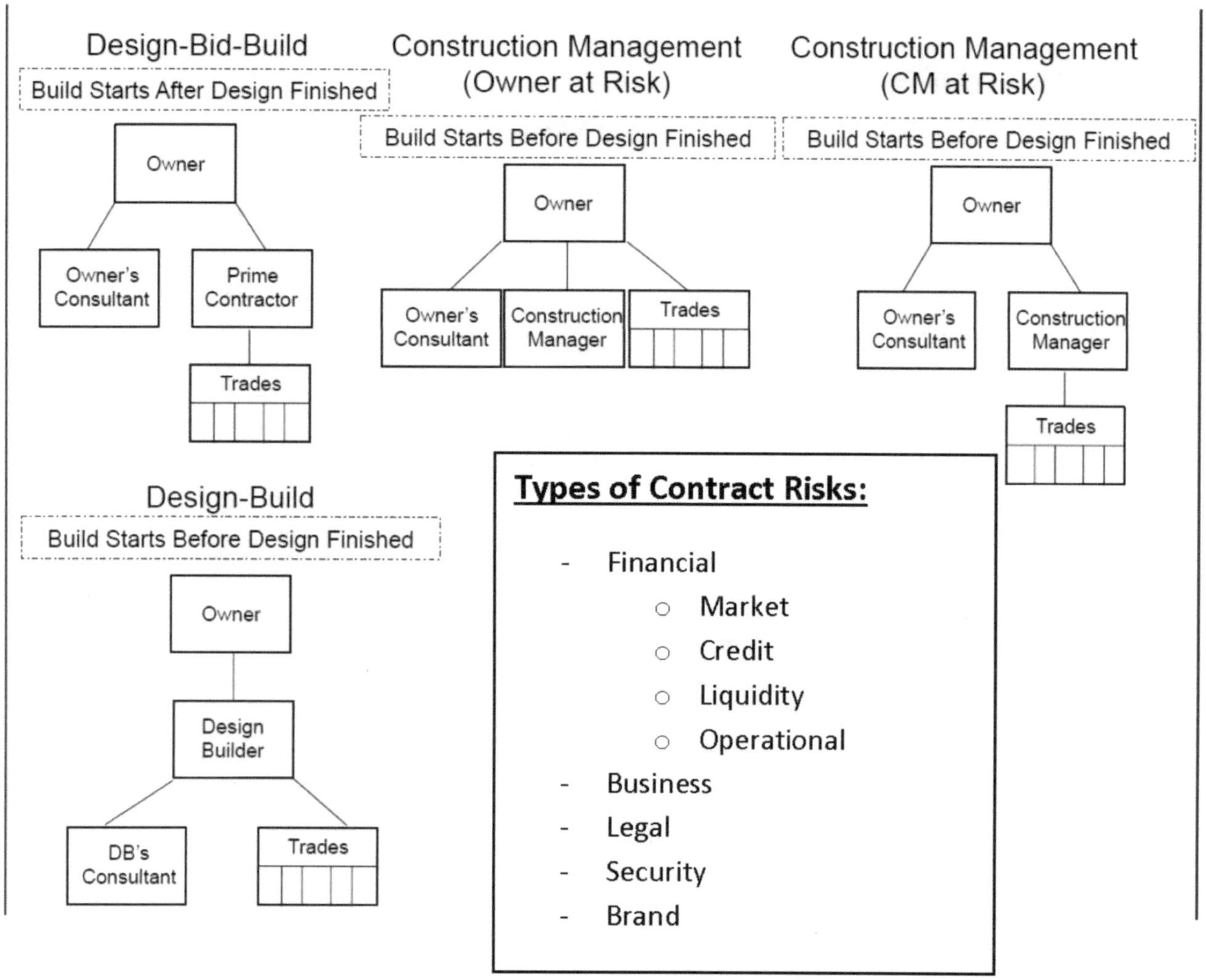

Issuing the Contract Documents

Ultimately, the professional committee should meet, discuss the results (points), and agree on each score to ensure that the assessment is conducted fairly and consistently for all proposers. For bidders who have passed the scoring point in the rated criteria that the company has established, their proposals (RFQ/RFP) can be opened and compared. The Client will then choose the best winner for the execution of the work.

The project team can enter into contracts by approving and signing the RFQ/RFP. Larger contracts may require a CCDC contract form.

CCDC Contract Documents

To find a complete set of CCDC contracts, you can visit:

https://www.ccdc.org/documents/

Figure 7. CCDC 2 Stipulated Price Contract Sample

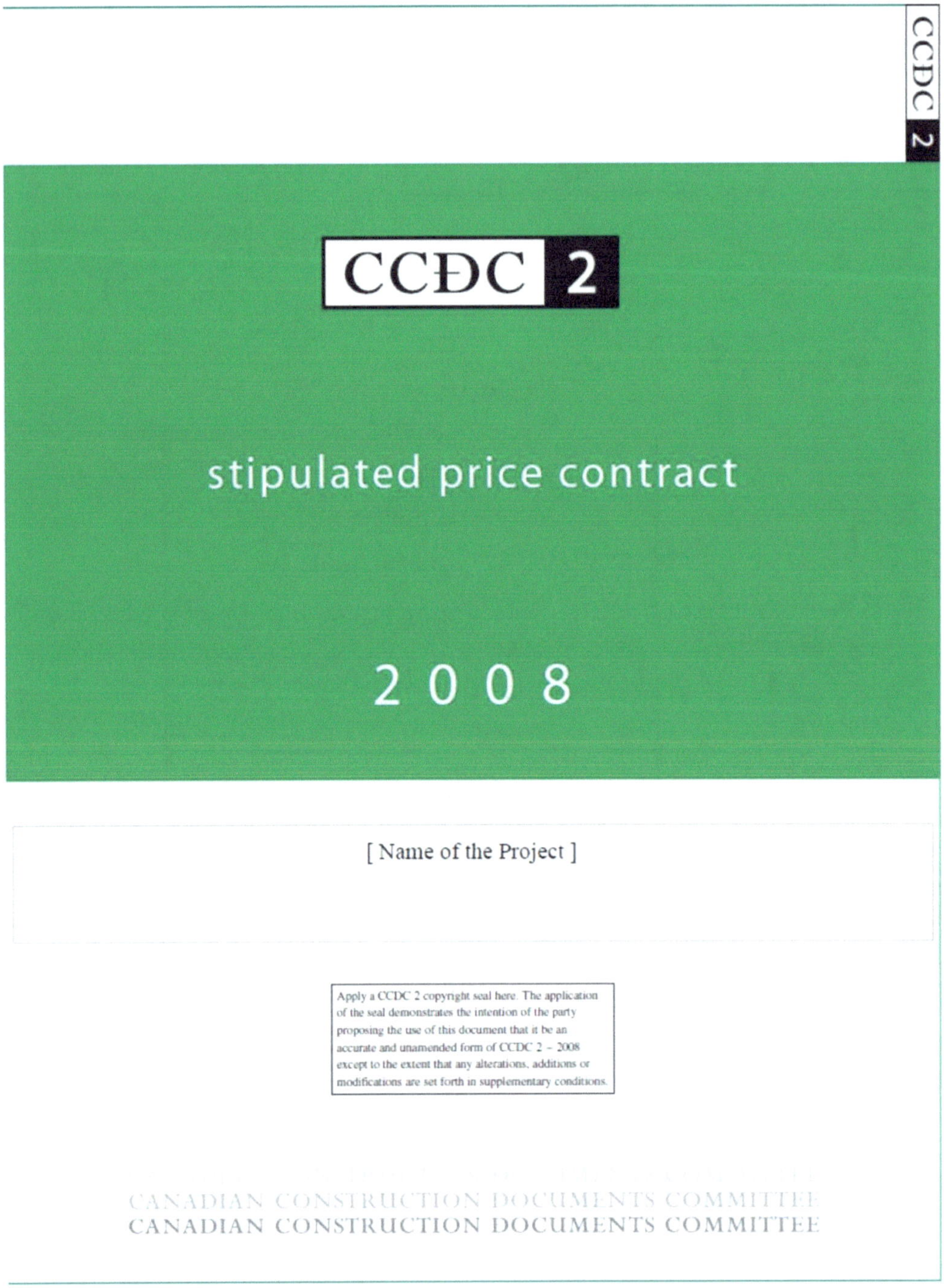

CCDC 2

CCDC 2

stipulated price contract

2008

[Name of the Project]

Apply a CCDC 2 copyright seal here. The application of the seal demonstrates the intention of the party proposing the use of this document that it be an accurate and unamended form of CCDC 2 – 2008 except to the extent that any alterations, additions or modifications are set forth in supplementary conditions.

CANADIAN CONSTRUCTION DOCUMENTS COMMITTEE
CANADIAN CONSTRUCTION DOCUMENTS COMMITTEE

Standard Construction Document CCDC 2 – 2008

AGREEMENT BETWEEN OWNER AND CONTRACTOR
For use when a stipulated price is the basis of payment.

This Agreement made on the ____________ day of ________ in the year _____ .

by and between the parties

____

hereinafter called the "*Owner*"

and

____

hereinafter called the *"Contractor"*

The *Owner* and the *Contractor* agree as follows:

ARTICLE A-1 THE WORK

The *Contractor* shall:

1.1 perform the *Work* required by the *Contract Documents* for

____
insert above the name of the Work

located at

____
insert above the Place of the Work

for which the Agreement has been signed by the parties, and for which

____
insert above the name of the Consultant

is acting as and is hereinafter called the "*Consultant*" and

1.2 do and fulfill everything indicated by the *Contract Documents*, and

1.3 commence the *Work* by the ____________ day of ________ in the year _____ and, subject to adjustment in *Contract Time* as provided for in the *Contract Documents*, attain *Substantial Performance of the Work*, by the ____________ day of ________ in the year _____ .

ARTICLE A-2 AGREEMENTS AND AMENDMENTS

2.1 The *Contract* supersedes all prior negotiations, representations or agreements, either written or oral, relating in any manner to the *Work*, including the bidding documents that are not expressly listed in Article A-3 of the Agreement - CONTRACT DOCUMENTS.

2.2 The *Contract* may be amended only as provided in the *Contract Documents*.

CCDC 2 – 2008 File 005213 1

ARTICLE A-3 CONTRACT DOCUMENTS

3.1 The following are the *Contract Documents* referred to in Article A-1 of the Agreement - THE WORK:

- Agreement between *Owner* and *Contractor*
- Definitions
- The General Conditions of the Stipulated Price Contract

*

* *(Insert here, attaching additional pages if required, a list identifying all other Contract Documents e.g. supplementary conditions; information documents; specifications, giving a list of contents with section numbers and titles, number of pages and date; material finishing schedules; drawings, giving drawing number, title, date, revision date or mark; addenda, giving title, number, date)*

CCDC 2 – 2008 File 005213 2

ARTICLE A-4 CONTRACT PRICE

4.1 The *Contract Price*, which excludes *Value Added Taxes*, is:

____/100 dollars $ ____________

4.2 *Value Added Taxes* (of ________ %) payable by the *Owner* to the *Contractor* are:

____/100 dollars $ ____________

4.3 Total amount payable by the *Owner* to the *Contractor* for the construction of the *Work* is:

____/100 dollars $ ____________

4.4 These amounts shall be subject to adjustments as provided in the *Contract Documents*.

4.5 All amounts are in Canadian funds.

ARTICLE A-5 PAYMENT

5.1 Subject to the provisions of the *Contract Documents*, and in accordance with legislation and statutory regulations respecting holdback percentages and, where such legislation or regulations do not exist or apply, subject to a holdback of Ten percent (10 %), the *Owner* shall:

.1 make progress payments to the *Contractor* on account of the *Contract Price* when due in the amount certified by the *Consultant* together with such *Value Added Taxes* as may be applicable to such payments, and

.2 upon *Substantial Performance of the Work*, pay to the *Contractor* the unpaid balance of the holdback amount when due together with such *Value Added Taxes* as may be applicable to such payment, and

.3 upon the issuance of the final certificate for payment, pay to the *Contractor* the unpaid balance of the *Contract Price* when due together with such *Value Added Taxes* as may be applicable to such payment.

5.2 In the event of loss or damage occurring where payment becomes due under the property and boiler insurance policies, payments shall be made to the *Contractor* in accordance with the provisions of GC 11.1 – INSURANCE.

5.3 Interest

.1 Should either party fail to make payments as they become due under the terms of the *Contract* or in an award by arbitration or court, interest at the following rates on such unpaid amounts shall also become due and payable until payment:

(1) 2% per annum above the prime rate for the first 60 days.

(2) 4% per annum above the prime rate after the first 60 days.

Such interest shall be compounded on a monthly basis. The prime rate shall be the rate of interest quoted by

N/A

(Insert name of chartered lending institution whose prime rate is to be used)

for prime business loans as it may change from time to time.

.2 Interest shall apply at the rate and in the manner prescribed by paragraph 5.3.1 of this Article on the settlement amount of any claim in dispute that is resolved either pursuant to Part 8 of the General Conditions – DISPUTE RESOLUTION or otherwise, from the date the amount would have been due and payable under the *Contract*, had it not been in dispute, until the date it is paid.

CCDC 2 – 2008 File 005213 3

ARTICLE A-8 SUCCESSION

8.1 The *Contract* shall enure to the benefit of and be binding upon the parties hereto, their respective heirs, legal representatives, successors, and assigns.

In witness whereof the parties hereto have executed this Agreement by the hands of their duly authorized representatives.

SIGNED AND DELIVERED
in the presence of:

WITNESS	**OWNER**
	name of owner
signature	_signature_
name of person signing	_name and title of person signing_
signature	_signature_
name of person signing	_name and title of person signing_

WITNESS	**CONTRACTOR**
	name of Contractor
signature	_signature_
name of person signing	_name and title of person signing_
signature	_signature_
name of person signing	_name and title of person signing_

N.B. *Where legal jurisdiction, local practice or Owner or Contractor requirement calls for:*
(a) proof of authority to execute this document, attach such proof of authority in the form of a certified copy of a resolution naming the representative(s) authorized to sign the Agreement for and on behalf of the corporation or partnership; or
(b) the affixing of a corporate seal, this Agreement should be properly sealed.

CCDC 2 – 2008 File 005213 5

Figure 8. CCDC Contract Forms

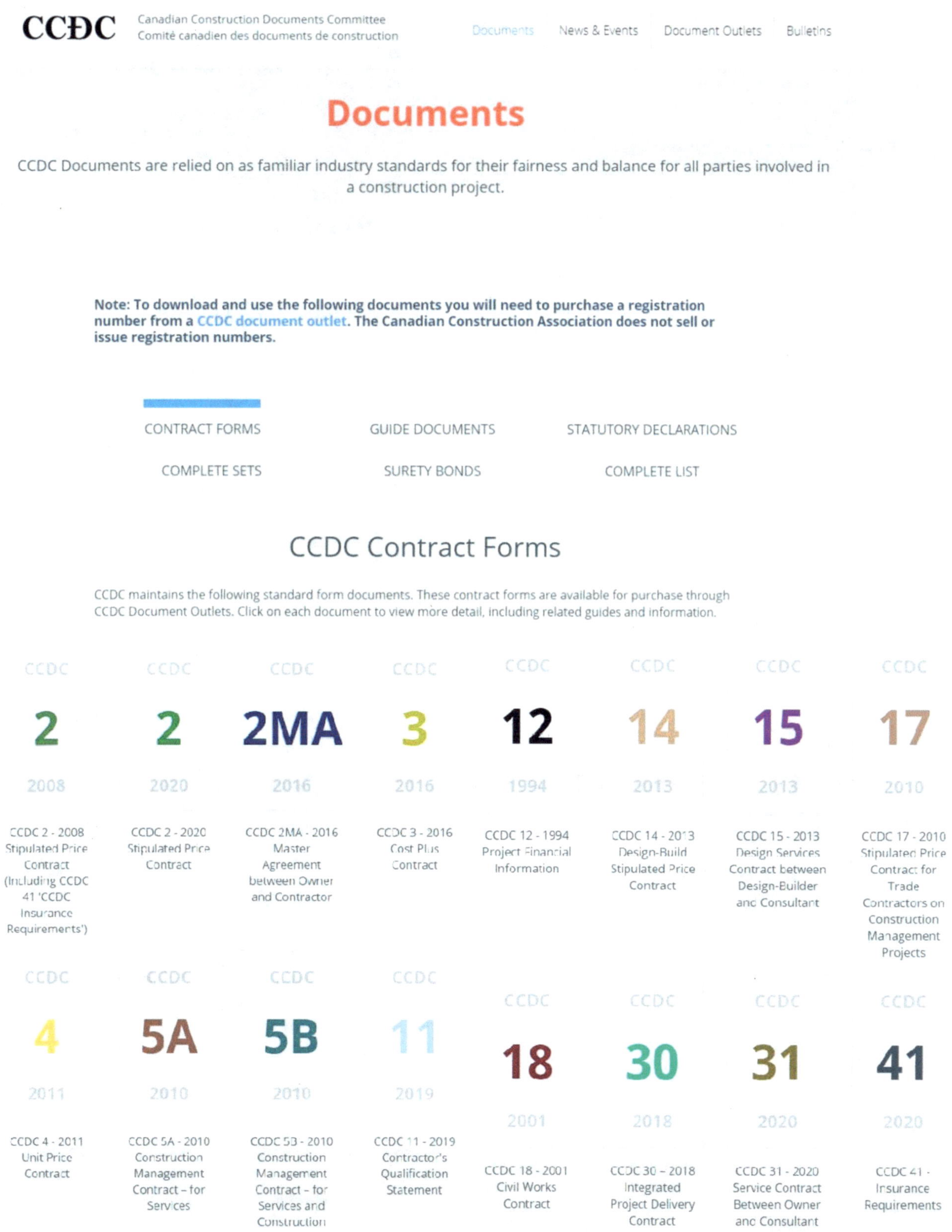

CCDC Canadian Construction Documents Committee
Comité canadien des documents de construction

Documents News & Events Document Outlets Bulletins

Documents

CCDC Documents are relied on as familiar industry standards for their fairness and balance for all parties involved in a construction project.

Note: To download and use the following documents you will need to purchase a registration number from a CCDC document outlet. The Canadian Construction Association does not sell or issue registration numbers.

CONTRACT FORMS GUIDE DOCUMENTS STATUTORY DECLARATIONS

COMPLETE SETS SURETY BONDS COMPLETE LIST

CCDC Contract Forms

CCDC maintains the following standard form documents. These contract forms are available for purchase through CCDC Document Outlets. Click on each document to view more detail, including related guides and information.

- CCDC 2 2008 — CCDC 2 - 2008 Stipulated Price Contract (Including CCDC 41 'CCDC Insurance Requirements')
- CCDC 2 2020 — CCDC 2 - 2020 Stipulated Price Contract
- CCDC 2MA 2016 — CCDC 2MA - 2016 Master Agreement between Owner and Contractor
- CCDC 3 2016 — CCDC 3 - 2016 Cost Plus Contract
- CCDC 12 1994 — CCDC 12 - 1994 Project Financial Information
- CCDC 14 2013 — CCDC 14 - 2013 Design-Build Stipulated Price Contract
- CCDC 15 2013 — CCDC 15 - 2013 Design Services Contract between Design-Builder and Consultant
- CCDC 17 2010 — CCDC 17 - 2010 Stipulated Price Contract for Trade Contractors on Construction Management Projects
- CCDC 4 2011 — CCDC 4 - 2011 Unit Price Contract
- CCDC 5A 2010 — CCDC 5A - 2010 Construction Management Contract – for Services
- CCDC 5B 2010 — CCDC 5B - 2010 Construction Management Contract – for Services and Construction
- CCDC 11 2019 — CCDC 11 - 2019 Contractor's Qualification Statement
- CCDC 18 2001 — CCDC 18 - 2001 Civil Works Contract
- CCDC 30 2018 — CCDC 30 – 2018 Integrated Project Delivery Contract
- CCDC 31 2020 — CCDC 31 - 2020 Service Contract Between Owner and Consultant
- CCDC 41 2020 — CCDC 41 - Insurance Requirements

Figure 9. Table of Content for a CCDC Contract

TABLE OF CONTENTS

AGREEMENT BETWEEN OWNER AND CONTRACTOR
A-1 The Work
A-2 Agreements and Amendments
A-3 Contract Documents
A-4 Contract Price
A-5 Payment
A-6 Receipt of and Addresses for Notices in Writing
A-7 Language of the Contract
A-8 Succession

DEFINITIONS
1. Change Directive
2. Change Order
3. Construction Equipment
4. Consultant
5. Contract
6. Contract Documents
7. Contract Price
8. Contract Time
9. Contractor
10. Drawings
11. Notice in Writing
12. Owner
13. Place of the Work
14. Product
15. Project
16. Provide
17. Shop Drawings
18. Specifications
19. Subcontractor
20. Substantial Performance of the Work
21. Supplemental Instruction
22. Supplier
23. Temporary Work
24. Value Added Taxes
25. Work
26. Working Day

GENERAL CONDITIONS OF THE STIPULATED PRICE CONTRACT

PART 1 GENERAL PROVISIONS
GC 1.1 Contract Documents
GC 1.2 Law of the Contract
GC 1.3 Rights and Remedies
GC 1.4 Assignment

PART 2 ADMINISTRATION OF THE CONTRACT
GC 2.1 Authority of the Consultant
GC 2.2 Role of the Consultant
GC 2.3 Review and Inspection of the Work
GC 2.4 Defective Work

PART 3 EXECUTION OF THE WORK
GC 3.1 Control of the Work
GC 3.2 Construction by Owner or Other Contractors
GC 3.3 Temporary Work
GC 3.4 Document Review
GC 3.5 Construction Schedule
GC 3.6 Supervision
GC 3.7 Subcontractors and Suppliers
GC 3.8 Labour and Products
GC 3.9 Documents at the Site
GC 3.10 Shop Drawings
GC 3.11 Use of the Work
GC 3.12 Cutting and Remedial Work
GC 3.13 Cleanup

PART 4 ALLOWANCES
GC 4.1 Cash Allowances
GC 4.2 Contingency Allowance

PART 5 PAYMENT
GC 5.1 Financing Information Required of the Owner
GC 5.2 Applications for Progress Payment
GC 5.3 Progress Payment
GC 5.4 Substantial Performance of the Work
GC 5.5 Payment of Holdback upon Substantial Performance of the Work
GC 5.6 Progressive Release of Holdback
GC 5.7 Final Payment
GC 5.8 Withholding of Payment
GC 5.9 Non-conforming Work

PART 6 CHANGES IN THE WORK
GC 6.1 Owner's Right to Make Changes
GC 6.2 Change Order
GC 6.3 Change Directive
GC 6.4 Concealed or Unknown Conditions
GC 6.5 Delays
GC 6.6 Claims for a Change in Contract Price

PART 7 DEFAULT NOTICE
GC 7.1 Owner's Right to Perform the Work, Terminate the Contractor's Right to Continue with the Work or Terminate the Contract
GC 7.2 Contractor's Right to Suspend the Work or Terminate the Contract

PART 8 DISPUTE RESOLUTION
GC 8.1 Authority of the Consultant
GC 8.2 Negotiation, Mediation and Arbitration
GC 8.3 Retention of Rights

PART 9 PROTECTION OF PERSONS AND PROPERTY
GC 9.1 Protection of Work and Property
GC 9.2 Toxic and Hazardous Substances
GC 9.3 Artifacts and Fossils
GC 9.4 Construction Safety
GC 9.5 Mould

PART 10 GOVERNING REGULATIONS
GC 10.1 Taxes and Duties
GC 10.2 Laws, Notices, Permits, and Fees
GC 10.3 Patent Fees
GC 10.4 Workers' Compensation

PART 11 INSURANCE AND CONTRACT SECURITY
GC 11.1 Insurance
GC 11.2 Contract Security

PART 12 INDEMNIFICATION, WAIVER OF CLAIMS AND WARRANTY
GC 12.1 Indemnification
GC 12.2 Waiver of Claims
GC 12.3 Warranty

The Canadian Construction Documents Committee (CCDC) is a national joint committee responsible for the development, production and review of standard Canadian construction contracts, forms and guides. Formed in 1974 the CCDC is made up of volunteer representatives from:

Public Sector Owners
Private Sector Owners
Canadian Bar Association (Ex-Officio)
* The Association of Canadian Engineering Companies
* The Canadian Construction Association
* Construction Specifications Canada
* The Royal Architectural Institute of Canada

*Committee policy and procedures are directed and approved by the four constituent national organizations.

CCDC 2 is the product of a consensus-building process aimed at balancing the interests of all parties on the construction project. It reflects recommended industry practices. CCDC 2 can have important consequences. The CCDC and its constituent member organizations do not accept any responsibility or liability for loss or damage which may be suffered as a result of the use or interpretation of CCDC 2.

CCDC-2(2008)

Appendices and attachments

The project management team adds annexes and attachments to the CCDC contract document in this section. Some of these appendices might be the RFP/RFQ Documents and some or all of the following documents if they were not part of the RFP documents.

Conflict of Interest Declaration Form

Confirmations

- I hereby confirm reading, acknowledging, and agreeing to the above items.
- I confirm that each of the Forms listed below have been reviewed and/or completed (as indicated) and are enclosed with the submission. Example Addenda, Forms Code of Conduct- Agreement to Bond, etc.
- I confirm that the Proponent, or any of its shareholders, directors, officers, subsidiaries, or affiliates, is not a party to any current litigation, anticipated litigation, or any other formal dispute resolution procedure with The Company or its subsidiaries.
- I confirm that I have authority to bind the Proponent and attest to the accuracy of the information provided in this Proposal.
- Etc.

Submission Form – Agreement To Bond

Used For Bids Over $Value Limits (Example Over $500,000.00)

1. Agreement to Bond

The Proponent must submit a completed Agreement to Bond (copy below) with their submission only if the bid submission is over $500,000.00. If the bid submission is less than $500,000.00, Proponents are not required to submit the Agreement to Bond.

2. Performance Security upon Award

Upon award for greater certainty, the successful Proponent will be required to provide the following performance security:

3. A Performance Bond

Issued by a Surety Company authorized to transact the business of suretyship in the Province of Ontario under the Owner's approved form, which is attached hereto and shall be in an amount equal to 50% of the Contract Price.

4. A Labour and Material Payment Bond

Issued by a Surety Company authorized to transact the business of suretyship in the Province of Ontario under the Owner's approved form attached hereto and shall be in an amount equal to 50% of the Contract Price.

SAMPLE 11. Agreement to Bond

Appendix I: Agreement to Bond

To:	THE CLIENT NAME	The Client
And to:	THE CONTRACTOR NAME	The Contractor

We, the undersigned, hereby undertake and agree to become bound as Surety for the Contractor in:

(a) a performance bond totaling **50%** of the total price and;
(b) a labour and material bond totaling **50%** of the total price
For the following bid:

RFP #	Description of the work and the Complete address
Name of the Bidder	

If THE COMPANY NAME accepts the bid mentioned above, the undersigned will execute the bond within seven (7) days of notification of acceptance of the bid.

Dated this _________ Day _________ 20 __

Name Of Surety Company:	
Name of Authorized Person:	
Signature of Authorized Person Signing for Surety) Attorney-in-Fact)	

SAMPLE 12. List Of Subcontractors

APPENDIX G – LIST OF SUBCONTRACTORS	
SUBCONTRACTOR 1	
COMPANY NAME:	
ADDRESS:	
CONTACT PERSON:	
CONTACT NUMBER:	
SCOPE OF WORK PERFORMED BY THIS SUBCONTRACTOR:	

SAMPLE 13. Scope Of Work Appendix

APPENDIX A – DELIVERABLES, SCOPE OF WORK and SPECIFICATIONS

A. Description of Deliverables

The RFP is an invitation to submit Proposals for the provision of Deliverables as described below:

Description of Deliverables required	Complete Project Description
Locations/Address(es) for delivery of Deliverables required	
Deliverables Start Date	
Deliverables End Date	

B. Material Disclosures

Proponents shall refer to Part 4 - Material Disclosures for additional information pertaining to the Deliverables, additional contractual requirements, and other factors that could impact their Proposals.

C. Scope of Work, Specifications, and Drawings

The Scope of Work, relevant specifications, and drawings are attached to this RFP as Appendix A. Please reference accordingly.

Please see the attached files indicated in Appendix A listed as follows:

1. Tender Drawings
2. Specification Documents Vol1
3. Specification Documents Vol 2
4. Communications Contractor's roster
5. Preferred List of Vendors
6. Etc.

Pricing Form

Pricing that is not adequately structured can trigger significant problems in evaluating offers and the contract results. Given the importance of price in the procurement process, purchasing agencies should fully integrate pricing into their procurement documents. The pricing is directly related to the goods and services required and how the customer would pay under the contract.

Submission Form of Pricing

Each Proponent must fully complete Submission Form - Pricing, which is attached as a separate file that summarizes the work scope with the quantities of deliverables.

Table 6. Quote Submission Form

LOGO	Submission Form – Pricing RFP # project #
Project Description	
Address	

ACTIVITY	UNIT OF MEASUREMENT	QTY	UNIT PRICE	SUBTOTAL
Division 01- General Conditions				
Mobilization & Demobilization	L.S.	1		
Bondings, Insurances, Health & Safety, Samples, Permits, Warranties, As-built DWG, etc.	L.S	1		
Division 03- Concrete				
Footing and foundation walls	M3			
S.O.G.	M3			
Exterior Blocks	EA			
Division 04- Masonry				
As per Plans and Specs	L.S.			
Division 06- Wood				
Wood Framings	L.S.			
Division 22- Plumbing				
Demolition associated with plumbing and drainage work.	L.S.	1		
Supply and installation of all other piping, plumbing equipment, and accessories as specified, including cut and patch repairs as required	L.S.	1		
Division 26- Electrical				
Electrical Distribution Major Equipment (Switchboard, ATS, Panels, Disconnect Switches)	L.S.	1		
Major Equipment Cabling and Wiring including cut and patch where required)	L.S.	1		
Allowances				
Brick Repairs	M2	50	$10	$500
Patch, repair and make good	M2	150	$100	$15,000
Total				

Vendor Evaluation Form

A Vendor can be a Contractor, Consultant, or Supplier, as the case demands. The purpose of the Vendor Performance Evaluation (VPE) Form is to provide an evaluative record, both positive and negative, of a vendor's performance throughout the project's life cycle.

The Vendor Performance Evaluation VPE is a standardized internal tool to encourage vendors to improve their performance. It will be used consistently across all the Company's divisions to assess performance and consider a vendor's eligibility for future awards.

VPE evaluations are conducted by the Company's Management staff with oversight from Senior Division Management and the Purchasing & Materials Management Division.

Many companies include the VPE model in their tender documents as a reminder tool for suppliers to do their work in the customer's best interest.

The expected frequency of performing a CPE (For Contractors) will be communicated to the contractor at the pre-construction meeting. Only the determined number of CPE reports will be issued to the contractor for CPE evaluation purposes.

An appropriate measure of weight has been allocated to each criterion and used in the evaluation process to calculate the score.

Example: Safety 25%; Quality 25%; Organization 12.5%; Execution 25%; Administration 12.5%.

SAMPLE 14. Contractor Performance Evaluation

CPE Performance Contractor Evaluation Form

Contractor Name: ☐Final ☐Progressive

Project Name:

Description:

Contract No: Contract Value: **Date:**

Start Date: Completion Date:

Rate on a scale of 1 to 4 for the following 10 criteria:

Passing Score >70%

1: Unsatisfactory (does not meet the expressed needs) Provide Justification Documents 25%

2: Acceptable (partially meets the expressed needs) 50%

3: Satisfactory (meets all expressed needs) 75%

4: Very satisfactory (meets all expressed needs and sometimes exceeds them). Provide Justification Documents 100%

N/A: not applicable

Description	1	2	3	4	N/A
1. **Schedule:** Respect the required deadlines and deliveries.					
2. **Safety Compliance:** Comply with Safety requirements.					
3. **Quality Compliance:** Comply with Drawings and Specs.					
4. **Quality Compliance:** Correct defective work as the project progresses.					
5. **Safety Compliance:** Comply with Safety requirements.					
6. **Change Management:** Timely Request for Information.					
7. **Change Management:** Timely Quotations and Reasonably Change order values. Seek Authorization to perform additional work.					
8. **Communication:** Properly communicate with the project team and respond to all site and management inquiries.					
9. **Communication:** Present in all meetings.					
10. **Closeout Documents:** Submit all required end-of-contract documents as described in the specifications and contract documents.					

Position	Name	Signature	Date

Occupational Health and Safety

Appendices are attached to the contract documents to ensure the parts that the contractor is responsible for the safety of the project.

Site Applications for Contract Documents

The Owner shall provide the Contractor, without charge, sufficient copies of the Contract Documents to perform the Work.

Models made by a sub-trade for the consultant's approval remain the property of the owner. The Consultant will have authority to act on behalf of the Owner only to the extent provided in the Contract Documents.

In a contract between the owner and a General Contractor (GC), this contract will not contain a relationship between the Owner and the subcontractor.

In a contract between the General Contractor (GC) and a Subcontractor, this contract will not contain a relationship between the Consultant and the Contractor.

The Contractor has to give access to the owner or the owner's consultant during construction.
If work is designated for tests, inspections, or approvals in the Contract Documents, or by the Consultant's instructions, or by the laws or ordinances of the Place of the Work, the Contractor shall give the Consultant reasonable notification of when the work will be ready for review and inspection. The Contractor shall arrange for and shall provide the Consultant reasonable notification of the date and time of inspections by other authorities.

The contractor has to remove defective work from the place of work.

If the Consultant's opinion is not practical to correct defective work or work is not performed as provided in the Contract Documents, the Owner may deduct from the amount otherwise due to the Contractor's difference in value between the work as performed and that called for by the Contract Documents. If the Owner and the Contractor do not agree on the difference in value, they shall refer the matter to the Consultant for a determination.

The Contractor shall have total control of the Work and shall effectively direct and supervise the Work to ensure conformity with the Contract Documents.

The Contractor shall be solely responsible for construction means, methods, techniques, sequences, and procedures and coordinating the various parts of the Work under the Contract.

The Owner reserves the right to award separate contracts connected with other parts of the Project to other contractors and perform work with their forces.

Conflict In the Contract Documents

If there is a conflict within the Contract Documents, the order of priority of documents, from highest to lowest, shall be:

- The Agreement between the Owner and the Contractor,
- The Definitions, – Supplementary Conditions,
- The General Conditions, – Division 1 of the Specifications,
- Technical Specifications – material and finishing schedules,
- The Drawings

SECTION 3
PROJECT STAKEHOLDER MANAGEMENT

In this section, the book will deal with internal and external stakeholder management.

An example of the roles and responsibilities of the consultant and the constructor (builder) will be described.

CHAPTER 4 - STAKEHOLDER MANAGEMENT

Background

Projects do not exist in isolation. Even if there is a defined brief, budget, program, and scope of work, the project is still subject to external influences. The project exists within a 'political' environment, populated by all those with a particular stake or interest in the project's outcome. This political environment and the expectations of stakeholders represent a significant risk to a project.

In construction projects, stakeholders can include:

- Users of a building
- Funders
- Neighbours
- Regulatory bodies
- General public
- Tenants
- Etc.

The checklist of stakeholders in a construction project is often extensive. It includes the owners and facility users, project management, team members, facilities managers, designers, shareholders, public administration, workers, subcontractors, services suppliers, competitors, banks insurance companies, media, community representatives, neighbors, the general public, clients, regional development agencies. Each one of these could influence the course of the project.

Defining stakeholders from the start of the project is crucial to improve communication. For example, the customer representative should liaise with the appropriate stakeholder channels. If this task is not done correctly, approving the design at different stages results in a lengthy process.

Internal Stakeholders

Internal stakeholders are the team members of the project or those who provide for its financing. Internal stakeholders are entities within a business (e.g., employees, managers, the board of directors, investors).

Managing internal stakeholders is often more problematic than managing external stakeholders. In construction projects, it is often difficult to identify who the customer is. There may be a single designated point of contact, but this person is not really the "customer," just the organization's representative.

External Stakeholders

External stakeholders are people or organizations who are not part of the client organization but are interested in the project. These are perhaps the most easily recognized stakeholder groups. For publicly funded projects, the number of stakeholders that can be identified is high. These generally consist of:

Funders, whether a government department, grant provider, or private sector partner.

- Users, whether they are passengers for a transport project or visitors to a museum.
- Regulatory authorities. Most often, planning authorities and specialized regulatory authorities, for example, those involved in railway projects.
- People affected, who may be neighbors or people working or living nearby.
- The press and media are other important groups that can significantly influence the perception of the project and its perceived and, in some cases, actual success.

It is relatively easy to identify forty individual stakeholder groups for a large public project, although private sector projects tend to have fewer. One of the main issues with stakeholder management is the large number of people involved; their levels of power and interest differ considerably.

Managing Stakeholders

Managing the stakeholder environment is a highly complex management task. Like all business models, the main advantage of stakeholder analysis is that it helps understand a complicated situation and thus helps project managers and teams to manage and communicate with stakeholders in the most effective manner.

A typical format for a project communication plan is given below. The project manager can use the results of the stakeholder analysis exercise to help define the recommended approach and course of action. This makes it possible to determine the communication channels' clarity and ensure consistency on a large project.

Table 7. Stakeholder Communication Plan

COMMUNICATION PLAN				
Stakeholder	**Reason Consultation/ Communication**	**Likely Impact on the project**	**Recommended Action Plan**	**Owner**
Organization or Individual.	The reason we need to communicate with them. For example, to get their approval.	Supportive or otherwise. Whether they have a particular interest in the project.	Who needs to talk to whom, what information needs to be provided? Who is responsible for doing this?	Responsible

CHAPTER 5 - ROLES AND RESPONSIBILITIES

To understand how to develop a plan for stakeholders, it is crucial to know the rights and responsibilities of each stakeholder. This book takes a look at the most common stakeholders involved in the construction and design industry.

The principal parties involved in a Construction Contract are:

- **The Owner**, an individual, firm, or corporation commissions a construction work and pays for its cost.
- **The ARCHITECT or ENGINEER** representing the OWNER furnishes the professional and technical skills required for planning the work and preparing the drawings and specifications for its construction, administration of the contract, and to review the construction work.
- **The Contractor** who, together with those sub-trades he elects to employ, provides the materials, labour, equipment, and skills for the physical accomplishment of the project, taking financial risks an OWNER will not usually take.

This Chapter aims to consider both the duties and liabilities of the Architect or Engineer not only to the Owner but also to the Contractor.

What is a consultant?

A Consultant is the architect, the engineer, or entity licensed to practice in the province or territory of the Place of the Work and engaged by the Client to provide all or part of the Design Services.

The architect must economically plan a building. They must be highly technical and knowledgeable in the structural type of buildings, building materials, and construction methods. As buildings have become more complicated over the past 75 years, engineers have become specialists in structural design, heating-ventilation-cooling, and electrical. The engineer must apply scientific principles to the design of developing structures, machines, or manufacturing processes.

Architects will contract the services of specialty engineers, but the architect is responsible for the coordination and design of the entire project. Architects and engineers are subject to duties imposed on them by Statute Law; therefore, they are subject to violation of Public Rights (criminal nature) and Private Rights (civil nature).

Duties of the Consultant

1. **Programming/Deciding What to Build**
   The owner and architect discuss the requirements for the project, including:
   - the function of the spaces
   - size requirements
   - testing the fit between the owner's needs, wants, and budget

2. **Schematic Design/Rough Sketches**
   - The architect prepares a series of rough sketches, known as schematic design, which show the general arrangement of rooms and the site. Some architects also prepare models to help visualize the project.
   - The owner approves these sketches before proceeding with the next phase.

3. **Design Development/Refining the Design**
   - The architect prepares more detailed drawings to illustrate other aspects of the proposed design. Floor plans show all the rooms in the correct size and shape. Outline specifications are prepared, listing the principal materials and room finishes.

4. **Preparation of Construction Documents**
   - Once the homeowner has approved the design, the architect prepares detailed drawings and specifications, which the contractor will use to establish actual construction costs and build the project.
   - These drawings and specifications become part of the building contract.

5. **Tender the Project**
   - Once the architect has prepared the bidding documents and invitations to bid and instructions to bidders, the project can be put out to tender. The architect recommends the contractor likely from among several contractors they've asked to submit bids on the project on behalf of the owner.

6. **Construction Administration**
   While the contractor will physically build the project, the architect can assist the owner in making sure that the project is built according to the plans and specifications. The architect can make site visits to:
   - confirm the quality of work performed by the contractor
   - observe construction, review and approve the contractor's applications for payment
   - generally, keep the owner informed of the project's progress.

Authority of The Consultant

Extracted From CCD - GC 2.1:

- The Consultant will have authority to act on behalf of the Owner only to the extent provided in the Contract Documents.
- The duties, responsibilities, and limitations of authority of the Consultant as outlined in the Contract Documents shall be modified or extended only with the written consent of the Owner, the Contractor, and the Consultant.
- The Consultant will provide administration of the Contract as described in the Contract Documents.
- The Consultant will visit the Place of the Work at intervals appropriate to the progress of construction to become familiar with the progress and quality of the work and to determine if the Work is proceeding in general conformity with the Contract Documents.
- If the Owner and the Consultant agree, the Consultant will provide at the Place of the Work one or more project representatives to assist in carrying out the Consultant's responsibilities. The duties, obligations, and limitations of authority of such project representatives shall be as outlined in writing to the Contractor.
- The Consultant will promptly inform the Owner of the date of receipt of the Contractor's applications for payment.
- The Consultant will be, in the first instance, the interpreter of the requirements of the Contract Documents.
- Matters in question relating to the performance of Work or the interpretation of the Contract Documents shall be initially referred in writing to the Consultant by the party raising the question for interpretations and findings and copied to the other party.
  The Consultant's interpretations and findings will be given in writing to the parties within a reasonable time.
- With respect to claims for a change in Contract Price, the Consultant will make findings as set out in GC 6.6 – CLAIMS FOR A CHANGE IN CONTRACT PRICE.
- The Consultant will have authority to reject work that, in the Consultant's opinion, does not conform to the requirements of the Contract Documents.
- During the progress of the Work, the Consultant will furnish Supplemental Instructions to the Contractor with reasonable promptness or in accordance with a schedule for such instructions agreed to by the Consultant and the Contractor.
- The Consultant will review and take appropriate action upon Shop Drawings, samples, and other Contractor's submittals, in accordance with the Contract Documents.
- The Consultant will prepare Change Orders and Change Directives.
- The Consultant will conduct reviews of the Work to determine the date of Substantial Performance of the Work.
- The Consultant will receive and review written warranties and related documents required by the Contract and provided by the Contractor, and will forward such warranties and documents to the Owner for the Owner's acceptance.

Pros and Cons for Employee versus External Consultant

Some of the advantages and disadvantages for an employee versus an external consultant from an employer's point of view are as below.

Table 8. Internal Employee VS. Hiring a Consultant

EMPLOYEE	EXTERNAL CONSULTANT
Usually works for only one employer.	Generally provides consulting services to more than one company.
Works the hours set by the employer	Sets his or her own hours.
Usually works at the employer's place of business.	Works out of his or her own office or home.
Often receives employment benefits, such as health and disability insurance.	Does not receive employment benefits from the employer.
Works under the control and direction of the employer.	Works relatively independently.
Accomplishes tasks in the manner the employer has requested.	Has the authority to decide how to go about accomplishing tasks and does so without the employer's input.

Who is a constructor?

The Occupational Health and Safety Act intends to have one person with overall authority for health and safety matters on a project. This person is the constructor of the project.

Section 1 of the Act defines a "constructor" as "a person who undertakes a project for an owner and includes an owner who undertakes all or part of a project by himself or by more than one employer." The dictionary definition for "undertake" is "make oneself responsible for," which means a constructor is a person who is responsible for a project. The definition of "employer" in section 1 of the Act includes contractors and subcontractors.

The constructor is the party with the most significant degree of control over health and safety during the entire project. He is ultimately responsible for the health and safety of all workers. The constructor must ensure that all the employers and workers on the project comply with the Act and its regulations.

The Client adds clauses and agreements for the general contractor to become the project's constructor. The contractor is entitled to additional charges if he is prepared to take on more safety responsibilities.

SECTION 4
PROJECT INTEGRATION MANAGEMENT

Project Integration Management includes the processes and activities needed to be created to develop a Project Charter, develop a Project Management Plan, direct and manage Project Execution, monitor and control project work and close the project.

Project integration management is high-level work that the project manager does, and it involves managing interdependencies among the other knowledge areas.

The project management processes do not happen independently. For example, a new resource added to the project may require changes in cost or schedule, or both.

In dealing with such situations, the project manager integrates the processes of project management. The need for integration drives much of the communication and the work of the project manager.

CHAPTER 6 - INTEGRATION MANAGEMENT

Project Charter

A project charter is a formal document based on the Statement Of Work (S.O.W.) submitted for authorization. It gives the project manager the authority to spend the project budget on delivering the project. Project charter objectives address the "why, who, what, when, where, and how" of the project.

Figure 10. S.O.W VS Project Charter

	STATEMENT OF WORK S.O.W	PROJECT CHARTER
WHAT IS IT?	A document to set an agreement between a client and agency. It's the project Contract.	A formal document based on the Statement of Work.
PURPOSE?	Addresses the business need for the project and what's included or not included.	It gives the Project Manager the authority to spend the budget.
WHAT'S IN IT?	For the Project. Includes : - Scope - Proposed deliverables - Project Assumptions - Proposed Exclusions - Proposed Criteria for acceptance	For the Project. Includes: -Why? - Who? - What? - When? - Where? - How?

The Benefits of Project Charters for Project Managers & Teams

- **Helps determine project value:** helps you decide whether it's worthwhile to carry out or propose the project.
- **Saves time down the road:** The time spent at the start of the project, defining the project charter will reduce troubleshooting during project execution.
- **Gives you budget clarity:** ensures that funding is available and will be released on time. Settle your spending authority and budgets before starting the project.
- **Helps you give clear guidelines to your team**: The milestones and criteria for measurement provide invaluable guidance to your team as you begin to brief out the project.
- **Inspires confidence:** gives the team assurance that they're working under an effective and well-organized project manager.
- **Boosts team morale:** A team working under a sloppy charter will repeatedly find themselves confused, with their hard work wasted or headed in the wrong direction. A well-written charter gives clear guidelines for success that your team can feel motivated and confident to work toward.

Project Charter Examples

SAMPLE 15. Project Charter- Notice of Contract

Notice of Contracts/Project Charter	
Title	Justice Facility
Address	San Francisco
Owner	Government of USA
Reference	Project Number 1496
Value	$3,000,000
Bond	Yes
Tender	Bid RFP# 123
Type	Building
Project Manager	Ihab Antabli
Project Director	John Smith
General Director	Jack Balance
Date Awarded	2019-01-17
Start date	2019-04-15
End date	2019-12-31
# Employees (Internal)	8
Authorization Purchase ($) Superintendent	$10,000
Authorization Purchase ($) Project Manager	$40,000
Authorization Purchase ($) Director	$250,000
Authorization Purchase ($) General Director	>$250,000
Plans and Specs	DWG-A1-A36. E1-E20. P1-P16. M001-M015. File No. DSL002256

Date Issued 2019-01-25

Signed in .... by the General Director ...

..Jack Balance.........

Table 9. Project Charter

<table>
<tr><th colspan="4">PROJECT CHARTER</th></tr>
<tr><th>ITEMS</th><th colspan="2">DESCRIPTIONS</th><th>REFERENCE(1)</th></tr>
<tr><td>PROJECT NAME</td><td colspan="2">JUSTICE FACILITY IN SUDBURY</td><td>Bidding Process</td></tr>
<tr><td>PROJECT OBJECTIVES</td><td colspan="2">A new construction project including earthworks, civil and landscape works, Structural and Mechanical construction</td><td>Cost Estimation</td></tr>
<tr><td>PROJECT CONSIDERED SUCCESSFUL WHEN</td><td colspan="2">- The project is completed on time and budget considering 12% of profit and overhead,
- Conformity log is answered on time,
- Lessons Learned are well documented, saved, and communicated,
- Client Satisfaction > 95%</td><td>Quality Plan</td></tr>
<tr><td rowspan="2">PROJECT PARTICIPANTS</td><th>Title:</th><th>Name:</th><td rowspan="2">Communication Plan

Stakeholder Plan</td></tr>
<tr><td>Owner
Project Manager
Project Director
Consultants:
1-Architect
2-Engineer
3- Etc.
Approvals:
1- Municipality Project Manager:
2- Region Project Manager:
3- Etc.
Account Payable
Team Member:
Superintendent:
Etc.</td><td></td></tr>
<tr><td>AVAILABLEBLE RESOURCES</td><td colspan="2">Budget : $10,000,000</td><td></td></tr>
<tr><td rowspan="3">MILESTONES</td><td>Project Start Date:</td><td></td><td rowspan="3">Time Management Plan.</td></tr>
<tr><td>Project End Date:</td><td></td></tr>
<tr><td>Project Close out Date:</td><td></td></tr>
<tr><td>POTENTIAL RISKS</td><td colspan="2">1- The team may not meet deadlines due to the unforeseen COVID 19 Waves
2- Over budget due to extending project schedule (See Risk Management Plan for corrective action and preventive measures)</td><td>Risk Management Plan</td></tr>
<tr><td rowspan="4">APPROVALS AND AUTHORITIES</td><th>Title and Name:</th><th>Thresholds</th><td rowspan="4">Procurement Management</td></tr>
<tr><td>Project Manager</td><td>$20,000</td></tr>
<tr><td>Project Director</td><td>$250,000</td></tr>
<tr><td>V.P.</td><td>> $250,000</td></tr>
</table>

Some companies perform integration management through their system while existing processes are in place. If the company has a quality department, the quality department creates methods for all the principal administrative and management elements. We will see more examples in the Quality Management section. Small businesses, however, can send a PDF file with information as the company finds it necessary to present the stakeholders and responsibilities of the project. A project charter usually focuses on the project manager for spending and control. However, a more complicated example is explained below, which some companies use to ensure project integration, communication, and responsibilities for the main stages of the project.

Table 10. Contract Review (Project Charter)

Contract Review					
Project Number 005	Building a Justice Facility	Address: Toronto–	Start Date:	Completion Date:	
Internal Stake Holders					
Project Manager:	Ihab	Construction Super:	Emile	Foreman:	Martin
Project Director:	Kevin:	Buyer:	Chris	Estimator:	Luis
Accountant:	John	Design and Engineer:	Construction Only project	Etc.	
External Stake Holders					
Client:	ABC Company:	Client Representative:	Conrad	Consultant Company:	SYZ
Consultant Rep.:	To come	Etc.			

Description	Completed Yes/No	Responsibility	Comments
Budget	Yes	Project Manager (PM)	Working on the Forecasting
Schedule	No	PM	
Quality Plan Including the list for close-out documents, warrantees, Manuals, etc...	No	PM	
Prevention Program (Health and safety)	No	Safety Consultant and PM	

Notice of Project/Project Opening with the Ministry of Labor	No	PM	
Pre-Construction Meeting/ Kick-off meeting	No	PM	Invitation sent to all stakeholders
Employee On-Board	No	Quality Dep. & PM	3 new employees
Training ISO	NO	Quality Dep.	3 new employees
Other Training	No	Quality Dep.	3 new employees: -Health and Safety Basic Training - Fall Protection Training - System Training - etc.
Purchasing Materials	No	Site Super/Project Manager	Through requisition form to be sent to the buyer, follow project charter for authorization limits
Sub-contractor List	Yes	Estimator	To be updated by the PM
List of labor required	NO	PM	
Signature Specimen	Yes		
Authorization limits	Yes	Project Director	Sent with the Project Charter
Request for Insurances	N/A		
Received Insurances	Yes	Estimator and Design/Engineering	
Request Bonds	N/A		
Received Bonds	Yes	Estimator and Design/Engineering	
Client Satisfaction Form	No	PM	At the end of the Project
Closeout documents	No	PM	At the end of the Project
Post Mortem Report	No	PM	At the end of the Project
Contractor/Subcontractor Evaluation Form	No	PM	At the end of the Project
Consultant Evaluation Form	No	PM	At the end of the Project

Date Issued 2019-01-25

Signed in .... by the General Director

..Jack Balance........

SECTION 5
PROJECT SCOPE MANAGEMENT

CHAPTER 7 - SCOPE MANAGEMENT

Project Scope Management includes the processes required to ensure that the project consists of all the work required and only the work necessary to complete the project.

Example of real-life Scope Management.

Collect Requirements

Defining and documenting stakeholders' needs to meet the project objectives.

A. Understand the Project Charter for the project – Examples are given in the Project Integration Management section.
   i. You know the spending authorization levels of the project team.
   ii. Super $10K; PM $40K; etc.
B. General project responsibilities are defined and will be further monitored and tested in the Project Management Quality section; Example:
   i. Superintendent can request materials using a specific form or through the system.
   ii. The Project Manager should prepare a site budget
   iii. The Project Manager should prepare a schedule
   iv. The Project Manager should negotiate and award the contract
   v. Etc.

Define Scope

A. The Project Charter provides a high-level project description. It also contains project approval requirements.
B. Create a project organization chart inside your company chart.

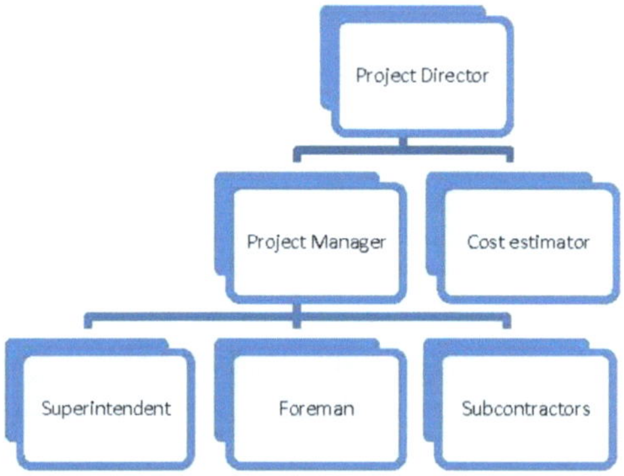

C. Progressively elaborate the **schedule**

   i. Use MS Project or other available software

   ii. Create a Work Breakdown Structure **(WBS)** for your Project.

   Activities need to be well defined, have clear start and end dates.

   1. Example Cladding EIFS system, 45 days
   2. Example of WBS

Create Work Breakdown Structure (WBS)

SAMPLE 16. WBS Contractor

Example :

1.0 Infrastructure Facility

1.1 Civil Work

1.1.1 Site Preparation

1.1.1.1 Clear Site

1.1.1.2 Survey & Layout

1.1.1.3 Rough grade

1.1.2 Excavation

1.1.2.1 Excavate for sewer

1.1.2.2 Excavate elec. Manholes.

1.1.2.3 Drill well

   iii. Identify **Milestones**. (with Zero time) Examples

   1. Foundation walls ready for City's inspection
   2. Appointing Sub-Contractor
   3. Completing design Stage
   4. Client approvals
   5. Draw time (the date that the contractor will issue).
   6. Etc.

SAMPLE 17. Schedule MS PROJECT

In the example schedule below, the customer requires invoices to be sent at the end of specific items and not monthly.

Read the plans and specifications and get a clear idea of the main things to follow; Identity Milestones; Examples: inspection milestones, shop drawing requirements, creation of a list of necessary guarantees, warrantees, list of subcontractors, list of equipment, list of employees, a complete list of stakeholders, frequency of meetings, notices and invitations to get and others to be sent, etc.

Figure 11. Schedule by Microsoft Project

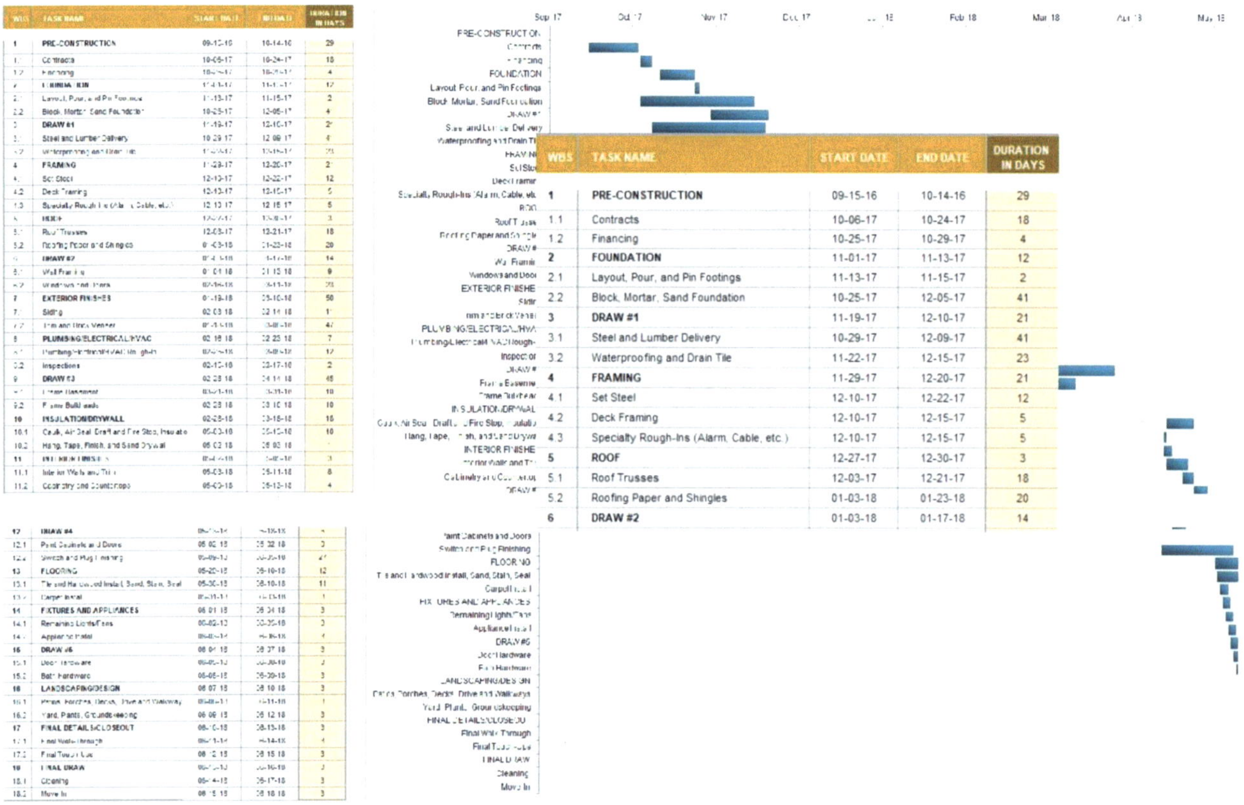

WBS	TASK NAME	START DATE	END DATE	DURATION IN DAYS
1	PRE-CONSTRUCTION	09-15-16	10-14-16	29
1.1	Contracts	10-06-17	10-24-17	18
1.2	Financing	10-25-17	10-29-17	4
2	FOUNDATION	11-01-17	11-13-17	12
2.1	Layout, Pour, and Pin Footings	11-13-17	11-15-17	2
2.2	Block, Mortar, Sand Foundation	10-25-17	12-05-17	41
3	DRAW #1	11-19-17	12-10-17	21
3.1	Steel and Lumber Delivery	10-29-17	12-09-17	41
3.2	Waterproofing and Drain Tile	11-22-17	12-15-17	23
4	FRAMING	11-29-17	12-20-17	21
4.1	Set Steel	12-10-17	12-22-17	12
4.2	Deck Framing	12-10-17	12-15-17	5
4.3	Specialty Rough-Ins (Alarm, Cable, etc.)	12-10-17	12-15-17	5
5	ROOF	12-27-17	12-30-17	3
5.1	Roof Trusses	12-03-17	12-21-17	18
5.2	Roofing Paper and Shingles	01-03-18	01-23-18	20
6	DRAW #2	01-03-18	01-17-18	14
6.1	Wall Framing	01-04-18	01-13-18	9
6.2	Windows and Doors	02-16-18	03-11-18	23
7	EXTERIOR FINISHES	01-19-18	03-10-18	50
7.1	Siding	02-03-18	02-14-18	11
7.2	Trim and Brick Veneer	01-18-18	03-06-18	47
8	PLUMBING/ELECTRICAL/HVAC	02-16-18	02-23-18	7
8.1	Plumbing/Electrical/HVAC Rough-In	02-25-18	03-09-18	12
8.2	Inspections	02-15-18	02-17-18	2
9	DRAW #3	02-28-18	04-14-18	45
9.1	Frame Basement	03-21-18	03-31-18	10
9.2	Frame Bulkheads	02-28-18	03-10-18	10
10	INSULATION/DRYWALL	02-28-18	03-18-18	18
10.1	Caulk, Air Seal, Draft and Fire Stop, Insulatio	05-03-18	05-13-18	10
10.2	Hang, Tape, Finish, and Sand Drywall	05-02-18	05-03-18	1
11	INTERIOR FINISHES	05-02-18	05-05-18	3
11.1	Interior Walls and Trim	05-03-18	05-11-18	8
11.2	Cabinetry and Countertops	05-09-18	05-13-18	4
12	DRAW #4	05-13-18	05-18-18	5
12.1	Paint Cabinets and Doors	05-02-18	05-02-18	0
12.2	Switch and Plug Finishing	05-09-18	06-05-18	27
13	FLOORING	05-29-18	06-10-18	12
13.1	Tile and Hardwood Install, Sand, Stain, Seal	05-30-18	06-10-18	11
13.2	Carpet Install	05-31-18	06-03-18	3
14	FIXTURES AND APPLIANCES	06-01-18	06-04-18	3
14.1	Remaining Lights/Fans	06-02-18	06-05-18	3
14.2	Appliance Install	06-03-18	06-06-18	3
15	DRAW #5	06-04-18	06-07-18	3
15.1	Door Hardware	06-05-18	06-08-18	3
15.2	Bath Hardware	06-06-18	06-09-18	3
16	LANDSCAPING/DESIGN	06-07-18	06-10-18	3
16.1	Patios, Porches, Decks, Drive and Walkway	06-08-18	06-11-18	3
16.2	Yard, Plants, Groundskeeping	06-09-18	06-12-18	3
17	FINAL DETAILS/CLOSEOUT	06-10-18	06-13-18	3
17.1	Final Walk-Through	06-11-18	06-14-18	3
17.2	Final Touch-Ups	06-12-18	06-15-18	3
18	FINAL DRAW	06-13-18	06-16-18	3
18.1	Cleaning	06-14-18	06-17-18	3
18.2	Move-In	06-15-18	06-18-18	3

Verify Scope

Once the scope is well defined according to the above steps, check and revise at any point in the project. For example, the schedule can be created when all contracts are not awarded, and then when more contracts are in place, a project manager will do more revisions to the schedule. Another example is the continuous reading of plans and specifications and observing necessary modifications or milestones. A project manager can redo these steps throughout the project. A business-quality plan that reminds the project manager of all the steps to take is helpful if it exists.

Control Scope

The process of monitoring the status of the project and product scope and managing changes to the scope baseline. The book will provide illustrations in the Quality, Time, and Cost Management Sections.

SECTION 6
PROJECT TIME MANAGEMENT

Project time management includes the processes necessary to manage the timely completion of the project.

Time management is the management of the time spent and progress made on project tasks and activities. Excellent time management requires planning, scheduling, monitoring, and controlling of all project activities.

Managing time is an integral part of task management. It helps to break down projects, assigning tasks, and completing the projects on time. Fortunately, with a bit of effort, you can implement time management strategies that not only make you more efficient but might make your working life more enjoyable.

CHAPTER 8 - TIME MANAGEMENT

Calculating Activity Duration (PERT)

PERT (Program Evaluation Review Technique), which breaks down individual project tasks for analysis, is usually explained during the introduction to time management.

When you estimate activity duration, you consider either an optimistic or a pessimistic approach. You can also consider both for different stakeholders. PERT suggests a formula to estimate each activity better. Duration = (optimistic time + 4 * most likely time + pessimistic time) / 6. (OT + 4 * MLT + PT) / 6.

Controlling the timeline (Schedule)

Time Management interacts with all other knowledge areas. Project Managers are controlling the schedule by updating it regularly.

Real-Life Examples:

Preconstruction meeting

When awarding contracts (the main subcontractors are on board), the project manager can call a pre-construction meeting or kick-off meeting to introduce the stakeholders to the other contractors and ask for deadlines to update the schedule. This task will speed up the project and start as soon as possible. Note any conflict between major contractors and call for a separate meeting to coordinate between them. Everything should be recorded at the pre-build meeting and progress meetings afterward.

SAMPLE 18. Preconstruction Meeting

Sample general contractor pre-construction meeting template

Preconstruction meeting minutes
Construction of a road with a New Training Center Structure. Parking areas and Landscaping around the facility.
Project Name and Number:...................................
Address:...
Date:...
Attendance:..
Distribution..
1. Project Team
General Contractor:...........................
Project Manager (PM):..........Tel......................E-mail..............
Superintendent:..........Tel......................E-mail..............
Foreman:..........Tel......................E-mail..............
Accountant:..........Tel......................E-mail..............
Project Manager Back-up:..........Tel......................E-mail..............

Owner Representative:
Project Manager ....Tel.......................E-mail...............

Safety Consultant: ....
Project Manager: ....

Civil engineering Consultant:
Project Manager: ....
Structure Consultant:
Project Manager: ....
Landscape Consultant:
Project Manager: ....
Architectural Consultant:
Project Manager: ....
Project Description:
Construction of a road with a New Training Center Structure. Parking areas and Landscaping around the facility.

Correspondences:
Points of contact for all correspondence and queries – Consultant. And cc'd to PM

<u>**2. Notification to Agencies**</u>
Ministry of Labor – Notice of Project (to be posted on-site)

Public Works
Project Manager: ....Tel.......................E-mail...............

Municipality
Project Manager: ....Tel.......................E-mail...............
Engineer: ....Tel.......................E-mail...............

Cable TV Company (e.g., Rogers)
...........Tel.......................E-mail...............

Gas Company (e.g., Enbridge):
...........Tel.......................E-mail...............

Internet Company (e.g., Bell Canada):
...........Tel.......................E-mail...............

Police
Phone:...............................
Fax:.................................
After Hours:...............................
Emergency: 911

Fire Department
Phone:...............................
Fax:.................................
Emergency: 911

Ambulance:
Phone:...............................
Fax:.................................
Emergency: 911

3. Work Schedule/ Working Hours.
Work Schedule –
Proposed start date: For Civil Works....................For Building..............
Proposed Substantial Completion date:..................
Working hours: Monday – Friday from 8:00 am to 5:00 pm. Noisy construction activities shall not start before 8:30 a.m.
THE PM MUST APPROVE ANY AFTER-HOURS WORK.

4. Completion Date:...

5. Construction process:
Types of equipment....................................
Schedule explanation..............................
Note 1: Bell, Rogers, and Civil Contractor must hold a separate meeting on site.

Note 2: The concrete block contractor and the steel structure contractor must coordinate the drawings. When the shop drawings are ready at the draft stage, an electronic invitation will be sent to meet at the steel structure contractor's office. The concrete block contractor asked if he could charge all site visits to the steel fabricator as an extra; PM has asked the contractor to send an RFI (inquiry), and it will be answered after reviewing the terms of the contract. If it is not covered in the contractual document, PM will send a quotation to the contractor.

Note 3: The wood structure contractor is willing to rent equipment from the steel structure company and save on mobilization costs; the lumber company can send a credit invoice to the general contractor when savings are known. Besides, the timeline for the Wood structure contractor can be brought forward by one week if the general contract accepts this proposal. (Saving one week on schedule- to update).

6. Subcontractor List:

PM will send the list of subcontractors to all subcontractors with contact details and addresses.

7. Site Meetings:

PM will send out recurring invitations for bi-weekly meetings starting at two weeks.

8. Layout Work:

Contractor's Site Layout plan –

Detailing the locations of construction work areas, propose a temporary location for the garbage enclosure, propose temporary Parking Spots space need to be used, propose the shout area, propose the trailer and washroom spots. Suggest the location of the storage container and the disposal bin in a site plan of the work area. Public work Staff can also suggest some places.

- Any other relevant site reservation required.

9. Material Suppliers:

Sand and Gravel will be hauled using the north route. Municipality accepted.

Wood Structure will be delivered on................ Types of equipment needed for unloading are................

10- Impo.tant tests:

The city's project manager requested to be contacted 48 hours before any required inspection.

A list of milestone items requiring inspections must be sent to the city for approval within 2 weeks.

11. Contingency Plans for Spills (to be posted at the site)

12. Traffic Control: Contractor to provide a copy of OTM Book 7 Certification.

13. Siltation and Erosion Control: As required.

14. Workplace Health and Safety:

Notice of Project

Contractor's OH&S Policy + COVID-19 Policy

Contractor's project-specific Health & Safety Plan

Emergency Plan, fall arrest, and Rescue Plan.

WHMIS, Fall Protection, Certificates of training, First Aid/CPR, Suspended Access Equipment, Elevating Work Platforms, Propane, Confined Space Entry, etc.

General Contractor is responsible for maintaining and complying with the health and safety rules.

At no point during the entire construction process, are residents or staff to be placed at risk. Refer all matters regarding residents' queries, complaints, and concerns to the superintendent.

Smoking is not allowed

Safety Consultant Pre-construction meeting minutes to be sent and followed by all subcontractors.

15. Payments:

Payments: Contractors send their demand for payment on the 25th of each month. Consultant approval time is 5 days—contractor to send the invoices accompanied with Statutory Declaration; WSIB; List of approved change orders.

16. Change Orders:

Change order procedures:

1. Contractor sends a Request For Information to the Consultant and copies the Contractor.
2. Consultant Sends Site Instructions recommending proper corrective actions and requesting a quotation if necessary.
3. Contractor sends the Quotation.
4. Consultant or Contractor approves, negotiates, modifies, or refuses.
5. Owner approves if needed.
6. The contractor starts the work.

17. Site Concerns:

Contractor to coordinate with Toronto Fire Services for any obstructions to the fire routes, egress, and lanes and obtain written approval.

Ensure that adequate warning signs are installed at the work areas; the safety consultant will review these signs. Contractors to use their portable washroom.

General Contractor will be using a generator installed by a qualified electrician.

18. Next Meeting:

After two weeks.

19. Other Business:

- Using the Washrooms
- Garbage bins
- Disposal of Materials.

Consultant noted:

Specifications for materials are to be adhered to strictly. Substitutes and deviations other than those submitted and accepted via Form of Bid will not be considered unless unusual circumstances prevail and such changes are approved in writing.
Photos to be taken for the site before starting the construction and sent to all parties involved. Closeout documents to be received. Etc.

Identifying The Critical Paths

Before and during the pre-construction meeting, most of the construction activities were defined. Now is the time to create WBS that identifies deliverables at the lowest level. Activities provide a basis for estimating, planning, executing, monitoring, and controlling project work.

By reading terms and conditions, contractor schedules, plans, quotes, tender documents, you can now identify which activities will take the most time and what other tasks depend on them. It is the good sense of the critical path. The ***critical path*** (or paths) is the longest path (in time) from Start to Finish; it indicates the minimum time necessary to complete the entire project.

As an example of a critical path, work cannot begin for a 6-month project duration until the structural framing shop drawing is approved, which is expected to take 3 months. The shop drawing approval activity will likely be on the critical path of this project. As a project manager, start calling the steel framing company and help as much as possible to complete this activity within 3 months. If this activity takes 4 months to complete, your entire project would be delayed by one month. If you, the contractor, could complete the shop drawings, get them approved within two months, find the other critical paths for the project, and keep pushing.

Critical paths must be identified at the very start of the project. Bar charts are commonly used and easily developed in MS Project. It is the project manager's responsibility to identify critical paths and update them. The project manager is also responsible for how many details to show for each stakeholder. The client's schedule may differ from the internal schedule; for example, the internal team schedule, including subcontractors, can be one month shorter to push to finish the project ahead of schedule.

Sequence Activities

There are four types of dependencies or logical relationships between activities.

1. **FS: Finish-to-Start**: The initiation of the successor activity depends upon the completion of the predecessor activity.
2. **FF: Finish-to-Finish**: The completion of the successor activity depends upon completing the predecessor activity.
3. **SS: Start-to-Start**: The initiation of the successor activity depends upon the initiation of the predecessor activity.
4. **SF: Start-to-Finish**: The completion of the successor activity depends upon the initiation of the predecessor activity.

There are some Mandatory Dependencies; a project manager has to decide when creating the schedule. Subcontractors can confirm mandatory dependencies during the pre-construction or progress meetings. For example, it is impossible to erect the superstructure until after the foundation has been built.

Applying Leads and Lags

A lead accelerates the activity of the successor. For example, excavations can begin before the building permit's issuance within a week (confirmation from the city that the building permit will be ready within a week will be sent at that time). **This would be shown as a finish-to-start with a 1-week lead.**

A lag directs a delay in the successor activity. For example, the erection of a steel structure can only begin after 3 days of a concrete slab on **grade** has been poured and hardened. **This could be shown as a finish-to-start relationship with a 3-day lag.**

In the schedule baseline below, you can notice the critical path bar chart in red color, milestones, relationships (dependencies) between activities, planned start and end dates, duration of activities. This planning was carried out using MS Project software.

Figure 12. MS Project Schedule

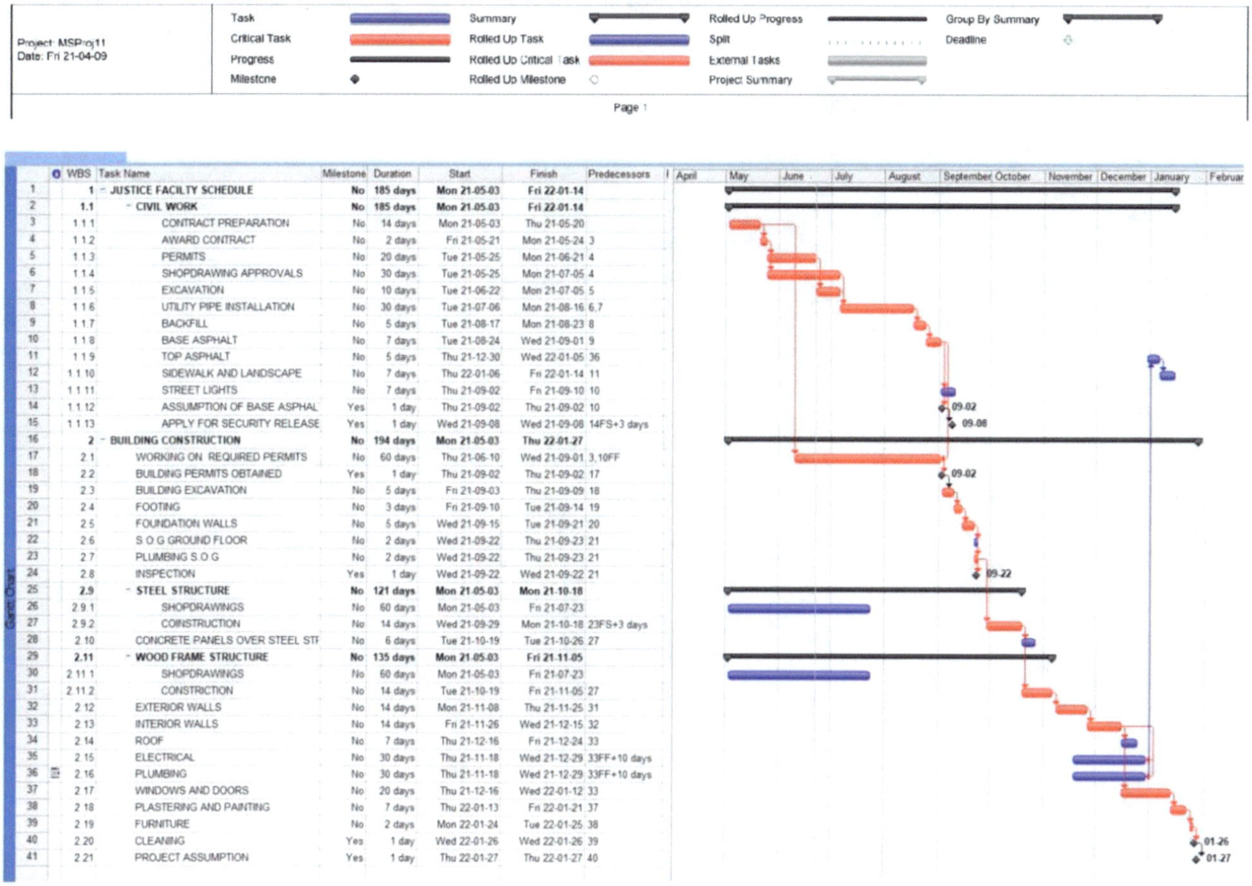

	WBS	Task Name	Milestone	Duration	Start	Finish	Predecessors
1	1	− JUSTICE FACILTY SCHEDULE	No	185 days	Mon 21-05-03	Fri 22-01-14	
2	1.1	− CIVIL WORK	No	185 days	Mon 21-05-03	Fri 22-01-14	
3	1.1.1	CONTRACT PREPARATION	No	14 days	Mon 21-05-03	Thu 21-05-20	
4	1.1.2	AWARD CONTRACT	No	2 days	Fri 21-05-21	Mon 21-05-24	3
5	1.1.3	PERMITS	No	20 days	Tue 21-05-25	Mon 21-06-21	4
6	1.1.4	SHOPDRAWING APPROVALS	No	30 days	Tue 21-05-25	Mon 21-07-05	4
7	1.1.5	EXCAVATION	No	10 days	Tue 21-06-22	Mon 21-07-05	5
8	1.1.6	UTILITY PIPE INSTALLATION	No	30 days	Tue 21-07-06	Mon 21-08-16	6,7
9	1.1.7	BACKFILL	No	5 days	Tue 21-08-17	Mon 21-08-23	8
10	1.1.8	BASE ASPHALT	No	7 days	Tue 21-08-24	Wed 21-09-01	9
11	1.1.9	TOP ASPHALT	No	5 days	Thu 21-12-30	Wed 22-01-05	36
12	1.1.10	SIDEWALK AND LANDSCAPE	No	7 days	Thu 22-01-06	Fri 22-01-14	11
13	1.1.11	STREET LIGHTS	No	7 days	Thu 21-09-02	Fri 21-09-10	10
14	1.1.12	ASSUMPTION OF BASE ASPHAL	Yes	1 day	Thu 21-09-02	Thu 21-09-02	10
15	1.1.13	APPLY FOR SECURITY RELEASE	Yes	1 day	Wed 21-09-08	Wed 21-09-08	14FS+3 days
16	2	− BUILDING CONSTRUCTION	No	194 days	Mon 21-05-03	Thu 22-01-27	
17	2.1	WORKING ON REQUIRED PERMITS	No	60 days	Thu 21-06-10	Wed 21-09-01	3,10FF
18	2.2	BUILDING PERMITS OBTAINED	Yes	1 day	Thu 21-09-02	Thu 21-09-02	17
19	2.3	BUILDING EXCAVATION	No	5 days	Fri 21-09-03	Thu 21-09-09	18
20	2.4	FOOTING	No	3 days	Fri 21-09-10	Tue 21-09-14	19
21	2.5	FOUNDATION WALLS	No	5 days	Wed 21-09-15	Tue 21-09-21	20
22	2.6	S O G GROUND FLOOR	No	2 days	Wed 21-09-22	Thu 21-09-23	21
23	2.7	PLUMBING S.O.G	No	2 days	Wed 21-09-22	Thu 21-09-23	21
24	2.8	INSPECTION	Yes	1 day	Wed 21-09-22	Wed 21-09-22	21
25	2.9	− STEEL STRUCTURE	No	121 days	Mon 21-05-03	Mon 21-10-18	
26	2.9.1	SHOPDRAWINGS	No	60 days	Mon 21-05-03	Fri 21-07-23	
27	2.9.2	COINSTRUCTION	No	14 days	Wed 21-09-29	Mon 21-10-18	23FS+3 days
28	2.10	CONCRETE PANELS OVER STEEL STF	No	6 days	Tue 21-10-19	Tue 21-10-26	27
29	2.11	− WOOD FRAME STRUCTURE	No	135 days	Mon 21-05-03	Fri 21-11-05	
30	2.11.1	SHOPDRAWINGS	No	60 days	Mon 21-05-03	Fri 21-07-23	
31	2.11.2	CONSTRICTION	No	14 days	Tue 21-10-19	Fri 21-11-05	27
32	2.12	EXTERIOR WALLS	No	14 days	Mon 21-11-08	Thu 21-11-25	31
33	2.13	INTERIOR WALLS	No	14 days	Fri 21-11-26	Wed 21-12-15	32
34	2.14	ROOF	No	7 days	Thu 21-12-16	Fri 21-12-24	33
35	2.15	ELECTRICAL	No	30 days	Thu 21-11-18	Wed 21-12-29	33FF+10 days
36	2.16	PLUMBING	No	30 days	Thu 21-11-18	Wed 21-12-29	33FF+10 days
37	2.17	WINDOWS AND DOORS	No	20 days	Thu 21-12-16	Wed 22-01-12	33
38	2.18	PLASTERING AND PAINTING	No	7 days	Thu 22-01-13	Fri 22-01-21	37
39	2.19	FURNITURE	No	2 days	Mon 22-01-24	Tue 22-01-25	38
40	2.20	CLEANING	Yes	1 day	Wed 22-01-26	Wed 22-01-26	39
41	2.21	PROJECT ASSUMPTION	Yes	1 day	Thu 22-01-27	Thu 22-01-27	40

When we anticipate cost contingencies, we also anticipate schedule contingencies. These contingencies should cover changes during project execution.

Performance Review

Schedule data for the project schedule include at a minimum milestone activity description, activity attributes, and documentation of all identified assumptions and constraints. In addition, the data can consist of resource requirements per period, often in the form of a resource histogram.

As the project progresses, determine the current state of the project schedule, the factors that create schedule changes, and manage actual changes as they occur.

Schedule data is updated and compiled into the schedule to reflect the actual progress of the project and the remaining work to be completed. At this stage, identify and document the causes of variances, corrective action chosen, and lessons learned from the project schedule control.

An essential part of schedule control is to decide if the schedule variation requires corrective action. For example, a significant delay on any activity not on the critical path may have little effect on the overall project schedule, while a much shorter delay on a critical activity may require immediate action.

Project management software for scheduling such as MS Project, Primavera, Excel, and others can track planned dates against actual dates and predict the effects of changes to the project schedule.

Figure 13. Baseline Vs Actual

		WBS	Task Name	Milestone	Baseline Start	Baseline Finish	Baseline Duration	Actual Duration	Actual Start	Actual Finish	Predecessors
1		1	– JUSTICE FACILITY SCHEDULE	No	Mon 21-05-03	Mon 22-01-31	190 days	58.66 days	Mon 21-05-03	NA	
2		1.1	CIVIL WORK	No	Mon 21-05-03	Mon 22-01-31	190 days	58.66 days	Mon 21-05-03	NA	
3	✓	1.1.1	CONTRACT PREPARATION	No	Mon 21-05-03	Thu 21-05-20	14 days	21 days	Mon 21-05-03	Mon 21-05-31	
4	✓	1.1.2	AWARD CONTRACT	No	Fri 21-05-21	Mon 21-05-24	2 days	4 days	Tue 21-06-01	Fri 21-06-04	3
5	✓	1.1.3	PERMITS	No	Tue 21-05-25	Mon 21-06-21	20 days	21 days	Mon 21-06-07	Mon 21-07-05	4
6		1.1.4	SHOPDRAWING APPROVALS	No	Tue 21-05-25	Mon 21-07-05	30 days	0 days	NA	NA	4
7		1.1.5	EXCAVATION	No	Wed 21-07-07	Tue 21-07-20	10 days	0 days	NA	NA	5
8		1.1.6	UTILITY PIPE INSTALLATION	No	Wed 21-07-21	Tue 21-08-31	30 days	0 days	NA	NA	7,6
9		1.1.7	BACKFILL	No	Wed 21-09-01	Tue 21-09-07	5 days	0 days	NA	NA	8
10		1.1.8	BASE ASPHALT	No	Wed 21-09-08	Thu 21-09-16	7 days	0 days	NA	NA	9
11		1.1.9	TOP ASPHALT	No	Fri 22-01-14	Thu 22-01-20	5 days	0 days	NA	NA	36
12		1.1.10	SIDEWALK AND LANDSCAPE	No	Fri 22-01-21	Mon 22-01-31	7 days	0 days	NA	NA	11
13		1.1.11	STREET LIGHTS	No	Fri 21-09-17	Mon 21-09-27	7 days	0 days	NA	NA	10
14		1.1.12	ASSUMPTION OF BASE ASPHLAT WORK WORK	Yes	Fri 21-09-17	Fri 21-09-17	1 day	0 days	NA	NA	10
15		1.1.13	APPLY FOR SECURITY RELEASE	Yes	Thu 21-09-23	Thu 21-09-23	1 day	0 days	NA	NA	14FS+3 days

Figure 14. Critical Path and Free Float

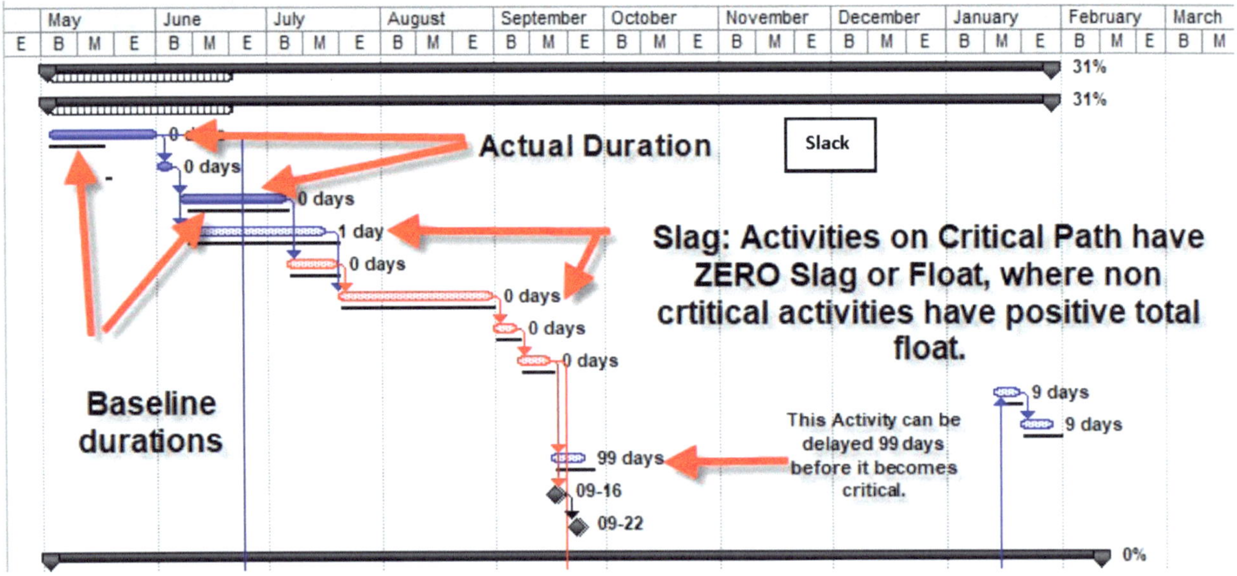

In the bar chart above, the option to show the float for each activity has been chosen in MS Project. Other options are also available, such as displaying start and end dates, activity names, or resource names.

Free Float: The length of time for an activity can be delayed without delaying any immediate successor activity's early start date. Activity with floating zero is critical path activity.

A buffer: is the contingency added to an activity to account for the uncertainty of the duration.

Free floats and buffers are different. The first is not part of the activity's duration, but it gives an indication showing the time required for each activity to be on a critical path; while the buffers are included in the duration of the activities.

The example above shows that the contract's preparation (activity number 4) slipped by 7 working days (21-14). Most of the activities in this schedule have a mandatory dependency relationship with the civil contract preparation. In other words, it is on the critical path of the project. The project is delayed by seven working days. In addition to this delay, the contract award took more than 2 days than expected (4 days - 2 days), and the permit took an additional day. In total, the project is 10 days late (excluding weekends and holidays), and we have not yet started the shop drawing process.

Plan Corrective Actions for Delays

The shop drawing approval activity cannot start until the contract has been awarded in the example above. Another actual start date is delayed. Instead of June 9, it will be after July 5. What are the options to mitigate this risk?

Option 1:
When the client or consultant has addressed the request for quotation to the civil contractor, it confirms the preliminary schedule to be sent, including the shop drawings' processing time. And this is how the project manager developed the duration of this activity. A call, formal letter/ e-mail, or a meeting with the contractor, in this case, is the first choice to use. The project manager can send a letter to try to catch up with the delays. Sample Letter below:

SAMPLE 19. Letter to Subcontractor and Suppliers Regarding Baseline Schedule Confirmation

LETTERHEAD

Distribution
....
....
....
....
....

Date: June 4, 2021
Project:...
Project No:..
RFQ Number & Date:............................
Contractor Name:................................
Contractor Address:................................

Subject: Respecting Shop-drawing Schedule.

Dear (name),

This is to draw your attention to the fact that the delay in returning the signed copy of the contract can be used as an excuse to delay the deadline for shop drawing approval. The original schedule submitted in quote no .... indicated that the shop drawing is expected to be finalized and approved by July 5, 2021.

We believe that one month period is sufficient to get the drawings approved by our consultant. Increase your workforce or resources if necessary to complete the pending work on time. So it is highly recommended and advised that you sort out the mentioned issue as soon as possible to boost up the work speed per the Contract Agreement between us.

If the completion date is still acceptable as mentioned in the schedule, please confirm by signing one copy, noting "approved," and returning it to my attention.

Your response is required by.........................., 2021.

We are looking forward to quick action.

Very truly yours,

COMPANY

....

Director,
Cc: file: Baseline Schedule.

Option 2:

Fast Tracking Technique

A schedule compression technique in which phases or activities typically performed in sequence are to perform in parallel. An example is the construction of the foundation for a building before completing all the architectural drawings. Fast-tracking may result in rework and increased risk. Fast-tracking only works if activities can be overlapped to shorten the duration.

Projects can be fast-tracked where construction can begin before all design decisions are finalized. Other activities can be fast-tracked by doing them in parallel or overlapping them.

Figure 15. Fast Tracking

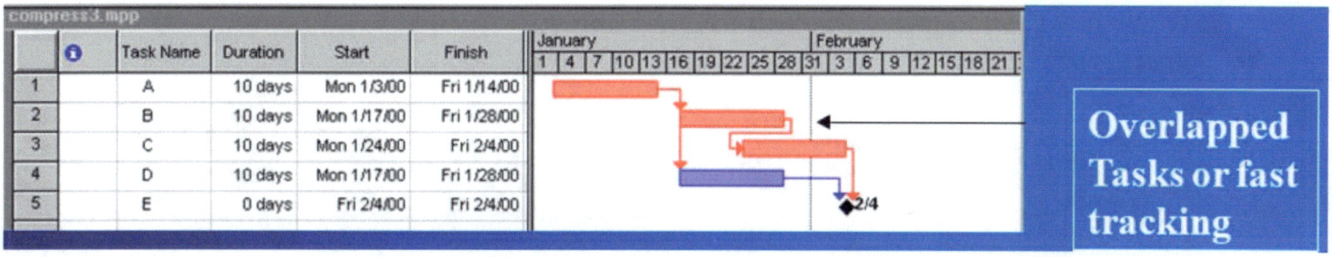

For example, the rest of the baseline activities (From WBS SHOP DRAWING APPROVALS till the end of the schedule).

SAMPLE 20. Baseline VS. Actual Durations

		WBS	Task Name	Milestone	Baseline Start	Baseline Finish	Baseline Duration	Actual Duration	Actual Start	Actual Finish	Predecessors
1		1	- JUSTICE FACILTY SCHEDULE	No	Mon 21-05-03	Mon 22-01-31	196 days	58.66 days	Mon 21-05-03	NA	
2		1.1	- CIVIL WORK	No	Mon 21 05 03	Mon 22-01-31	196 days	58.66 days	Mon 21-05-03	NA	
3	✓	1.1.1	CONTRACT PREPARATION	No	Mon 21-05-03	Thu 21-05-20	14 days	21 days	Mon 21-05-03	Mon 21-05-31	
4	✓	1.1.2	AWARD CONTRACT	No	Fri 21-05-21	Mon 21-05-24	2 days	4 days	Tue 21-06-01	Fri 21-06-04	3
5	✓	1.1.3	PERMITS	No	Tue 21-05-25	Mon 21-06-21	20 days	21 days	Mon 21-06-07	Mon 21-07-05	4
6		1.1.4	SHOPDRAWING APPROVALS	No	Tue 21-05-25	Mon 21-07-05	30 days	0 days	NA	NA	4
7		1.1.5	EXCAVATION	No	Wed 21-07-07	Tue 21-07-20	10 days	0 days	NA	NA	5
8		1.1.6	UTILITY PIPE NSTALLATION	No	Wed 21-07-21	Tue 21-08-31	30 days	0 days	NA	NA	7,6
9		1.1.7	BACKFLL	No	Wed 21-09-01	Tue 21-09-07	5 days	0 days	NA	NA	8
10		1.1.8	BASE ASPHALT	No	Wed 21-09-08	Thu 21-09-16	7 days	0 days	NA	NA	9
11		1.1.9	TOP ASPHALT	No	Fi 22-01-14	Thu 22-01-20	5 days	0 days	NA	NA	36
12		1.1.10	SIDEWALK AND LANDSCAPE	No	Fri 22-01-21	Mon 22-01-31	7 days	0 days	NA	NA	11
13		1.1.11	STREET LIGHTS	No	Fri 21-09-17	Mon 21-09-27	7 days	0 days	NA	NA	10
14		1.1.12	ASSUMPTION OF BASE ASPHLAT WORK WORK	Yes	Fri 21-09-17	Fri 21-09-17	1 day	0 days	NA	NA	10
15		1.1.13	APPLY FOR SECURITY RELEASE	Yes	Thu 21-09-23	Thu 21-09-23	1 day	0 days	NA	NA	14FS+3 days

We can try to Fast-track a few activities and convince the contractor in our preconstruction meeting that the activities highlighted in green may overlap with their predecessors, as shown below:

SAMPLE 21. Schedule Fast-Tracking

ID		WBS	Task Name	Milestone	Baseline Start	Baseline Finish	Baseline Duration	Revised Start/New Baseline	Revised Finish/New Baseline	Actual Duration	Actual Start	Actual Finish	Predecessors	Resource Names
1		1	JUSTICE FACILITY SCHEDULE	No	Mon 21 05 03	Mon 22 01 31	196 days	Mon 21 05 03	Wed 22 01 12	58.5 days	Mon 21 05 03	NA		
2		1.1	CIVIL WORK	No	Mon 21-05-03	Mon 22-01-31	196 days	Mon 21-05-03	Wed 22-01-12	58.5 days	Mon 21-05-03	NA		
3	✓	1.1.1	CONTRACT PREPARATION	No	Mon 21-05-03	Thu 21-05-20	14 days	Mon 21-05-03	Mon 21-05-31	21 days	Mon 21-05-03	Mon 21-05-31		OWNER
4	✓	1.1.2	AWARD CONTRACT	No	Fri 21-05-21	Mon 21-05-24	2 days	Tue 21 06 01	Fri 21 06 04	4 days	Tue 21-06-01	Fri 21-06-04	3	OWNER
5	✓	1.1.3	PERMITS	No	Tue 21-05-25	Mon 21-06-21	20 days	Mon 21-06-07	Mon 21-07-05	21 days	Mon 21-06-07	Mon 21-07-06	4	OWNER
6		1.1.4	SHOPDRAWING APPROVALS	No	Tue 21-05-25	Mon 21-07-05	30 days	Mon 21-06-07	Fri 21-07-16	0 days	NA	NA	4	CONSULTA
7		1.1.5	EXCAVATION	No	Wed 21 07 07	Tue 21 07 20	10 days	Tue 21 07 06	Mon 21 07 19	0 days	NA	NA	6	CONTRACT
8		1.1.6	UTILITY PIPE INSTALLATION	No	Wed 21-07-21	Tue 21-08-31	30 days	Tue 21-07-13	Mon 21-08-23	0 days	NA	NA	7FS-5 days	CONTRACT
9		1.1.7	BACKFILL	No	Wed 21-09-01	Tue 21-09-07	5 days	Fri 21-08-20	Thu 21-08-26	0 days	NA	NA	8FS-2 days	CONTRACT

Note that the baseline start and end dates are not updated because this is the first baseline. When the contractor accepts the fast-track proposal, the project manager can update the baseline to show savings over 7 days in Civil Construction works.

For the Construction of buildings part. The highlighted cells represent the proposals, which translate into a saving of 12 business days- which are, in fact, more than that when you count the holidays, including the Christmas holidays. That was just an example of how you can still catch up and even improve the preliminary schedule regardless of matching how many days of savings we achieved.

10	1.1.8	BASE Asphalt	No	Wed 21-08-18	Thu 21-08-26	7 days	Fri 21-08-27	Mon 21-09-06	0 days	NA	NA	9
11	1.1.9	TOP Asphalt	No	Fri 22-01-14	Thu 22-01-20	5 days	Tue 21-12-28	Mon 22-01-03	0 days	NA	NA	[illegible]
12	1.1.10	SIDEWALK AND LANDSCAPE	No	Fri 22-01-21	Mon 22-01-31	7 days	Tue 22-01-04	Wed 22-01-12	0 days	NA	NA	11
13	1.1.11	STREET LIGHTS	No	Fri 21-09-17	Mon 21-09-27	7 days	Tue 21-09-07	Wed 21-09-15	0 days	NA	NA	10
14	1.1.12	ASSUMPTION OF BASE Asphalt WORK WORK	Yes	Fri 21-09-17	Fri 21-09-17	1 day	Tue 21-09-07	Tue 21-09-07	0 days	NA	NA	10
15	1.1.13	APPLY FOR SECURITY RELEASE	Yes	Thu 21-09-23	Thu 21-09-23	1 day	Mon 21-09-13	Mon 21-09-13	0 days	NA	NA	14FS+3 days
16	2	BUILDING CONSTRUCTION	No	Mon 21 05 03	Fri 22 02 11	206 days	Mon 21 05 03	Fri 22 01 11	0 days	NA	NA	
17	2.1	WORKING ON REQUIRED PERMITS	No	Fri 21 06 25	Thu 21 09 16	60 days	Tue 21 06 15	Mon 21 09 06	0 days	NA	NA	3,10FF
18	2.2	BUILDING PERMITS OBTAINED	Yes	Fri 21-09-17	Fri 21-09-17	1 day	Tue 21-09-07	Tue 21-09-07	0 days	NA	NA	17
19	2.3	BUILDING EXCAVATION	No	Mon 21-09-20	Fri 21-09-24	5 days	Wed 21-09-01	Tue 21-09-07	0 days	NA	NA	18FS-5 days
20	2.4	FOOTING	No	Mon 21-09-27	Wed 21-09-29	3 days	Wed 21-09-08	Fri 21-09-10	0 days	NA	NA	19
21	2.5	FOUNDATION WALLS	No	Thu 21-09-30	Wed 21-10-06	5 days	Mon 21-09-13	Fri 21-09-17	0 days	NA	NA	20
22	2.6	S.O.G GROUND FLOOR	No	Thu 21 10 07	Fri 21 10 08	2 days	Mon 21 09 20	Tue 21 09 21	0 days	NA	NA	21
23	2.7	PLUMBING S.O.G	No	Thu 21 10 07	Fri 21 10 08	2 days	Mon 21 09 20	Tue 21 09 21	0 days	NA	NA	21
24	2.8	INSPECTION	Yes	Thu 21 10 07	Thu 21 10 07	1 day	Mon 21 09 20	Mon 21 09 20	0 days	NA	NA	21
25	2.9	STEEL STRUCTURE	No	Mon 21-05-03	Tue 21-11-02	132 days	Mon 21-05-03	Thu 21-10-14	0 days	NA	NA	
26	2.9.1	SHOPDRAWINGS	No	Mon 21-05-03	Fri 21-07-23	60 days	Mon 21-05-03	Fri 21-07-23	0 days	NA	NA	
27	2.9.2	CONSTRUCTION	No	Thu 21-10-14	Tue 21-11-02	14 days	Mon 21-09-27	Thu 21-10-14	0 days	NA	NA	23FS+3 days
28	2.10	CONCRETE PANELS OVER STEEL STRUCTURE	No	Wed 21-11-03	Wed 21-11-10	6 days	Fri 21-10-15	Fri 21-10-22	0 days	NA	NA	27
29	2.11	WOOD FRAME STRUCTURE	No	Mon 21 05 03	Mon 21 11 22	146 days	Mon 21 05 03	Wed 21 11 03	0 days	NA	NA	
30	2.11.1	SHOPDRAWINGS	No	Mon 21 05 03	Fri 21 07 23	60 days	Mon 21 05 03	Fri 21 07 23	0 days	NA	NA	
31	2.11.2	CONSTRUCTION	No	Wed 21 11 03	Mon 21 11 22	14 days	Fri 21 10 15	Wed 21 11 03	0 days	NA	NA	27
32	2.12	EXTERIOR WALLS	No	Tue 21-11-23	Fri 21-12-10	14 days	Thu 21-11-04	Tue 21-11-23	0 days	NA	NA	31
33	2.13	INTERIOR WALLS	No	Mon 21-12-13	Thu 21-12-30	14 days	Wed 21-11-24	Mon 21-12-13	0 days	NA	NA	32
34	2.14	ROOF	No	Fri 21-12-31	Mon 22-01-10	7 days	Tue 21-12-14	Wed 21-12-22	0 days	NA	NA	33
35	2.15	ELECTRICAL	No	Fri 21-12-03	Thu 22-01-13	30 days	Tue 21-11-16	Mon 21-12-27	0 days	NA	NA	33FF+10 days
36	2.16	PLUMBING	No	Fri 21-12-03	Thu 22-01-13	30 days	Tue 21-11-16	Mon 21-12-27	0 days	NA	NA	33FF+10 days
37	2.17	WINDOWS AND DOORS	No	Fri 21-12-31	Thu 22-01-27	20 days	Tue 21-12-14	Mon 22-01-10	0 days	NA	NA	33
38	2.18	PLASTERING AND PAINTING	No	Fri 22 01 28	Mon 22 02 07	7 days	Fri 21 12 31	Mon 22 01 10	0 days	NA	NA	37FS-7 days
39	2.19	FURNITURE	No	Tue 22-02-08	Wed 22-02-09	2 days	Tue 22-01-11	Wed 22-01-12	0 days	NA	NA	38
40	2.20	CLEANING	Yes	Thu 22-02-10	Thu 22-02-10	1 day	Thu 22-01-13	Thu 22-01-13	0 days	NA	NA	39
41	2.21	PROJECT ASSUMPTION	Yes	Fri 22-02-11	Fri 22-02-11	1 day	Fri 22-01-14	Fri 22-01-14	0 days	NA	NA	40

Continue to speed up other activities and communicate with subcontractors as needed to ensure that these fast tracks are possible.

Option 3:

Crashing Technique

Crashing is a time-cost trade-off. It is used to shorten activity duration.

Procedure for crashing:

- Crash the project one period at a time
- Only activity on the critical path should be crashed
- Crash the least expensive activity

Figure 16. Crashing & Fast Tracking

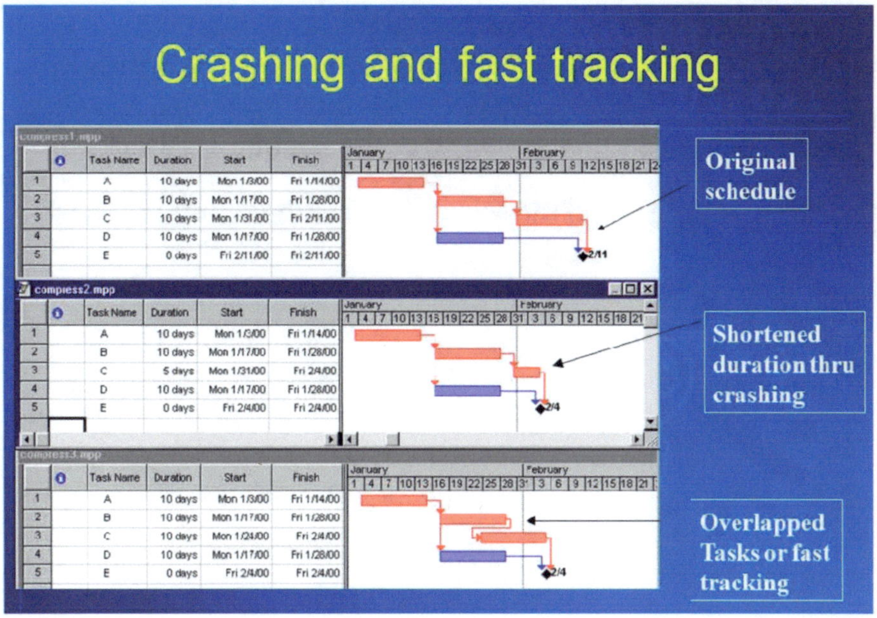

It is often possible to complete activities faster than usual by using more resources (better equipment, overtime, etc.). This is called "crashing" the project.
We might want to determine the optimal way to crash a project to complete it faster than initially planned and keep it on schedule if critical activities have been delayed.

How we apply the crash technique to our example: We have seen that the steel structure is on the critical path for this project from the sample timeline. Besides, the subcontractor's shop drawing schedule is 60 days. A project manager can send a letter to the contractor asking them to crash this activity by strengthening the team with more staff or working overtime. The PM will indeed receive a quote associated with this change. In light of the work's progress and management direction, the general contractor accepts or rejects the proposal.

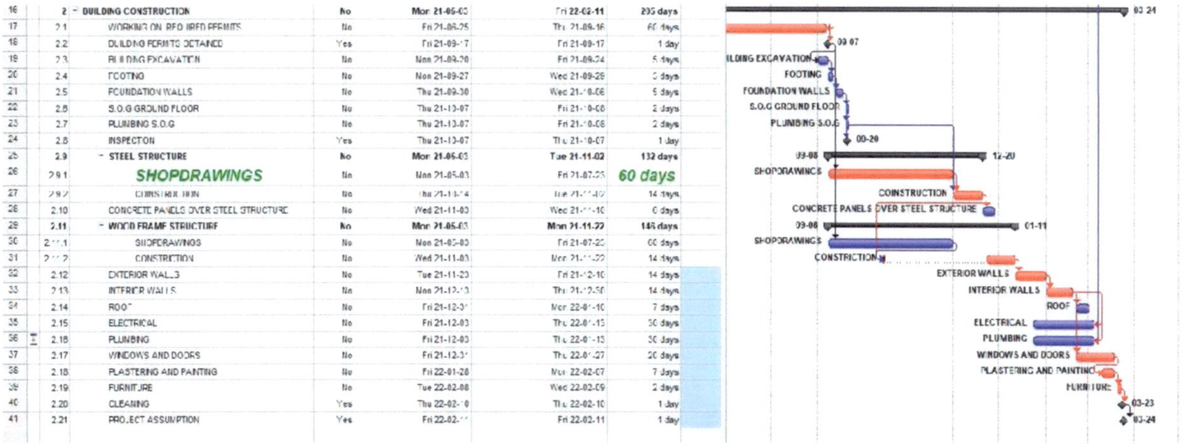

Crashing and fast-tracking often cause more problems and change orders; the project manager must strictly control costs and deadlines to avoid more extended deadlines.

Variance Analysis

If earned value management (EVM) is utilized, the schedule variance (SV) and Schedule performance index (SPI) are used to assess the magnitude of schedule variations. A sample example will be discussed in the Project Cost Management section, including SV and SPI.

An essential part of schedule control is to decide if the schedule variation requires corrective action.

SECTION 7
PROJECT COST MANAGEMENT

Project Cost Management includes the process involved in **estimating, budgeting, and controlling costs** to complete the project within the approved budget.

An essential part of a project manager's job is managing money. All organizations must spend their money well to fulfill their mission, including not-for-profit and government organizations. The tools and methods used to manage money on a project vary depending on the phase and complexity of the project.

Cost management starts from the procurement and contracting phase, so procurement and cost management are linked.

CHAPTER 9 - COST ESTIMATION

Cost estimates are influenced by numerous variables such as labor rates, material costs, inflation, risk factors, and other variables.

The Project Management Institute defines cost estimate as "The development of an approximation (estimate) of costs of the resources needed to complete project activities."

A project goes through different levels of estimates based on its development stage. Calculations are performed throughout a project's life, beginning with the first estimate and extending through the various design phases and construction. There are three primary stages or steps in project development, and for each of them, estimates are made:

1 | **The Planning Stage** can include Preliminary, Order of magnitude (Guesstimates), and other higher-level estimates.

Order of Magnitude estimate or Rough Order of Magnitude (ROM) is the estimate used at the early stage of the project where the variation between estimated and actual costs can easily be plus or minus fifty percent. Anyone preparing a ROM estimate should be sure to indicate that the accuracy of the estimate can vary greatly, especially if it is in the early stages of a project.

This stage can be when deciding to take the project or do a Go or No Go analysis for the general contractor.

2 | **The Basic design stage** will include the prepared budget with more details, but it is still considered a preliminary estimate.

3- **Detailed engineering construction stage** includes definitive and detailed estimates based on plans and specifications. It can also contain Lump sum costs if contractors receive these costs. An example will be given for this type of estimate.

For the general contractor, this step can be at estimating the offer (bid estimate). The contractor must submit either a call for tenders (competitive bidding) or negotiation to the owner.

The direct construction cost is derived from Subcontractor Quotations, Quantity Takeoffs, Construction processes, and General Conditions Division 01.

Many businesses use simple Excel sheets to calculate and estimate quantities. For general contractors, many companies depend on their subcontractors' price and add overhead, profit, and contingency on the overall cost and submit their price to the customer. If the business is the client, such as the owner of 200 homes who wants to build the land and homes with contractors, or if the business is government business, they can use this estimate as a baseline to create the project budget. And forecast cash flow—outputs (Spending of money) for each month or quarter.

Medium General Contractors mainly use Excel sheets – Quantity take-off and RS means to estimate each activity cost.

SAMPLE 22. Master Format Divisions

Master Format Divisions

MasterFormat was first released in 1975 and only had 16 Divisions until the new 50-Division MasterFormat 2004 was released in late 2004. Divisions that are not listed are reserved for future use (including Division 49.)

- Division 00 - Procurement and Contracting Requirements
- Division 01 - General Requirements
- Division 02 - Existing Conditions
- Division 03 - Concrete
- Division 04 - Masonry
- Division 05 - Metals
- Division 06 - Wood, Plastics, Composites
- Division 07 - Thermal and Moisture Protection
- Division 08 - Openings
- Division 09 - Finishes
- Division 10 - Specialties
- Division 11 - Equipment
- Division 12 - Furnishings
- Division 13 - Special Construction
- Division 14 - Conveying Equipment
- Division 21 - Fire Suppression
- Division 22 - Plumbing
- Division 23 - Heating, Ventilating, and Air Conditioning (HVAC)
- Division 25 - Integrated Automation
- Division 26 - Electrical
- Division 27 - Communications
- Division 28 - Electronic Safety and Security
- Division 31 - Earthwork
- Division 32 - Exterior Improvements
- Division 33 - Utilities
- Division 34 - Transportation
- Division 35 - Waterway and Marine Construction
- Division 40 - Process Integration
- Division 41 - Material Processing and Handling Equipment
- Division 42 - Process Heating, Cooling, and Drying Equipment
- Division 43 - Process Gas and Liquid Handling, Purification and Storage Equipment
- Division 44 - Pollution and Waste Control Equipment

- Division 45 - Industry-Specific Manufacturing Equipment
- Division 46 - Water and Wastewater Equipment
- Division 48 - Electrical Power Generation

Uses of the Estimate

The estimates are used to:

- Form a planning and control basis by defining the scope of the work (a budget is an estimate),
- Provide the basic information (hours, resources, etc.) necessary for the preparation of a schedule,
- Indicate the general resource requirements (labor, material, equipment, and subcontractor) or what is called the 4 M (labor, material, machinery, and money)
- Provide a financial contribution (cash flow),
- Provide the basis for assessing productivity and risks.

The most important element that governs a construction company's success is the ability to prepare fully detailed and accurate estimates of the cost of performing work.

An example shows how midsize companies manually estimate their projects.

To sum up the estimate, we can create excel sheets like this

Now start reading the general requirements section in the RFP, specification, or contract document. Usually, it is called GC01. Write down all the information considered to have an associated cost and create your first sheet.

SAMPLE 23. Estimation Tables

Training Center Sudbury		Section: 001			General Requirements	
Work Begins:		Completion of the Work:			Page:	1 Of 2
Description	**Quantity**	**Man-power**	**Materials**	**Equipment**	**Sub-Contractor**	**Subtotal**
Building Permits:	1				$ 2,000	$ 2,000
Liability Insurance:	2				$ 2,500	$ 5,000
Execution bonds:	1				$ 4,000	$ 4,000
Temporary Electricity:						
Trailer Connection	2		$ 500		$ 1,000	$ 3,000
Construction Trailer						
Rental /Month	10				850	$ 8,500

Add all costs associated with general conditions for the period of the project such as Truck Rentals, Phone & Communications, Waste Containers, Project Manager and Foreman, Night Watchman, Cleaning, Snow Removal, Surveyor, Laboratory, Protection, Safety, trailers, Insurances, Bonds, Permits, etc.

For example, the annual salary of the Project Manager + Benefits is $120,000. The duration of the project is 12 months. The project manager will be responsible for two projects at the same time. Therefore, a project manager's cost to complete this project is $120,000 for 12 months divided by two projects = $60,000.

Start the estimation for each division.

Figure 17. Estimation Sheet

	A	B	C	D	E
1	description	Quantity		Unit Price	TOTAL
2					
3	building:				
4	*excavation:*				
5	- miscellaneous sub-slab	1200	m³	$3.75	4,500 $
6	- materials to come out:	1200	m³	$6.00	7,200 $
7	embankment under slab:				
8	- sand MG-112, upgrade	0	m³	$21.53	0 $
9	- stone MG-20	600	m³	$41.00	24,600 $
10	- machinery - compaction	600	m³	$4.50	2,700 $
11	- labour	600	m³	$1.00	600 $

Assume that the estimated excavation cost is $40,000 for this project. At this point, most midsize businesses compare this cost with quotes received by contractors (standard minimum selection of 3) and then decide which numbers to choose as the basis for the estimate. Let's say the best contractor's award is $35,000, and the second-best is $50,000. It may be wise to use the $40,000 estimated internally. If the business wins the offer, save $5,000 on one side and count towards any future contingencies for that activity.

When contracts are awarded to vendors under competitive processes, additional cost estimating work can be required to examine the price of individual deliverables and derive a cost supporting the final total project cost.

Do the same for all divisions and accumulate the results in one sheet.

SAMPLE 24 Breakdown of Bid Price.

	A	B	C
1	**Training Center**		
2	**Lot1- General**		
3			
4	**Consultant Project number ....**		
5			
6	**BID Form**		
7			
8	Breakdown of Bid Price		
9			
10		Price	Total
11	**Division 1 - Terms and Conditions**		
12	Transportation of materials	52,513.71 $	
13	Transportation of the workforce	32,400.00 $	
14	Construction organization including the costs of mobilizing and demobilizing equipment	91,625 $	
15	Camp (houses and covered)	337,950 $	
16	Energy (electricity, heating)	4,050 $	
17	Work Directorate (superintendent)	265,200 $	
18	communication	2,250 $	
19	Chanier insurance	82,500 $	
20	Bonds	51,750 $	
21	Final site clean-up	12,000 $	
22	Administration and profit	218,155 $	
23	Others (specify)		
24		SubTotal Division 1	**1,150,393.33 $**
25			
26	**Division 3 - Concrete**		
27	formwork	25,690 $	
28	frame	39,700 $	
29	concreting	247,050 $	
30	Prefabricated concrete cracks	459,000 $	
31	Others (specify)		
32		SubTotal - Division 3	**771,440 $**

136	**Division 26 - Electricity**		
137	Electrical entrance and ground socket	35,000.00 $	
138	Electrical distribution	80,000.00 $	
139	lighting	110,000.00 $	
140	Lighting ds parking lots	15,000.00 $	
141	Taken and services	40,000.00 $	
142	heating	55,000.00 $	
143	Connecting mechanical equipment	35,000.00 $	
144	klaxon	70,000.00 $	
145	Control security system	inclus dans alarm	
146	Other (specify) miscellaneous	8,100.00 $	**448,100 $**
147		**Sous-total - Division 26**	
148			
149	**Division 32 - Outdoor facilities**	955,700 $	
150	Parking lots and path		
151	excavation	Included	
152	insulation	Included	
153	Granular infrastructure	Included	
154	Borders	Included	
155	paving	Included	
156	Sidewalk and concrete slabs	Included	
157	Marking the pavement	Included	
158	Signage on pole	Included	
159	Drainage (including insulation when indicated)	Included	
160	Setting up vegetable soil and finishing leveling	Included	
161	Planting trees, shrubs and plant cover	Included	
162	Others (specify)		
163		**Sous-total - Division 32**	**955,700 $**
164			
165		SubTotal Divisions 1 to 32	**7,490,267.56 $**

Details of the cost estimate are usually provided to the project manager to compare with the actual cost and learn lessons from underestimated or overestimated activities, if applicable.

Bid Management

Cost estimators (including the project management team) should ensure that all offers are well documented. Confirmation from all contractors is received, confirming compliance with quotes provided per plans and specifications.

Some companies ask a contract administrator to write contracts with suppliers; others require the project manager to award contracts. In either case, the project manager should fully understand the estimate, match plans and specifications with contracts, and ensure no component is left behind in the estimate phase. For example, the project manager drafting the steel frame contract must include all the steel divisions mentioned in the specifications -

for example (The agreement consists of the complete division 5- Metals and drawings A00-A31).

A letter to invite a contractor to quote can be like the below example.

LOGO	Company Letter Head, Logo, and Address

SAMPLE 25. Letter Of Invitation To Tender

Letter Of Invitation To Tender

ABC LTD. Invites submissions for Request for Proposal 14-221
Construction of a new Training Center at Sudbury Ontario

Here is the information for the "Construction of the training center lot 1" project currently presented to our office in Toronto. This project will be carried out in the north of Ontario, in Sudbury (380 km from Toronto).

This project under tender is a public call for tenders. This RFP is for constructing a new steel and wood-frame building that requires you to provide the material, labor, equipment, and transportation necessary to achieve the scope of the specific discipline of work for which your business submits.

The ABC ltd. will act as general contractor for the project. The project closing date for ABC is Wednesday, March 19, 2014.

The project file number at ABC is B14-221. You can find information about the project (plans, specifications, addenda, and others - if applicable) on the following FTP site: ftp://www.ABC.ON.ca??

Identification: B14-221
Password: ABC-B14-221

ABC transfers all official documents received and issued by professionals to the FTP site within a maximum of 24 hours after receiving them at our technical offices in Toronto. You are entirely responsible for consulting our FTP site to ensure you have the documents from the owner and/or professionals (addenda and others) via the FTP site.

ABC will issue, if time permits, an informative e-mail to inform you of the presence of new documents for the project being submitted. You have access at all times to all documents via the FTP site. You must make sure you have all the documents issued during the professionals' tender period to have a complete tender when your price is closed.

Questions and requests for clarifications from proponents will be received until March 01, 2014. Responses to received questions will be posted as an addendum to the RFP.

You must include in your quote the cost for room and board for your employees working on this project to achieve the full scope of your work.

You must send your submission to our Toronto office by email before Monday, March 10, 2014, or file at the public tender website www.publicname.ca on the required date and under the terms and conditions if applicable.

You can call me anytime if you have any questions about the project.

Have a good day.

Commonly, a contractor or subcontractor will submit a construction RFI while the building is underway to ask the designer or engineer to clarify a drawing or specification. Similarly, during bidding, a contractor may submit an RFI to understand the project's details fully and fine-tune a quote.

Example of Contractor RFI during the tender stage:

SAMPLE 26. Bid Request For Information (RFI)

SubContractor LOGO and Complete Contact Information
BID REQUEST FOR INFORMATION (RFI)

RFI NO:001	RFI Date:	February 19, 2014
RFP # 14-221	Bid #	B14-221
Submitted By: SUB's PM	Submitted To:	General Contractor's PM
RFI Reference:	Date:	February 25, 2014

Request For Information Description

1. We are experiencing issues reading the drawings (pages D8 and D9), and our trades are asking questions. Can you please provide an updated set of drawings that fixes the writing on the last two pages?
2. Bird Netting Section 10 81 13, 2.2.5 calls for ¾" and 2" Mesh size. Please clarify the size.
3. Please confirm if any of the following alternative railing suppliers will be considered:
   - Norstar Cresco?

Thank you
Subcontractor Project Manager Name and Signature.

Responding to the RFI's received by the consultant, here is a Sample Addenda prepared and sent by the owner or the owner's consultant.

Sample Addenda

SAMPLE 27. Addenda

Consultant Name and Logo

Addendum Number	1
Addendum Date of Issue	August 15, 2019
RFP Number	14-221
RFP Description	Construction of a new Training Center at Sudbury Ontario
Pages	3
Attachment(s)	8

This Addendum forms part of the RFP mentioned above document and is to be read, interpreted, and

coordinated with all other parts. The following revisions supersede the information in the

original RFP documents issued for the project mentioned earlier to the extent referenced and shall become part thereof.

The following information supplements and/or supersedes the RFP document issued on February 19, 2014.

Changes to item number 6.5 in the submission bid form. A note has been added (a square mesh of 3/4" (19 mm) must be used at all locations).

Section 10 81 13, Clause 2.2.5: Corrected to (a square mesh of 3/4" (19 mm) must be used at all locations).

REVISED SECTION 07 42 55 – FIBER-REINFORCED CEMENT PANELS:

Item 2.2.1 revised to: "Tectiva Surface Coloured and Textured High-Density Fiber- Cement Panels by Engineered Assemblies".

Item 2.2.1.16.1.1 revised to: "Basis of Design Product: Tectiva High-Density Fiber- Cement Reinforced Cement Panels...".

DELETE Drawings – 'D8' only in its/their entirety and replace with the attached revised file Drawings –D8- D8.rev01.Issued.214.03 .05'.

Questions and Answers

Q1) We are experiencing issues reading the drawings (pages D8 and D9), and our trades are asking questions. Can you please provide an updated set of drawings that fixes the writing on the last two pages?

A1) Please refer to D8 and D9, which have been attached as part of this Addendum.

Q2) Bird Netting Section 10 81 13, 2.2.5 calls for ¾" and 2" Mesh size. Please clarify the size.

A2) A square mesh of 3/4" (19 mm) must be used at all locations.

Q3) Please confirm if any of the following alternative railing suppliers will be considered: - Norstar Cresco?
A3) Alternative aluminium railing manufacturers may be considered if they are able to meet the project specifications.

Q4) As requested in the site meeting, please provide the contact details for the Rogers, Bell, and Freedom Mobile persons aware of this project for the cable relocation.

A4) Please see contact information in the attached Document (Contact Info).

All other terms and conditions remain the same.

Signature

Now all requests for information have been answered, and addenda have been published. Subcontractors can send their bids. The clients, general contractors in this example, will analyze the quotes received.

Price Analysis

Example1: Concrete Company
See Table of Comparison-Price Analysis
Sub= Subcontractors or Contractors sending quotes to the General Contractors

The Estimator, Project Manager, or Contract Administrator can make his recommendations to the upper management.

According to the table, SUB1 may have a better chance of winning the contract if the general contractor or owner decides to rent a place for employees to eat and sleep (lodge and board).

SUB 2 offers a better price overall, but there is a risk associated with hiring another contractor to pour and finish the slab at grade.

SUB3 does not offer a pump. If no accommodation is provided for lodge and boarding, this entrepreneur may be the best among all the rest.

Example 2: Pond Cleaning
A home builder sends a request for proposal to Pond Cleaning Contractors.

See Table of Comparison- Price Analysis-Pond Cleaning
Below is the Form of Tender to be filled by Contractors:

Section 1. Pond Cleaning
1.1 Supply and install siltation control fence as per detail on engineering drawings (incl. removal after pond cleaning operations have been completed and all applicable restoration)—installation of ESC as per attached detail.

1.2 Supply and install the pump and related appurtenances to drain the remainder of the pond (incl. multiple setups, removal of pump and appurtenances, and all efforts to keep the water pumped downstream as clean as possible, i.e., filter bags, clear stone, elevated pumps, etc.). Pumps are to be noise-contained (silent) based on the proximity of works to existing residential dwellings.

1.3 Clean out Vegetation as per cleanup Drawings (2 stages).

1.4 Excavate and remove Fill/ sediment off-site to an approved disposal site provided by the contractor: see Sediment analysis and bathymetric drawing details as attached.
a- Forebay 420m3
b- Main Pond 380 m3

1.5 Restore Rip-Raps.

1.6 Collect all Marine Life: By others. Not to Price.

1.7 Layout Pond below Permanent pool elevation: By others. Not to Price.

Result of Analysis:
Contractor 1:the lowest proponent.

Below is a sample of Project Manager's recommendations to higher management. Assume that the cost estimation was 30%higher than the price received.

1. The submitted price is 30 %lower than the cost estimate and 20%lower than the second-best proponent. A confirmation meeting (Vendor Committee Meeting: to ensure that contractor 1 understands the scope of work) is required and should be scheduled before sending the results to all contractors.
2. Contractor 1 evaluation form was consulted (The evaluation form show contractor's old performance) to assume the results are as following:
   a. The score is above 75%(acceptable to good).
   b. Contractor change orders do not exceed 10%(acceptable).
   c. Delay in most projects by 10%.

SAMPLE 28. Table of Comparison-Price Analysis- Concrete Companies

Subs	3100 Form Work		3350 S.O.G. Pouring, finishing, and Curing		Comments	New Total
	Amount	Exclusions	Amount	Exclusions		
SUB1	$40,000	Lodge and Board. (Cost from estimation -$10,000	$20,000	Lodge and Board. (Cost from estimation $5,000	$30,000 Add $10,000 L&B. Add $10,000 SOG Add $5,000	$75,000
SUB2	$55,000	Include all	Does not do slabs	$15,000 Missing	$45,000 New contract needed for S.O.G – Estimation $15,000	$70,000
SUB 3	$60,000	Include all	$5,000	Does not offer the Pump	Pump renting with 1 day's Manhours needed (5m.h)- $5,000	$70,000
SUB 4	$75,000	Lodge & Board - $10,000		PUMP $5,000	Pump renting with 1 day's Manhours needed (5m.h)- $5,000	$90,000

Related to Example 1: Concrete company

Table 11. Table of Comparison- Price Analysis-Pond Cleaning

Item	CONTRACTOR 1		CONTRACTOR 2	
	PRICE	COMMENTS	PRICE	COMMENTS
1.1	$15,000.00	Original Price $17,000	$5,000	Does not accept any kind of negotiation
1.2	$22,000.00		$13,500	
1.3	$7,000.00		$4,500	
1.4 a	$70,000.00	Original Price $81,000	$120,000	
1.4 b	$32,000.00		$45,000	
1.5	$15,000.00		$10,000	
Total	$161,000		$198,000	

Item	CONTRACTOR 3		CONTRACTOR 4	
	PRICE	COMMENTS	PRICE	COMMENTS
1.1	$17,000	Contractor requested 10% Upfront Payment	$2,000	
1.2	$30,000		$60,000	
1.3	$14,000		$20,000	
1.4 a	$90,000	Original price $125,000	$120,000	Price Not negotiated
1.4 b	$50,000		$65,000	
1.5	$7,000		$75,000	
Total	$208,000		$342,000	

Related to Example 2: Pond cleaning

After receiving all the offers, the CG (general contractor) adds them all together, adds contingencies, overheads, and profits from the general requirements section, and sends the client's final quote. Most clients ask general contractors to send in their quotes by following a pricing form sheet for better comparisons with other general contractors.

SAMPLE 29. General Contractor Proposal

Example of GC Proposal Submission Form

Company Letter Head and Address

Submission Form

Consultant Project NO. 1234 Date : 2014-03-19

Project: Training Center Sudbury

1. I declare, on my behalf or on behalf of the company I represent:
   a. I have received and taken cognizance of the complete estimate, plans, general conditions, and all addenda issued and instructions to bidders and other tender documents concerning the title project.
   b. I have taken the necessary information on the replacement status of the work, the nature of the services to be provided, and the contract requirements.
   c. to be satisfied with the documents made available to me, having understood all the conditions and their outcomes. To my knowledge, there is no other relevant and decisive information that the client could have.
2. I therefore undertake:
   a. to comply with all the conditions and specifications appearing in the tender documents, and to perform all the work required by the plans and specifications, as well as all those which, although not explicitly mentioned, are necessary in accordance with the spirit of the plans and specifications;
   b. to accomplish all this work for the lump sum of ....dollars ($) in legal money of Canada, including the cost of permits (except building permit), premiums, royalties as well as all applicable taxes;
   c. to complete all this work within the time limit prescribed in section 01 11 00 Summary of the work;
   d. to hire only subcontractors having an establishment comprising in Ontario or, having an intergovernmental agreement is applicable, in Quebec or in a province or territory covered by this agreement, permanent installations and the personnel required to carry out the work that are the subject of their mandate, except for specialties which are exempt from this obligation in the tender documents
3. I certify that the price submitted is valid for sixty days (60 days) from the deadline set for the submission of bids.

BID FORM

Price Ventilated

SAMPLE 30. Bid Form

	Price	Total
Division 1 - General conditions		
Site organization, including equipment mobilization and demobilization costs		
Construction management		
Site insurances		
Bonds		
Final site cleaning		
Others Specify		
Subtotal Division 1		
Division 3- Concrete		
Formwork		
Steel Rebars		
Concreting		
Precast Concrete Panels		
Others (Specify)		
Subtotal Division 3		
Division 4- Masonry		
Concrete blocks and accessories		
Others Specify		
Subtotal Division 4		
Division 5- Metals		
Steel Frame		
Metal post supporting frames		
Metallic structures		
Ladders and metal stairs		
Others Specify		
Subtotal Division 5		
Division 6- Wood and Plastic		
Laminated wood structure		
Wood Work		
Carpentry		
Cabinet		
Laminated Finish Coating		
Others Specify		
Subtotal Division 6		
Continue the same ... to Division 32		
Subtotal Divisions 1 to 32		$
Administration and Profit		

Award The Contract

SAMPLE 31. Award The Contract Letter of Intent

Letter Of Intent

The client reviews the price of all general contractors and decides who to work with; the client must send a letter of intent to the successful bidder stating the preliminary commitment to do business with the contractor. The letter of intent indicates the employer's attention to enter into a formal written contract for the work described in the letter or referred to (under the name RFQ#) and requesting the contractor to begin the work before executing the formal contract.

Letter Head: Owner/Client Logo, Name, and Complete address

April 29, 2014

Mr. xxxxxxx, Director
Name of the Contractor
complete address

Project: Training Center Sudbury-Lot1. F/N: Consultant or Client File Number

OBJECT: LETTER OF INTENT

Dear Sir/Madam,

We are pleased to inform you that the ***(Client/Owner Name)*** is awarding you a construction contract for the project as mentioned above, in the amount of your bid, which is ***7 500 000$.***

A construction contract will be prepared for signature by both parties in the amount of your proposed bid. Please send the required documents (see attached document) upon Fifteen days of receiving this letter of intent. Forms are to be forwarded to ***(Consultant or Owner name and address)*** or electronically ***(Email or Website).***

Please contact the consultant firm to plan a start-up meeting for this project (***mention the name and contacts of the person to communicate with).***

We thank you in advance for your collaboration and remain,

Sincerely yours,

cc:

List of documents required for signing the contract.

Project Title: Sudbury Training Center

Project number:

SAMPLE 32. List Of documents Required When Awarding the Contract

To Submit	Already Submitted	N/A	Document Title
☐	☒	☐	Letter of Intention
☐	☒	☐	Bidding Form
☐	☒	☐	Resolution for signing an authorization for the contract – original
☒	☐	☐	Performance bond - original or check vice representing 10% of the cost of the contract
☒	☐	☐	Guarantee of the contractor's obligations for pledges and services - original or check vice representing 10% of the cost of the contract
☒	☐	☐	Civil liability insurance certificate - Annex-A (in the case of a CCDC contract) completed by the insurer
☒	☐	☐	Site insurance certificate to be provided by the contractor - Annex 3-8 (in the case of a contract CCDC) completed by the insurer
☒	☐	☐	Entrepreneur's license
☐	☒	☐	Schedule of work
☐	☒	☐	Subcontractor List

Negotiation with Contractors

According to the type of contracts and following the RFQ documents, the Project management team can negotiate some contracts. The general contractor can obtain profit for the project before even starting the job.

However, before starting the negotiation techniques, keep in mind the following (from staff experience):

- Never Tell a Contractor They are the Only One Bidding on the Job.
- Don't Tell a Contractor Your Budget.
- Never Ask a Contractor for a Discount if You Pay Upfront.
- Don't Tell a Contractor That You Aren't in A Hurry.
- Do Not Let a Contractor Choose the Materials.

You may have provided the take-off item to subcontractors or have asked them to send you their take-off quantities while submitting their quotes. If so, your team would check if the project manager can remove specific portions from the quote and, accordingly, you can negotiate the cost difference.

You can get lower prices before mobilization simply by calling the contractors and asking them for a discount; again, if the tendering process allows the general contractors to choose the second or third lower price, you would be amazed knowing that subcontractors would lower their cost over the phone and the project manager could create more contingency or profit.

The following is an example of the actual real-life negotiation sheet.

Tip: Activities that are not on the critical path (review time management) and do not start immediately can be negotiated and improved first. As you can see, understanding all the tools and techniques of project management results in a better cost-benefit ratio and a better schedule. All these knowledge areas integrate during project execution, time management, cost management, resource management, integration management, communication management, etc.

Table 12. Negotiation Reporting

Specialty	Bidding Company name	Awarded company name	Budget Code	Bidding Price (1)	Revised price (2)	(1)-(2)
Asphalt	A	A	2530	$190,000	$190,000	
Fencing	B	C (Changed for the competitive price provided)	2620	$20,500	$16,000	$4,500
Formwork	D	D	3100	$26,000	$26,000	
Rebars	E	E	3200	$40,000	$35,000	$5,000
Prefabricated Concrete Blocks	F	F	3400	$470,000	$430,000	$40,000
Maconry	G	G	4100	$120,000	$100,000	$20,000
Steel Structure	H	H	5100	$320,000	$280,000	$40,000
Etc...						
Total to Date					**$1,077,000.00**	**$109,500**

CHAPTER 10 - DETERMINE BUDGET

Budget planning is building a budget and then using it to control a business's operations. The purpose of budget planning is to mitigate the risk that an organization's financial results will be worse than expected.

In mid-sized companies, a project manager/ senior project manager/ operations manager/ etc., who supervises and works closely with the estimation department, is usually responsible for creating a project budget.

In larger companies, a Design, Engineering, or Project Management Department can assign staff to estimate the project.

Activity Cost Estimates and Timelines

Cost estimates for each activity within a work package are aggregated to obtain a cost estimate for each work package.

As part of the project management plan, the project Schedule includes planned start and finish dates for the project activities, milestones, and work package. This information can be used to determine the budget.

Assigning resources for activities indicates resource costs throughout the project.

Applicable purchase orders, including services and renting equipment, are included when determining the budget.

Example of budget created (planned cost) - can be found in the company system to which the project management team has access. This budget will include all direct and indirect costs. This budget will be monitored by the project manager, the account payable, the director, the operation manager, and/ or any other person in an authorized position.

Planned Costs are determined for Insurances and Bonds, Supervisions, Electricity, Trailers, Telephones, Meals and Lodging, Transport, Cleaning, Equipment, Maintenance, Gas, Diesel, Transport, Concrete Work, Steel and Metal Works, Wood Works, Civil Works, etc.

Example:

Table 13 Budget.

Project: Training Center Sudbury, Ontario, Canada P. 014-221	Planned Construction Duration: May 2014-May 2015	Closeout Planned Duration June 2015-Sept 2015
Activity CODE & Description		
01041 Project Manager (PM)		
Comments		
12-month x $10,000 (Include Benefits) Full time + 4 months(June-Sept 2015) *25% of time (Close out)= $120K+$10K	Manpower	$130,000
	Equipment	PM Truck expenses can be found in code 01810
	S-Contractor	
	Material	$10,000
	Total	**$140,000**
01930 Mobilization/Demobilization		
Site Organization. Including Equipment and exterior surveying	Manpower	$25,000
	Equipment	$7,000
	S-Contractor	
	Material	$1,000
	Total	**$33,000**
02317 Gravel Infrastructure		
GC will be working on this activity with his forces. No Subcontractor. From Estimation calculation sheet.	Manpower	$20,000
	Equipment	$30,000
	S-Contractor	
	Material	$90,000
	Total	**$140,000**
02315 Excavation & Backfill		
15 m3 including waterproofing sys 120m2. Insulation etc. From the Estimation calculation sheet.	Manpower	$25,000
	Equipment	$50,000
	S-Contractor	
	Material	$5,000
	Total	**$80,000**
03100 Concrete and Formwork		
SUB1 Add $10,000 in Lodging & Meal Code 01595	Manpower	
	Equipment	
	S-Contractor	$60,000
	Material	$5,000
	Total	**$65,000**

Creating Subcontractor List for each job

The list of subcontractors is first created during the estimation phase; it may contain a few subcontractors for each discipline with recommendations. After that, the project manager or the contract administrator will re-evaluate the best bidder, which returns the best investment for the company, as explained before. Then the accountant and the project management team put everything into the system.

The list of subcontractors in the estimation phase may look like this:

Table 14. List of Subcontractors-Estimation

Specialty	Company	Contact Person	Tel/e-mail	Price	Recommendations
Asphalt Code 2530	A			$100,000	Less than 10% of the estimated price. Confirm the quantity before awarding the contract.
	B			$120,000	Used price in the tender document.
	C			$125,000	Previous experience with our company.
	D			$220,000	
Rebars Code 3200	E			$40,000	Used price in the tender document.
	F			$50,000	Price can be negotiated. Good reputation company. Good experience with our company. Contractor Evaluation Form shows more than 80% (Satisfaction rate)
	G			$52,000	
	H			$74,000	

The list of subcontractors, when the contracts are in the award phase (e.g., preparation of project manager or contract administrator) may look like this:

SAMPLE 33. List of Subcontractors

Specialty	Company	Contact Person	Tel/e-mail	Price	Recommendations
Asphalt Code 2530	A			$100,000	Price Confirmed and quantity verified
Rebars Code 3200	F			$38,000	Price Negotiated and went down $12,000

The accountant or management team may enter the costs into the system as follows:

SAMPLE 34. Account Job Cost Codes

Specialty	**Total Budgeted amount**	**Commitments**	**PO issued date**	**Contingency**	**Projected final Costs**
Asphalt	$117,500	$100,000	2014.08.15	$10,000	$107,500
	Manpower	Material	Equipment	Subcontractor	
Code 2530	$7,500	0	0	$100,000	
Rebars	**Total Budgeted amount**	**Commitments**	**PO issued date**	**Contingency**	$38,000
Code 3200	$40,000	$38,000	2014.08.20	$2,000	
	Manpower	Material	Equipment	Subcontractor	
	$0	0	0	$40,000	

The total budgeted amount for the asphalt is estimated at $117,500, including the estimated subcontractor price of $100,000, and the labor required to help the contractor is $7,500. The award of a $100,000 contract resulted in a savings of $10,000, which the project manager can use for any unforeseen situation. This $10,000 is not supposed to cover change orders unless those change orders are missing from the tender documents sent to subcontractors. If it is not used, the project manager will add this contingency to the project's profit.

The total budgeted amount for rebar is estimated to be $40,000; the subcontractor's price must cover everything. The award of a $38,000 contract resulted in savings of $2,000.

Creating Original Business Case (B.C.O.) & Contracts

A. Creating Original Business Case (B.C.O.)

When a budget is created for the project, a business case is developed in the system. It gets all the necessary approvals according to the standards of the company. In this book, the first business case set to create a project will be called a B.C.O. See Table –"Original Business Case." This B.C.O. for most companies looks like a questionnaire describing the costs and benefits of specific projects.

At the start of the construction stage, a budget for the whole project is opened. This budget contains contingencies. Not all contracts have been officially awarded. Construction work has not started. The design work, if any, is almost complete. According to the table, today's date should be around 5/25/2022. Allow approximately two weeks to 2 months for all contracts to be signed and awarded according to the company approval process.

Table- Original Business Case can have more than 50 lines for general contractors, including all the sub-trades. If applicable, the internal expenses of the general conditions' part and the rental of equipment, etc. Each element must be budgeted for and controlled during project execution, either manually or using the company program, or both.

B. Creating Contracts.

A project team is assigned. Contracts should be awarded to start the project. The project stakeholders can be made up of:

- Development team: Project managers for construction and project managers for design and engineering; Construction superintendents, buyers, etc.
- Team of consultants: Safety consultants, Other professionals (Engineers (Structures, Mechanics, Electrical, Civil, etc...), Architects, Landscapers, etc.),
- Team of general contractors: Project managers, superintendents, foreman, subcontractors, etc.
- Government team if necessary; for example, municipal and regional team, etc.
- Others.

Some companies may like to negotiate contracts to cut costs; this is an excellent time to close the deals. The project team is prepared for the next step. Everyone is waiting for the contract or purchase order to be issued and received.

Project Managers at different levels (Developers/ Owners/ consultants/ contractors/ municipalities) begin to prepare the project according to the level of responsibility. Read the plans and specifications of the project, understand the General Conditions, identify Critical Paths, anticipate errors, seek the best security measures, prepare for the pre-construction or kick-off meeting, purchase or rent of pieces of equipment, and any other necessary preparation.

Creating Purchase Orders and Sending Them to Vendors

The buyer sent all Purchase Orders (PO); the Project Manager can call for a pre-construction.

As the example in **Table** "Budgeted Contracts" shows, all contracts or purchase orders are issued. The system will also show which PO or contract is pending so that the responsible manager can follow up. In this case, I recommend whoever has read this manual to follow up and find the reason for the delay if she or he is in a decision-making position.

To further explain **Table** "Budgeted Contracts." The total approved budget from the management level for this project is $350,000. Apparently, after sending the contracts' $32,500 ($350,000- $317,500) is the contingency for this project. The project manager will use this additional funding to cover all change orders to come either from the contractor/ subcontractor part or the consultant part. Notice that for Consultant 2 (which can be the engineer, for instance), there is no contingency. The budget is $20K, and the contract is $20K. If an extra comes, the project manager either needs to transfer contingency from another discipline to cover this extra (change order) or create a business case amendment (B.C.) or any other similar synonym that the company uses to add more budgets (funding).

N.P: this table will possibly contain more columns, such as the Holdback release; Variance; Tax; deferred costs; Actual start and end dates; Etc. However, for ease of illustration, analyzing the items mentioned in the column table is sufficient to comprehend the system.

MasterFormat divisions are widely used for budgeting purposes. See **Table** "Budget and MasterFormat Divisions." Items such as Division 01 can be used to cover equipment rental, supervisions, surveyors, temporary electricity, etc. Division 03 can also be divided to cover formwork, reinforcing steel, concrete, precast concrete panels, etc.

The table can also be exhausted with many specialties; however, all businesses should estimate budgeted activities and compare them with actual activities to create better estimation tools and predict future job costs as lessons learned.

You can imagine that the displayed tables can be retrieved from an enterprise system. The system can also allow you to divide each code into subcategories such as manpower, equipment, material, and subcontractor.

Example:

Figure 18. Budgeting Distribution for Each Activity

Description	Code		Budget(Include Contingency)	Commitment (PO/Contract Issued)	%Completed	Cost to Date	Cost to come
Reinforcing Steel 03200	03200	Manpower	$20,000	$17,500	20%	$3,500	$14,000
	03200	Equipment	$5,000	$5,000	20%	$1,000	$4,000
	03200	Material	$10,000	$7,500	20%	$1,500	$6,000
	03200	S-Contract	0.00	0,00			
	S-Total		**$35,000**	**$30,000**		**$6,000**	**$24,000**

Table 15. Original Business Case/Budget

Project 001	Address: 123 Front street		Description: New Roof System		Project Manager: Tom Smith		Buyer: Hank		Superintendent: Luis			
Design Schedule Start 01/25/2022			Design Schedule complete 05/25/2022			Construction Start 07/25/2022		Construction Complete 012/25/2022				
Project Number 001	**Budget *(Planned)***	**Cumulative Change Orders**	**Pending revisions (Change Orders)**	**Revised budget**	**Contract Amount**	**Revised Contract Amount**	**Pending Contract Amount**	**Invoiced**	**% Completed Invoice**	**% Completed Actual on site**	**Forecast to Complete**	**Projected Final Cost**
	$350,000	$0.00	$0.00	$350,000	$0.00	$0.00	$0.00	$0.00	0	0	$350,000	$350,000

Table 16. Budgeted Contracts

Project 001	Address: 123 Front street		Description: New Roof System		Project Manager: Tom Smith.		Buyer: Hank		Superintendent: Luis			
Design Schedule Start 01/25/2022			Design Schedule complete 05/25/2022			Construction Start 07/25/2022			Construction Complete 012/25/2022			
Project Number 001	**Budget *(Planned)***	**Cumulative Change Orders**	**Pending revisions (Change Orders)**	**Revised budget**	**Contract Amount**	**Revised Contract Amount**	**Pending Contract Amount**	**Invoiced**	**% Completed Invoice**	**% Completed Actual on site**	**Forecast to Complete**	**Projected Final Cost**
Roofing Contractor	$300,000	$0.00	$0.00	$300,000	$275,000	$275,000	$0.00	$0.00	0	0	$300,000	$300,000
Safety Consultant	$10,000	$0.00	$0.00	$10,000	$7,500	$7,500	$0.00	$0.00	0	0	$10,000	$10,000
Consultant 1	$20,000	$0.00	$0.00	$20,000	$15,000	$15,000	$0.00	$0.00	0	0	$20,000	$20,000
Consultant 2	$20,000	$0.00	$0.00	$20,000	$20,000	**$20,000**	$0.00	$0.00	0	0	$20,000	$20,000
	$350,000	$0.00	$0.00	$350,000	**$317,500**	$317,500	$0.00	$0.00	0	0	$350,000	$350,000

Entering contract value - best used for a client

Table 17. Budget and MasterFormat Divisions

Entering contract value - best used for a client

Project 001	Description: New Roof System	Project Manager:	Buyer:	Superintendent
Address: 123 Front street		Tom Smith.		Luis
Design Schedule Start	Design Schedule complete	Construction Start		Construction Complete
01/25/2022	05/25/2022	07/25/2022		012/25/2022

Project Number 001	**Budget (*Planned*)**	**Cumulative Change Orders**	**Pending revisions (Change Orders)**	**Revised budget**	**Contract Amount**	**Revised Contract Amount**	**Pending Contract Amount**	**Invoiced**	**% Completed Invoice**	**% Completed Actual on site**	**Forecast to Complete**	**Projected Final Cost**
Division 00 - Procurement and Contracting Requirements												
Division 01 - General Requirements												
01007 Insurance												
01039 Supervisions												
01051 Surveyor												
01511 Temporary Electricity												
01514 Telephone (Cell & fix)												
01590 Trailer & toilette												
01710 Final Cleaning												
01810 Renting Equipment												
Division 02 - Existing Conditions												
02622 Drainage												
02410 Civil Work												
02317 Gravel												
02315 Excavation & Backfill												
02715 Gravel under a slab												
02620 Fences												
02715 Bollard, Bases for flag poles												
Division 03- Concrete												
Etc.												

Table 18. Budgeting for a HomeBuilder

A good start budgeting for Home Builders

Project 001	Address: 123 Front street		Description: New Roof System		Project Manager: Tom Smith.		Buyer: Hank		Superintendent: Luis			
Design Schedule Start			Design Schedule complete			Construction Start			Construction Complete			
01/25/2022			05/25/2022			07/25/2022			012/25/2022			
Project Number 001	**Budget (Planne d)**	**Cumulative Change Orders**	**Pending revisions (Change Orders)**	**Revised budget**	**Contract Amount**	**Revised Contract Amount**	**Pending Contract Amount**	**Invoiced**	**% Completed Invoice**	**% Completed Actual on site**	**Forecast to Complete**	**Projected Final Cost**
Site Maintenance												
Fencing (perimeter)												
Tree Removal												
Site Servicing												
Site Grading												
Electrical Site Servicing												
Hard & Soft Landscaping												
Entry Gate												
Driveway Paving												
Utility Connections												
Construction Management												
Site Superintendents & labours												
Building Permit												
Architect												
Interior Designer												
Site Servicing Engineer												
Structural Engineer												
Electrical Engineer												
Mechanical												
Landscape Architect												
Survey												
Tree Consultant												
Natural Heritage Consultant												
Geotechnical/Environmental/Record of Site Condition												
Etc.												

CHAPTER 11 – COST CONTROL

Goals of Project Cost Control:

- A timely, accurate comparison of actual cost against planned budget.
- A timely, accurate comparison of actual schedule against planned schedule.
- "Early Warning" of problems and identification of possible corrective actions.
- Control of changes.
- Valuable reports; keep everyone informed where they stand against their budget and schedule.
- Forecast for the cost and schedule at completion.

Figure 19. Cost Control Interaction

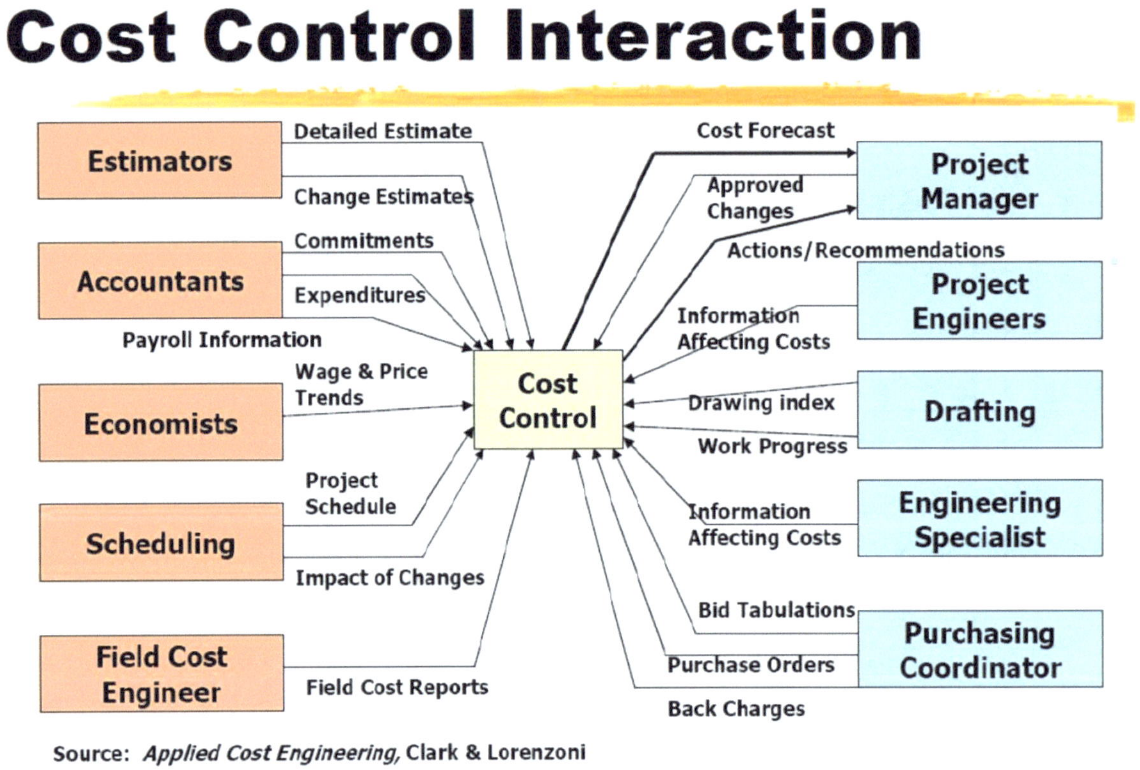

Actual Cost against Planned Budget

Project Management Department Cost Control

Control the budget at the level of the project management department, which may include in medium-sized companies, the team of the construction manager (for example, Project Directors, Project Managers, Estimators, Superintendents, Foreman, etc.). Each project manager should be given clear instructions on how to report on budget progress using specified tools and techniques.

Control the Cost Using Excel

After creating the estimate using simple software like Excel or more complicated software like Timberline or others, the project director, for example, adds the contingency (usually 5%-15%) and creates a detailed budget for the control of costs.

This budget will be distributed to the accounting department and the site manager, such as the project manager, for cost control purposes.

One example used among many of the budgets distributed to the project manager is the Control Budget and Cost distribution sample.

Note that each activity is divided into four sections (Remember the 4M's from PMBOOK) (Material, Money (Subcontractor), Machine, and Manpower).

In this example, a long database sheet has been created and **linked** to the cost distribution sheet to detail all expenses and the progress of payments. The planned budget can therefore be controlled and sometimes improved.

Companies create different datasheet entries and show how the cost is distributed and the project progresses. Most of the time, this is a system entry.

SAMPLE 35. Control Budget and Cost Distribution

Description	CODE		Cost	% Used	Cost Distribution: ManPower	Equipment	Materials	Sub-contractors	Others	S-Total	Budget Available ($)	Cost to Come $
Insurances & Bonds	01007	ManPower		0%	$0					$0	$0	$0
	01007	Equipment		0%		$0				$0	$0	$0
	01007	Material		0%			$0			$0	$0	$0
	01007	S-Contract	$134,250	93%				$124,422		$124,422	$9,828	
	01007	Transport		0%					$0	$0	$0	$0
		S - Total	$134,250									
Foreman	01039	ManPower	$160,980	31%	$50,305					$50,305	$110,675	$110,675
	01039	Equipment		0%		$0				$0	$0	$0
	01039	Material		0%			$0			$0	$0	$0
	01039	S-Contract		0%				$0		$0	$0	$0
	01039	Transport		0%					$0	$0	$0	$0
		S - Total	$160,980									
Project Managers	01041	ManPower	$106,470	26%	$28,000					$28,000	$78,470	$78,470
	01041	Equipment		0%		$0				$0	$0	$0
	01041	Material		0%			$0			$0	$0	$0
	01041	S-Contract		0%				$0		$0	$0	$0
	01041	Transport		0%					$0	$0	$0	$0
		S - Total	$106,470									
Surveyor	01051	ManPower		0%	$0					$0	$0	$0
	01051	Equipment		0%		$0				$0	$0	$0
	01051	Material		0%			$0			$0	$0	$0
	01051	S-Contract	$6,920	0%				$0		$0	$6,920	$6,920

Database sheet

	A	B	C	D	E	F	G	H	I	J	K	L	M	N	O	P	Q
1																	
2	Description	Descriptrion	P.O # / n° bon de cde	req date	Purchased Date / Date du bon de cde	Requis #	Invoice # / n° facture	Invoiced Date / Date de la facture	Act. Code	Amount Purchase Order / Montant bon de commande	COST Correction	COST Invoice with P.O / Facture avec bon de cde	COST Invoice without P.O / Facture sans bon de cde	SubContractor	Contact Name	Tel #	Fax #
2848							Material		16000	$ 150.00	-$ 150.00	$ -	$ -				
2849	NewTec Elctrique																
2850	Payment Request 1	2014-06-01			17-Jun-14		14099	25-May-14	16000	$ 69,215.00	-$ 69,215.00	$ -		NewTec Electrique	Martin Gagnon		
2851	Payment Request 2	2014-06-02			25-Jun-14		14110	25-Jun-14	16000	$ 7,962.00	-$ 7,962.00	$ -					
2852	Payment Request 3	2014-06-03					14120	25-Jul-14	16000	$ 6,893.00	-$ 6,893.00						
2853	Payment Request 4	2014-06-04					14139	25-Aug-14	16000	$ 154,295.00	-$ 154,295.00						
2854									16000		$ -						
2855									16000		$ -						
2856									16000		$ -						
2857	Transport 30,000$								16000		$ -						
2858	DDP # 1	mai 2014	164415				F14633		16000	$ 4,500.00	-$ 4,500.00			NewTec Electrique			
2859	DDP# 2	Juin 2014	164415				F14264		16000	$ 3,000.00	-$ 3,000.00	$ -	$ -				
2860	DDP 3	Jul-14							16000	$ 1,500.00	-$ 1,500.00	$ -	$ -				
2861	DDP#4	Aug-14							16000	$ 3,000.00	-$ 3,000.00						
2862									16000		$ -						
2863									16000		$ -						
2864									16000		$ -						
2865									16000		$ -						
2866									16000								
2867									16000	$ -	$ -	$ -	$ -				
2868							S-Contrat		16000	$ 250,365.00	-$ 250,365.00	$ -	$ -				

Control the Cost Using Complimentary Programs

Many of the materials explained in this section can be read in the Procurement Project Management Section.

Each company can use different project management and accounting control systems; however, they all achieve the same goal: cost control.

The project management and control system (Computer System) is created for the following fundamental reasons.

- Creating Original Business Case & Contract.
- Creating Purchase Orders and sending them to vendors.
- Creating Change Orders.
- Creating Business Case for Amendments.
- Following Invoice progress.
- Creating Subcontractor List for each job.
- Budget Control.

More advanced systems can cover the following control points:

- Schedule Control.
- Creating requisitions.
- Bid management.
- And others.

Regardless of the sophisticated appearance of any program or system used, they will all exhibit the same principles and perform similarly. General examples will illustrate some of the elements mentioned.

Budget Control by a System

The system will refuse the issuance of any purchase order exceeding the budgeted values. This is a way of alerting the team that the project cost will exceed the budget and that justifications are needed at this stage. As explained earlier, creating a business case in some companies is one way to justify budget overruns (adding the extra scope of the original design).

As a general rule, a general contractor should not exceed the budget submitted to the client since any addition over the budget is a change order, which the client will be willing to pay associated with the management fees. On the other hand, from the client's perspective, the allocated budget can be exceeded if the client is willing to add items over the scope of work.

As an example, you are a client, and you want to renovate your house. You ask a general contractor to send you the cost of these renovations following the plans and specifications completed by the consultants. At the start of the project, you realize that it would be beneficial for the market value of your house to create an open concept kitchen that requires additional construction materials and a new beam to substitute a load-bearing wall. This cost is extra for the client. He has to bring the funds for it; however, this cost is outside the scope of work for the general contractor. The client will pay additional fees for the contractor to execute the work as modified.

Schedule Control by a system

When the company depends on an automatic system as one way to control the cost and schedule, the company will require the project manager to update regularly the schedule in the system. When the business depends on an automatic system to control costs and schedule, the business will ask the project manager to periodically update the schedule in the system (project start and end dates). In the event of a delay, the system-generated reports will highlight projects that are falling behind, showing the baseline schedule and revisions. Based on company protocols, the project manager should identify the reasons for this delay (e.g., shop drawing approval process, lack of workforce in the company's staff, a subcontractor, change orders, etc.) Suppose the justification is not convincing, such as understaffing one subcontractor; in that case, the company should implement a preventive measure such as putting a detailed explanation in the evaluation form of that subcontractor for later review (lesson learned).

Creating Requisitions

A project manager or superintendent can create requisitions to buy materials or equipment for the site. Some companies offer some cash, "petty cash" for the site team to use; others offer credit cards for this purpose. In any way, these materials or equipment to be bought must be well ordered by formal requisitions.

Timely Accurate comparison of Actual Schedule Against Planned Schedule

The project manager is responsible for the progress of the project. This person should keep the next level informed of any project delays. One method of revising the completion date is to update the calendar in the system.

For example, today's date is 05/25/2024. Color is used in the system to measure actual versus planned; green to display the indication of the schedule ahead, red for the delay. Explanations must be noted by the project manager or a senior manager to explain the delay (reasons of force majeure, refusal of entry into the tenant accommodation, manufacturing delay, significant modifications to the project, etc.)

Construction Start Date	05/20/2024	Actual Start date	**04/30/2024**
Construction End Date	10/20/2024	Actual Complete date	**11/02/2024**

Early Warning of Problems and Identification of Possible Corrective Actions

As the project progresses, we need to monitor and control the project work to ensure that risks are identified early, their status is reported, and appropriate risk plans are being executed. Monitoring includes **status reporting, progress measurement, and forecasting.**

Performance Reports Real-Life Examples

Performance report provides information on the project's performance concerning scope, schedule, cost, resource, quality, and risk.

Performance report for a portfolio of many projects.

Example # 1

In this performance report, managers at the executive level want to know how projects are going in general. Usually, they may need to know which disciplines are not awarded contracts and how much is spent to date and planned to spend more.
The data provided in the table assumes that today's date is May 17, 2021. We need to get a cash flow of $4,874,356.40 for the first two projects by the end of 2023 and an additional $1,374,077.32 by 2022. There isn't much detail in this report, but it's important to get a general idea of how the project is going. Forecast reports will be more detailed for each quarter or month and explained later in this manual. However, this table will allow the executives to ask questions related to contract awards and progress. For example, why no noise study contract is yet ready for the first two projects? Isn't it necessary?

SAMPLE 36. Construction Global Performance Report (Land Development)

Construction Global Performance Report (Land Development cost)			
Short Project Description	67 Single Detached Houses. Land area 0.2 Hectare	60 Single Detached Houses. Land area 0.18 Hectare	18 Single Detached Houses. Land area 3 Acres
Approved Budget	**$5,000,000**	**$4,500,000**	**$1,500,000**
Reports List/ SCHEDULE	01/01/2021 - 12/31/2023	02/02/2021- 12/31/2023	05/03/2021- 12/31/2022
PLANNING	**$47,000**	**$40,000**	**$20,000**
CONSULTANT PLANNING PART	$12,000	$10,000	$6,000
ASI ARCHAELOGICAL STUDY	$0	$0	$2,000
NOISE STUDY	$0	$0	$1000
SURVEYING	$35,000	$30,000	$5,000
TOWN	$0,00	$0,00	$500
ENGINEERING & LANDSCAPING	**$229,850.00**	**$142,592.50**	**$105,922.68**
SUBDIVISON AGREEMENT			$16,824.09
TOWN ENGINEERING FEES			$18,616.84
LANDSCAPE FEES	$15,000.00		$6,080.25
REVIEW FEES	$85,000	$110,000.00	$0.00
AGREEMENT COST	$7,000.00	$1,650.00	$0.00
PERMITS	$850.00	$900.00	$0.00
APPLICATIONS	$2,000.00		$17,609.00
ENGINEERING SERVICES	$20,000.00	$30,042.50	$46,792.50
Distribution System Code HYDRO DISTRIBUTION	$100,000		$0.00
CIVIL CONSTRUCTION	**$2,177,981.50**	**$1,988,219.60**	**$0,00**
TREE SLASHING	$23,000.00	$63,000.00	
CUT & FILLS	$162,800.00	$268,000.00	
FILL MATERIALS IMPORTED	$400,000.00	$450,000.00	
Forcemain	$433,299.00		
Subdivision Servicing Contract	$998,013.75	$179,652.50	
STREET LIGHTS	$106,966.91		
UTILITY TRENCH & ROAD CROSSINGS FOR STREET LIGHTS	$45,000.00		
BRIDGE CONSTRUCTION		$1,027,567.10	
ETC.			
Total Project Cost	**$2,454,831.50**	**$2,170,812.10**	**$125,922.68**
Cost to come	**$2,545,168.50**	**$2,329,187.90**	**$1,374,077.32**

Example# 2

It is always good to have additional reports ready when creating a general report like the one explained above. For example, have a list of an updated list of subcontractors prepared for each project and another list for the progress of the contract, if necessary. As a project manager, be ready for explanations. Specify when items are underestimated or when savings can be obtained and identify the reasons. You can shine in this meeting if this exercise is done right. See the following example.

SAMPLE 37. Contractual Status Report

Project Name	67 Single Detached Houses. Land area 0.2 Hectare			
Contracts	**Contract awarded YES/No**	**Values**	**Vendor**	**Comments**
POND CONSTRUCTION AND CLEANING	No	$365,000	ABC	Draft contract sent for signature
POND TREES AND MAINTAINING	Yes	$66,000	XYZ	
BOULEVARD PLANTING	No	$64,000	C-VD	Received two quotes waiting for the third
LOT PAVING-DRIVEWAYS	Yes	$118,000	Asphalt	
LOT SODDING	NO	167,000	ABC	A confirmation meeting is required. The variance between the best two quotes is more than - 10% estimated cost.
UNDERGROUND CCTV AND REPAIRS	No			Working on the tender documents
TOP ASPHALT INSTALATION & SIDE WALKS	No			Working on the tender documents
CUT AND FILL	YES	$90,000	RANDY	Unit price contract. Estimated overrun for quantity variance cost by 20%. **10% more than the estimated budget.**
BRIDGE CONSTRUCTION	YES	$400,000	CCM	After negotiating with the Contractor, we save $100,000 from the original quote, **20% keeping under the estimated budget.**

Example #3

Brief Comparison of all projects as a summary.

SAMPLE 38. Project Portfolio Short Report

Project No. & Description	Original Contract Value	2020	2021	Future Years	Comments
1588 Justice Facility Sudbury	$20,000,000	$15,000,000	$5,000,000	$0.00	Ending June 2021
1590 Community Center Vaughn	$10,000,000	$5,000,000	$5,000,000	$0.00	Ending Dec 2021
1610 Repair of a garage roof in Montreal	$1,500,000	$250,000	$1,250,000	$0.00	Ending Nov 2021
1611 Supply and installation of 5 pre-fab buildings North York	$1,500,000	$1,500,000	$0.00	$0.00	Complete d
1620 Training Center Sudbury	$7,000,000	$0.00	$4,000,000	$3,000,00 0	Ending April 2022
Total	**$40,000,000**	**$21,750,000**	**$15,250,000**	**$3,000,00 0**	

Example#4

In this example, management should compare the actual completed values, money, and schedule to forecasted (planned). The management team can use a form that looks like this one.

Table 19. Planned Versus Actual - Cost Control

			Jan 2020	Feb 2020	Mar 2020	....	Dec2021
Project 1588 Justice Facility Sudbury $20,000,000 Budgeted Cost $18,000,000	Schedule	Planned	5%	7%	8%		
		Actual	7%	10%	12%		
	Invoicing	Planned	$1,000,000	$1,400,000	$1,600,000		
		Actual	$1,400,000	$2,000,000	$2,400,000		
	Cost	Planned	$900,000	$ 1,260,000	$1,440,000		
		Actual	$ 1,260,000	$1800,000	$2160,000		
		Profit	**$140,000**	**$200,000**	**$240,000**		
Project 1590 Community Center Vaughn $10,000,000 Budgeted Cost $9,000,000	Schedule	Planned	0%	2%	4%		
		Actual	0%	0 %	4%		
	Invoicing	Planned			$400,000		
		Actual			$400,000		
	Cost	Planned			$360,000		
		Actual	$20,000	$20,000	$360,000		
		Profit	**-$20,000**	**-$20,000**	**$40,000**		

Example# 5

The Cash-in and Cash-out report may look like the following figure. A project manager can do this for a portfolio of projects or a single project.

Figure 20. Cash-Ins Cash-Outs Report $$

	Oct-11	Nov-11	Dec-11	Jan-12	Feb-12	Mar-12	Apr-12	May-12
Expenses	$25,645.95	$24,521.00	$24,521.00	$61,872.36	$70,125.50	$80,747.50	$63,495.00	$29,525.00
Expenses Cumulative	$25,645.95	$50,166.95	$74,687.95	$136,560.31	$206,685.81	$287,433.31	$350,928.31	$380,453.31
Invoicing	51,020.95 $	$ 69,916.60	$ 33,269.26	$ 72,865.00	$ 106,088.75	$ 109,396.25	$ 104,185.00	$ 66,615.00
Invoicing Cumulative	$51,020.95	$120,937.55	$154,206.81	$227,071.81	$333,160.56	$442,556.81	$546,741.81	$613,356.81

Detailing Performance report for each project

A company can ask project managers to create their reports for each project. Most companies use a predefined template and teach managers how they require data to be entered.

Quick reminder, as explained previously, that the budget has already been created as a cost baseline and that protocols have been established to apply the contingency reserve.

The following is a real-life example of the type of reporting required by some businesses in the construction process.

Table 20. Project Cost Report

Project Number 001 Address: 123 Front Street		Construction of Training Center Actual Start Date: May 5, 2021 Planned end date Dec 31, 2022								
Description	**Budget**	**$Commitments/ Contracts**	**% Completed**	**Cost to date**	**Cost to come**	**Contingency**	**Contingency needed**	**Over/Under Budget$**	**Actual Start date**	**Actual end date**
Excavation	$20,000	$17,500	100%	$17,500	$ -	$2,500	$ -	**$2,500**	May 5, 2021	June 4, 2021
Concrete works	$100,000	$85,000	100%	$85,000	$ -	$15,000	$ -	**$15,000**	June 4, 2021	July 19, 2021
Frame work	$100,000	$90,000	90%	$81,000	$9,000	$10,000	$15,000	**-($5,000)**	July 19, 2021	October 17, 2021
Etc.										
Etc.										
Total Examples	**Total Budget = $7,490,267.95**		**Cost to date= $3,436,171.64**		**Cost to come= $ 3,799,047.61**			**Contingency needed = $100,000**		

This table can be expanded to show other essential items. Such as Invoices received, Invoices accrued, Change order values, Planned Start and End dates for each activity and/or for the whole project, Profit amount, Profit percentage, etc. Also, the invoices sent to the customers for collection are recorded. From the table above, we can extract the following information.

End of project Projection = Cost to date + Cost to come + Contingency needed = **$7,335,219.25**.
Assume that the Last Payment certificate, including the upcoming change orders, are **$7,512,872.52**. The profit for this project is the difference **($177,653.27)**.

As per the table above, each activity or contract is monitored in cost and schedule. Contingencies are also estimated and updated frequently as per company protocols, for example, monthly.

From the example explained, other reports can be extracted as needed. Sample of a monthly summary cost report is as follows.

SAMPLE 39. Monthly Summary Cost Report

	$ Previous Cumulative	**$ Current Period**	Cumulative	End of project Projection	Project Budget
Invoiced Amount	2,023,040.76 $	**1,820,182.16 $**	3,843,222.92 $	7,512,872.52 $(1)	7,490,267.95 $(2)
Cost	1,728,150.00 $ (3)	**1,708,021.64 $ (4)**	3,436,171.64 $	7,335,219.25 $(5)	7,272,112.95 $ (6)
Profit/loss	294,890.76 $	**112,160.52 $**	407,051.28 $	177,653.27 $	218,155.00 $
% Profit/Loss	14.58%	**6.16%**	10.59%	2.42%	3.00%

(1): = Budget + profit + Change orders approved by client and ready to invoice.

(2): = Original Budget + profit

(3): = The cost to date from the previous month report

(4): = The Cost to date from this month report – (1)

(5): = The Cost to date + The cost to come + Contingency

(6): = Original Budget

The invoiced amount corresponds to the invoices sent to the customer for payment. In other words, it is the amount of collections.

Each company generates different reports; however, if you understand the simple principles of the examples mentioned above, you will get the big picture.

CHAPTER 12 - CHANGE ORDERS

Managing change orders is considered an essential part of cost control. Because of the importance of addressing this activity, a new chapter has been devoted to change requests.

Creating Change Orders

A change order is a document used to record an amendment to your original construction contract. Change orders in construction create a record of additional services provided to the customer and the cost for those services.

Change orders exist because of the dynamic and complex nature of construction projects; for most projects, it's simply not possible to anticipate every challenge or variable from the outset.

Knowing who has the authority to agree to changes is one of the more important legal issues for a contractor. The person with the requisite authority to agree to changes, binds their party to that change. Any person who does not have the requisite power may not legally bind their party.

Depending on contractors and consultants, the process of creating a change order may be referred to as Change Notice, Project Change, Extra/Credit, Project Modification, or other synonyms. When the change notice is reviewed and approved by all parties, it is called a change order. The customer will then issue a purchase order for this change order. Most companies include these change order values in the original PO issued. For example, contract 4001 has been awarded for $100,000, and a change order 4001-01 of $5,000 is approved. The purchase order clerk will issue a revised purchase order of $105,000, including the amendments.

A standard change order should include the following:

- Name, address, and telephone number of the Job.
- Name of owner.
- A complete description of the new work to be done.
- Total price of materials and labor to complete the change.
- Revised completion date due to change request.
- Signatures of the representative of the company.

Managing change orders is a critical part of project success at various levels—the reason why the upper management should create a change order system in every company.

To enter a change order internally, the project manager must follow company procedures for entering a change order. An example of change request entry is described later.

Change Order Creating Example

Suppose the internal parties involved in issuing change orders are:

A. Project Manager (PM) Authority to approve change orders up to $10,000.
B. Senior Project Manager (SPM) Authority to approve change orders up to $25,000.
C. Project Director (PD) Authority to approve change orders from $25,000 to $250,000.
D. V.P Authority to approve change orders greater than $250,000.
E. The VP must approve cumulative change orders greater than $250,000 before being sent to the purchaser to issue a revised order.
F. No cumulative change order greater than 20% of the value of the awarded contract is eligible for issuance of a revised purchase order unless the President personally approves it.
G. The last person from the business unit who reviews and approves the contract (based on your unit's organizational structure, signing authority, and the workflow selected) can forward the contract to the PO Clerk for review and issue a revised PO, including the change order.

The project manager receives a third contractor modification order approved by the consultant, if necessary, at $20,000.

Summarize in a table the facts that the project manager must consider in his analysis before sending the change order to the next level, and secure against cost overruns for this activity.

After analyzing the Table (Change Order Workflow), the project manager can start writing the $20,000 change request, including all supporting documentation, explained later in this section.

The above table may be requested in some companies to ensure the project manager does due diligence, other companies can integrate all the data and encourage the project manager to create the change order via the system so that the thresholds are determined automatically.

Either way, as an apprentice, you should know that most businesses need the above information before pushing the change order to the next workflow level.

The management of change orders will significantly affect the project manager's assessment at the end of the year. Evaluation would have positive results if the change orders of a project are clear, well supported, and done before execution if possible.

Table 21. Change Order Workflow

Project Total budget:	**$7,500,000** (Including Contingency)	Contractor Name :	**ABC Contracting**
All Awarded contract values including change orders. N.P. ABC one Contract among a few others.		**$7,150,00000**	ABC Contract Value **$2,500,000**
Contingency = $7,500,000-$7,150,000= $350K		>$20,000. No need for amendment of the budget funding (B.C. Business Case)	
Project Start date:	2014-05-29	Project End Date:	2016-05-29
Approved CO's	**Value**	**Description**	**Reason**
Change Order 1	$230,000	Adding Steel Structure	Design Omission
Change order 2	$20,000	Additional Bracings	Safety Requirement- Following building Code new Compliance
Current change Order 3	**$20,000**	**Lodge and Boarding**	**Site conditions- Contractor is eligible for lodge and boarding as per contract document**
Cumulative CO's	**$270,000**	Workflow:	Send to SPM, PD & VP for approvals
Original ABC Award Contract Value	$2,500,000	% of cumulative change orders	$10.8% < 20% OK No Need for President Approval
Revised Completion date :	N/A- it doesn't affect the schedule	B.C. required?	NO (The original budget still has contingency = $350K-$20K = $330K)

Table 22. Creating a Change Order

COMPANY LOGO			
Vendor Name:	**Date(m/d/y):**	**RFQ/RFP#:**	**Change Order No:**
ABC Steel Contracting	01/15/2015	14-221	003
Project Number:	**PO Number:**	**Primary Contact:**	**Manager:**
1234	61778	PM's Name	PM's Name
Address:		**Work Description:**	
1234 Front Street, Ontario		Training Center	
Consultant:		**Internal Engineer/Architect:**	
DEF Consultant		Engineer Name	

Explanation of Change Orders – Add additional Pages if required

Description Of Change Order	Value of Change Order
ABC Contracting's initial scope of work did not include its employees' lodge and board. All the hotel rooms with which our company has contracted are reserved for the same period. An estimate of $20,000 is needed to cover the cost of the employee's lodge and board at another facility (see quote provided by contractor and hotel, with three meals per day). 4 employees x 20 days x $250/ day = $20,000	☐ Credit ☒ Extra ☐ Insurance required ☐ Bonding required **$20,000**

Reason for this Change Order				
☐ Missing in Design	☒ Requested by the Owner	☒ Request By Safety	☒ Site Condition	☐ Major Force
Others (Explain)				

Supporting Documentation attached					
☒ Consultant Change Order	☒ Receipt	☐ Report	☒ Quotation	☒ RFI	☒ E-mail
☐ Others (Specify)					

Status of work	
☐ Date of Start	
☐ Date of Completion	

If Started Explain why			
☐ Emergency	☒ Health and Safety	☐ Code Compliance	☒ Work Schedule
Others (Specify):	Complies with the terms of the contract. Division 1 Section xxx		
# of days for the delay :		**New Revised Schedule date:**	

Approvals:

Project Manager .... Date............................

Senior Project Manager .... Date............................

Project Director .... Date............................

V.P. .... Date............................

President .... Date............................

Creating a Business Case (B.C.) for Funding Amendments.

As the example explained before shows, if the change request values exceed the budgeted value of the project, some companies ask you to prepare a business case, break-even analysis, or amendment that describes the reason for exceeding the budget. In this book, we'll call it B.C. A B.C. should include the value of the budget change, the cost of making that decision (negative or positive), the risks of making that decision or not, and the expected benefits.

In accordance with the order change request, B.C.'s proposal must include a full explanation of the increased budget requirements. For example, B.C.O (Original Business Case) is created to design a pond with the help of a consultant when the design is complete. This BCO (Project) can be closed financially or extended to the construction phase by creating a B.C. to increase the budget to meet the financing needs and contingencies.

As noted above, the project manager can use the change request form and table to explain the need for additional funding.

Likewise, large companies could integrate all forms into their systems. Small businesses may require a faster chain of approval (for example, the project manager and manager or owner may close the deal).

Control of change Orders

The customer must approve change orders. "Emphasize this point during pre-construction meetings." Consultants and contractors should be aware that the client will evaluate them according to the management change guidelines.

The typical process used for change requests is as follows:

1. The contractor sends a request for information (RFI):
   - **Example (1)**: When opening the porch deck, the size of the support joists and space was found not to meet the minimum requirements of Ontario building codes. The contractor sends a request to the consultant (RFI) to request instructions on the site.
   - **Example (2)**: While excavating for the construction of a concrete ramp, the contractor accidentally found utility plastic pipes that cannot tolerate the additional loads of the ramp structure. The contractor sends a request to the consultant to request on-site instructions (RFI).
2. The consultant informs the owner, sends a site instruction report recommending the appropriate solutions, and requests a quote if this work falls outside the scope of the contractor's work.
3. The contractor sends an estimate for the additional work to be carried out.
4. The consultant reviews the proposal, compares it with previous projects, negotiates the price with the contractor, informs the owner, and obtains its acceptance, preferably in writing.
5. The consultant issues a change request form signed by the contractor, the consultant, and the owner.
6. The owner issues a purchase order (PO) for this change order and enters it into the system.
7. The consultant adds an item in the following progress payment report and presents it in the next payment certificate, which is generally between the 25th and the 5th of the following month.

Table 23. Adding 2 Change Orders to the Progress Payment Sheet

		Description	Value	% Completed	Previously invoiced	Current Month	Total Invoiced	To Come
Item Number	Change Orders							
45	Change order 1	Porch Joists to conform to OBC (Ontario Building Code)	$4,000	25%	$0,00	$1,000	$1,000	$3,000
46	Change Order 2	New utility System under Concrete Ramp	$10,000	100% (1)	$0,00	$10,000	$10,000	$0.00

*** The contractor could complete this change order before receiving a purchase order if this work was an emergency or essential for continuing the work. The contractor or the project manager should get the approval in writing form from the client representative. The project manager must inform his superiors of the urgency of doing this work. It wouldn't be easy for a project manager to defend himself for a site-approved potential highly estimated change order after completing the job. Do not put yourself in this situation. Obtain the required approvals before carrying out the work when possible.

CHAPTER 13 - INVOICING

SAMPLE 40. Invoice

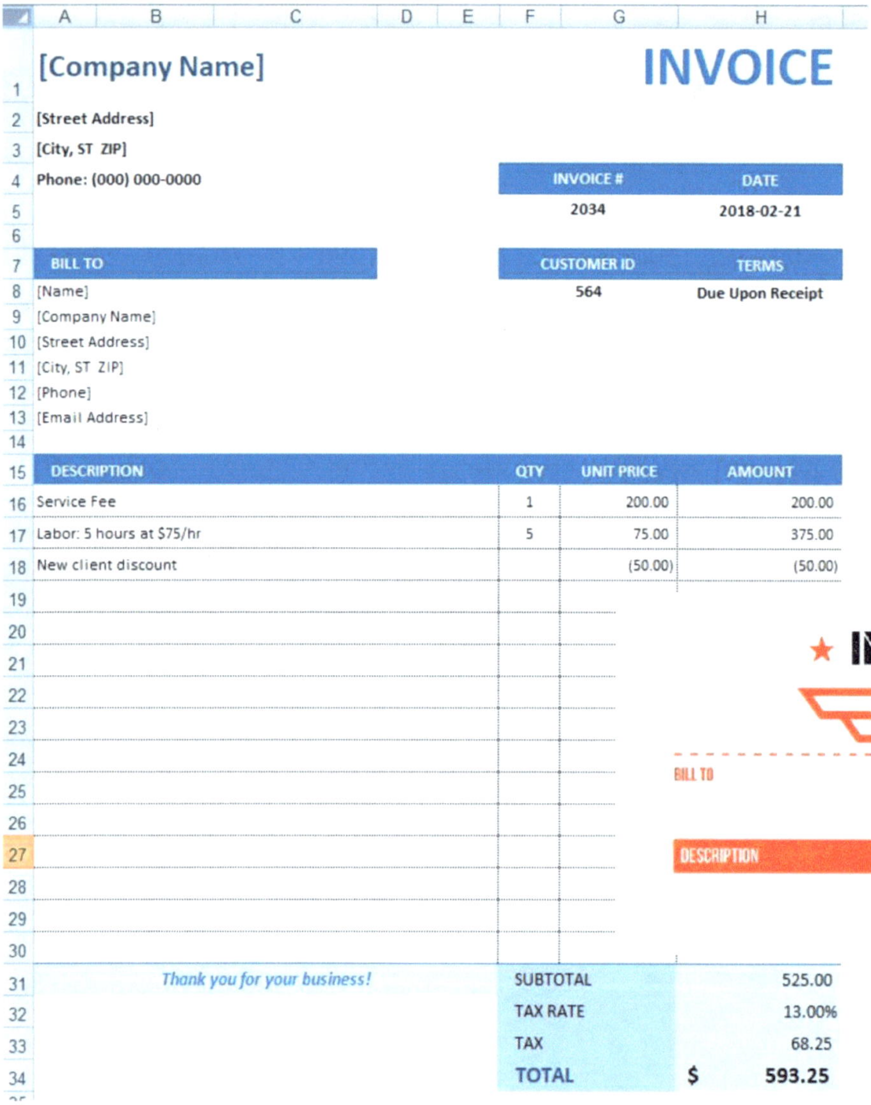

[Company Name]

INVOICE

[Street Address]
[City, ST ZIP]
Phone: (000) 000-0000

INVOICE #	DATE
2034	2018-02-21

CUSTOMER ID	TERMS
564	Due Upon Receipt

BILL TO
[Name]
[Company Name]
[Street Address]
[City, ST ZIP]
[Phone]
[Email Address]

DESCRIPTION	QTY	UNIT PRICE	AMOUNT
Service Fee	1	200.00	200.00
Labor: 5 hours at $75/hr	5	75.00	375.00
New client discount		(50.00)	(50.00)

Thank you for your business!

SUBTOTAL	525.00
TAX RATE	13.00%
TAX	68.25
TOTAL	$ 593.25

An important role of a project manager is the approval of invoices. Project managers sometimes create invoices. In either case, the project manager needs to understand the invoicing process in depth.

Before approving an invoice, the project manager should check that all the necessary documents are attached. The invoice is considered a proper invoice.

Approve Invoices

We will explain a method that some companies use for the invoice approval process.

1- For large contracts - This method illustrates how to approve invoices submitted by a general contractor or major subcontractors to their clients.

Payment Requests

- The typical way to create invoices for the main contractors is to follow the breakdown of the tender form. In the tender document, each item is priced, and, depending on the progress of the work, the contractor would create a payment request. The consultant would verify this payment request. The consultant visits the site and checks the progress of the work for each activity against the values claimed by the general contractor.
- The consultant modifies the percentage claimed for the actual advancement seen by the consultant.
- The contractor corrects the figures and sends the payment request for final review.

Table 24. Payment Request

Progress payment # 5							
Period: March 2021		Date:	April, 1 2021		P. Manager:		
Item No.	Description	Total/ Budget	% Completed	Previously Invoiced	Invoice Current Period	Total to date	Cost to Complete
Division 1- General Requirements							
1	Mobilization	$15,000	100%	$15,000	0	$15,000	0
2	Demobilization	$15,000	0%	0	0	0	$15,000
3	Bondings, Permits, H&S requirements, closeouts, etc.	$15,000	20%	$1,000	$2,000	$3,000	$12,000
Division 3- Concrete work							
4	Concrete	$30,000	100%	$25,000	$5,00	$30,000	0
5	Rebars	$10,000	100%	$8,000	$2,000	$10,000	0
Division 6- Wood Work							
6	Formworks	$10,000	90%	$5,000	$4,000	$9,000	$1,000
7	Framing	$90,000	30%	$70,000	$11,000	$81,000	$9,000
8	Wood structure	$250,000	10%	0	25,000	$25,000	$225,000
Division 22- Plumbing							
9	Demolishing associated with plumbing and drainage work	$15,000	100%	$12,000	$3,000	$15,000	0

10	Supply and install new pumps	$100,000	70%	$20,000	$50,000	$70,000	$30,000
11	Supply and install all plumbing equipment	$150,000	50%	$50,000	$25,000	$75,000	$75,000
	Etc.						
			Change Directives				
CO #1	Additional Concrete	$5,000	100%	$4,000	$1,000	$5,000	0
CO #2	Supply and Install Lighting Fixtures	$15,000	0%	0	0	0	$15,000
	Etc.						
Total Example:		$2,000,000	40%	$500,000	$300,000	$800,000	$1,200,000

Payment certificate.

- The Consultant approves the payment request and creates a Payment Certificate (C.O.P) for the client to process the invoice.
- The Customer's representative examines the payment certificate, the payment request, and the supporting documents to complete a proper invoice.
  See Sample Certificate Of Payment (C.O.P)

Payment of invoices

- The customer's representative approves the invoice.
- According to company protocols, the General Contractor can send the completed package to the client's account payable.
- The Account payable checks again whether the invoice received can be considered as a proper invoice.
- The account payable verifies the necessary workflow for invoice approvals. For example, for invoices over $250,000, the signature of an internal manager like a project director may be required.
- The Account Payable checks the budget code to find if there are enough funds to pay this invoice.
- After obtaining all required approvals, the accountant issues a check or pays the invoice electronically.
- As stated above, if the invoice is missing documents or shows an error detected by the accountant, the invoice will revert to the first person in the chain. In this case, the client's project manager will return the package to the contractor's project manager.

2- For small contracts - Invoices can be approved simply by stamping them and entering them into the system. They will go through the same workflow approval process, which depends on the approval thresholds of invoices received. For example, a geotechnical engineer sends an invoice asking for $2,000 for the service or part of the service he has rendered compared to the initial value of the contract or purchases order.

SAMPLE 41. Certificate Of Payment (C.O.P)

Consultant LOGO & address

CERTIFICATE OF PAYMENT

Based on CCDC-24-1996

Consultant: **Payment Certificate No. 5**

Owner: **Project Number:**

Contractor:
Work Description:
Location:
Plans and Specifications:

This is to certify that the value of work performed and products delivered to the place of work as of **April 5th, 2021**, is **$800,000** (exclusive of value-added taxes).

Certified by the Consultant

....

Name and title of person sig. signature date of issue

CONTRACT SUMMARY

Original Contract Price	$1,980,000.00 (1)
The current value of Change Directives included in the COP	$20,000.00 (2)
Value of Contract on the last day of the payment period (1+2)	$2,000,000.00 (3)
Value Added Taxes at 13%	$260,000.00 (4)

CERTIFICATE SUMMARY

Value of work performed and products delivered to the place of work	$800,000.00(5)
Total holdback at 10%	$80,000.00(6)
Holdback released	$0.00(7)
Holdback retained	$80,000.00(8)

Amount (value of work performed and products delivered

to the place of work less holdback retained) (5-8)	$720,000.00 (9)
Amount from the previous certificate for payment	$500,000.00(10)
Amount of Contract Price payable, current period (9-10)	$220,000.00(11)
Value Added Taxes at 13%	$28,600.00(12)
Total amount payable current period including Value-added Taxes(11+12)	**$ 248,600.00(13)**

Payment Cycle

Check that the payment runs according to the jurisdiction of the project where the contract is executed. For example, we will explain the terms of the payment cycle in Ontario in effect as of October 1, 2019:

28-day payment cycle effective from October 1st, 2019

The new bottom line on construction projects in Ontario: owners will have **28 days** to pay a contractor after receiving **a proper invoice**. Contractors will have **7 days** to pay their subcontractors after receiving payment from the owner.

Disputing invoices

Owners will be able to dispute all or parts of an invoice, but they will need to provide written notice of non-payment within strict timelines. Owners will be required to deliver a statement of non-payment within 14 days of receiving the proper invoice from the contractor. The notice of non-payment must set out all of the reasons for not paying. Any undisputed amounts will have to be paid.

Recommendations Regarding Invoice Payments

The project manager must pay the invoices as soon as possible. The reputation of the company can be at risk in the event of continued late payment. Consider reviewing the invoice once received, being proactive, and working with the team of consultants to have an entirely justifiable invoice from the start. Whereas before the company's reputation is damaged, the project manager's reputation will be first damaged.

Problems Associated With Slow Payments

The results are staggering. If you are slow at paying your bills, you:

- See higher construction costs
- Don't get bids from the best subcontractors
- Have projects delayed due to stopped work
- Miss out discounts for paying faster
- Subcontractors may file a lien due to slow payments.

CHAPTER 14 - EARNED VALUE MANAGEMENT ANALYSIS (EVM)

Earned Value Management (EVM) helps project managers to measure project performance. A systematic project management process is used to find variances in projects based on comparing work performed and work planned. EVM is used on cost and schedule control and can be very useful in project forecasting.

Primary Data Points

Budget At Completion (BAC)
The total cost of the project

Budgeted Cost for Work Scheduled (BCWS)/Planned Value (PV)
The amount expressed in Dollars (or hours) of work to be performed as per the scheduled plan
PV = BAC * % of planned work

Budgeted Cost for Work Performed (BCWP)/Earned Value (EV)
The amount expressed in Dollars (or hours) on the actual work performed
EV = BAC * % of Actual work

Actual Cost of Work Performed (ACWP)/Actual Cost (AC)
The sum of all costs (in Dollars) accrued for a task to date.

For example, say we should have completed \$1000 of work by today. We completed \$800 worth of work. The BCWP is \$800. The BCWS is \$1000. And if we actually paid \$900 then (ACWP) = \$900.

Derived Data Points

Cost Forecasting:

Estimate At Completion (EAC)
The expected TOTAL cost required to finish complete work
EAC = BAC / CPI
= AC + ETC
= AC + ((BAC - EV)/CPI) (typical case)
= AC + (BAC - EV) (atypical case)
Here atypical means it is assumed that similar variances will not occur in the future.

Estimate to Complete (ETC)

The expected cost required to finish all the REMAINING work
ETC = EAC – AC
= (BAC/CPI) - (EV/CPI)
= (BAC - EV)/CPI

Variances:

Cost Variances (CV)

How much under or over budget
CV = EV-AC
NEGATIVE is over budget, and POSITIVE is under budget

Schedule Variances (SV)

How much ahead or behind schedule
SV = EV-PV
NEGATIVE is behind schedule, and POSITIVE is ahead of schedule
Variance At Completion (VAC)

The variance of the TOTAL cost of the work and expected cost

VAC = BAC – EAC

Performance Indices:

Cost Performance Index

CPI = EV/AC
Over (< 1) or under (> 1) budget

Schedule Performance Index

SPI = EV/PV
Ahead (> 1) or behind (< 1) schedule

EVM Example 1

The best way to understand an EVM example is to solve it.

Problem: A project has a budget of $10M and schedule for 10 months. It is assumed that the total budget will be spent each month equally until the 10th month is reached. After 2 months, the project manager finds that only 5% of the work is completed and a total of $1M spent.

Solution:
PV = $2M
EV = $10M * 0.05 = $0.5M
AC = $1M

CV = EV-AC = 0.5-1 = **- 0.5M**
CV% = 100 * (CV/EV) = 100*(-0.5/0.5) = **-100% overrun (Overbudget)**

SV = EV-PV = 0.5-2 = **-1.5** months
SV% = 100 * (SV/PV) = 100*(-1.5/2) = **-75% behind**

Comments: (This project, after 2 months of work, was planned to finish 1 M $/month, or 2 M $/2 months and thus represents 20% of the completion of the project and not 5%)

CPI = EV/AC = 0.5/1 = 0.5
SPI = EV/PV = 0.5/2 = 0.25

EAC = BAC/CPI = 10/0.5 = $20M
ETC = (BAC-EV)/CPI = (10-0.5)/0.5 = $19M

Time to compete = (10-0.5)/0.25 = 38 Months

This project will take TOTAL $20M (19+1) and 40 (38+2) Months to complete if it continues the same way and no corrective actions are taken (e.g., fast-tracking or crashing)

EVM Example 2- Real-Life Example

A project manager can create something similar to this example with the use of Excel.

Table 25. EVM Earned Value Analysis Model

G	H	I	J	K	L	M	N	O	P	Q
Monthly Planned Value	$ 705,300.00	$ 51,600.00	$ 61,300.00	$ 52,800.00	$ 52,350.00	$ 74,075.00	$ 72,350.00	$ 71,300.00	$ 56,300.00	$ 81,300.00
Planned % completion		7.32%	8.69%	7.49%	7.42%	10.50%	10.26%	10.11%	7.98%	11.53%
Cumulative Planned Value	0	$ 51,600.00	$ 112,900.00	$ 165,700.00	$ 218,050.00	$ 292,125.00	$ 364,475.00	$ 435,775.00	$ 492,075.00	$ 573,375.00
Monthly Actual Cost		$25,645.95	$24,521.00	$24,521.00	$61,872.36	$70,125.50	$80,747.50	$63,495.00	$29,525.00	$49,744.76
% of Actual Work		3.64%	3.48%	3.48%	8.77%	9.94%	11.45%	9.00%	4.19%	7.05%
Cumulative Actual Costs	0	$25,645.95	$50,166.95	$74,687.95	$136,560.31	$206,685.81	$287,433.31	$350,928.31	$380,453.31	$430,198.07
Monthly earned value (EV) Example Invoices sent to client		$ 28,210.55	$ 26,973.10	$ 26,973.10	$ 68,059.60	$ 77,138.05	$ 88,822.25	$ 69,844.50	$ 32,477.50	$ 54,719.24
Cumulative Earned value (EV)	0	$28,210.55	$55,183.65	$82,156.75	$150,216.34	$227,354.39	$316,176.64	$386,021.14	$418,498.64	$473,217.88

Project EV as of	30-Jun-12			473.218					
Project PV as of	30-Jun-12		$	573,375.00					
Project AC as of	30-Jun-12			$430,198.07					
		CV=EV-AC	$	43,019.81	**Under Budget**				
		SV=EV-PV	-$	**100,157.12**	**Behind Schedule**				
		CPI=EV/AC	1.10		Under Budget				
		SPI=EV/PV	0.83		**Behind Schedule**				
		Estimated at completion(EAC) =	**BAC/CPI**	$ 641,181.82	(Original plan	$ 705,300.00	EAC= AC+(BAC-EV)/CPI =	$ 641,181.82	
		Estimated time to complete	**Months**	12.12	(Original plan months)	10	Months		
		ETC Estimated to Complete =	**EAC-AC=**	**210,983.75**					
				VAC= Variance at Completion =	BAC-EAC	$ 64,118.18	Under Budget		

Figure 21. EVM Earn Value Chart

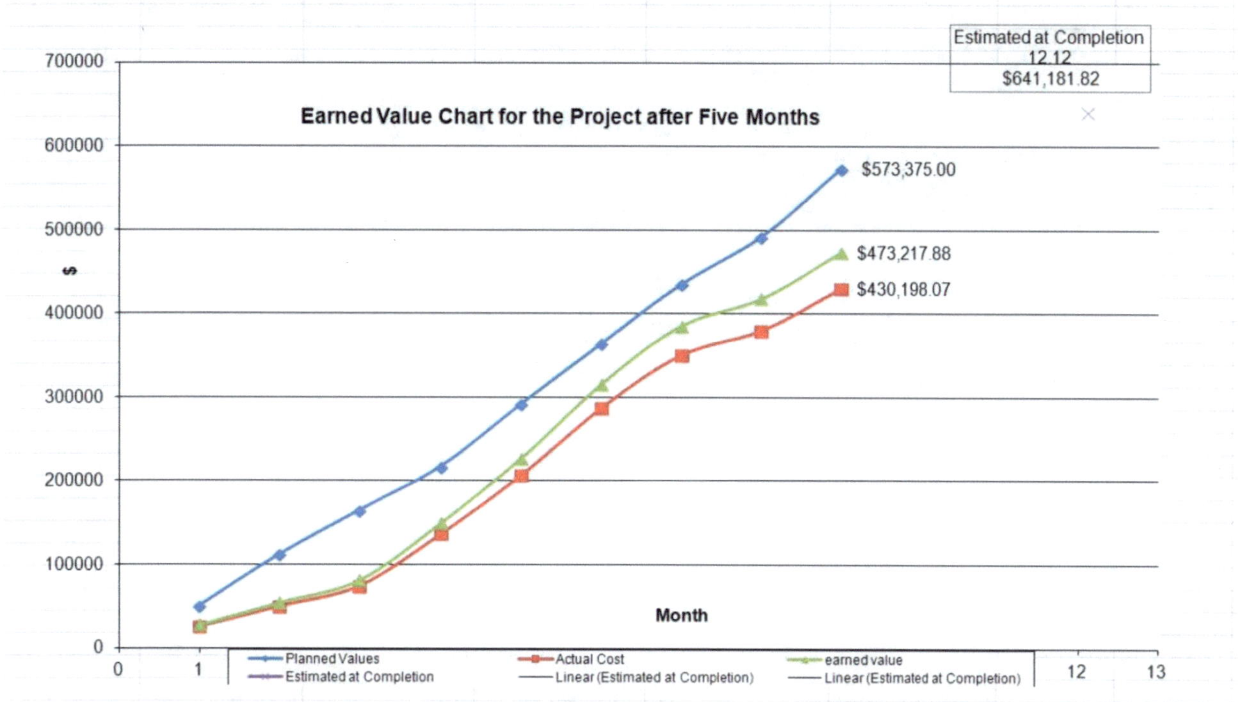

Forecast for the cost and schedule at completion

Forecasting & Estimated at Completion (EAC).

Know what is wrong early and why. Compare, analyze, and find out where and why cost or schedule deviation is occurring. Compare the forecast to the control estimate and schedule.

As the project progresses, the project team can develop a forecast for the completion (EAC) estimate that may differ from the budget at completion (BAC) based on the project performance. Besides, it is typical for businesses to know how much money they will be using each quarter (3 months). This is why quarterly forecasts are badly needed.

Table 26. Quarterly Forecast

Project No.	Q1 Forecast	Q2 Forecast	Q3 Forecast	Q4 Forecast	EAC 2021	EAC 2022
001	$500,000	$500,000	$500,000	$500,000	$2,000,000	$1,000,000
002	$300,000	$700,000	$700,000	$300,000	$2,000,000	$1,000,000
003	$150,000	$300,000	$700,000	$850,000	$2,000,000	0
Total	$950,000	$1,500,000	$1,900,000	$1,650,000	$6,000,000	$2,000,000

Some companies like to run a straight-line forecasting method that will evenly spread across all months or quarters. You may also create your spend curve.

- Project 001: The forecasting method used is a straight line. This project lasts for two years.
- Project 002: The forecasting method used is the curved method. This project lasts for two years.
- Project 003: The forecasting method used is the curved method. This project lasts for one year.

For the curved method, the estimated values can be used as benchmarks or references to assess the project's progress. These future forecasts/estimates will be compared to actual progress to date and/or the $ values of invoices received.

Table 27. Quarterly Forecasts Versus Actual Completed

	CUMULATIVE $ VALUES 2021								Project Manager Name	
P No	Q1 Forecast	Q1 ACTUAL	Q2 Forecast	Q2 Actual	Q3 Forecast	Q3 Actual	Q4 Forecast	Q4 Actual	**EAC 2021**	EAC 2022
1	$500,000	**$300,000**	$1,000,000	$700,000	$1500,000	$1,200,000	$2000,000	$1,600,000	**$2,000,000**	$1,000,000
2	$300,000	**$400,000**	$1,000,000	$1200,000	$1700,000	$2000,000	$2,000,000	$2,400,000	**$2,000,000**	$1,000,000
3	$150,000	$150,000	$450,000	$450,000	$1,150,000	$1,150,000	$2,000,000	$2,000,000	**$2,000,000**	$0.00
4	$0.00	$0.00	$0.00	$0.00	$0.00	$0.00	$0.00	$0.00	**$0.00**	$4,000,000
Total	**$950,000**	**$850,000**	**$2,450,000**	**$2,350,000**	**$4,350,000**	**$4,350,000**	**$6,000,000**	**$6,000,000**	**$6,000,000**	$6,000,000

To analyze the table above.
One Project Manager is a project lead for three projects. The Load work in 2021 is $6M and $6M in 2022. (Cumulative Q4 for 2021 = End of Year Spending for 2021 = EAC 2021).

Q1 = Quarter 1 from Jan. 01-Mar.

Q2 = Second Quarter from April-June.

Q3 = Quarter 3 from July-Sep.

Q4 = Quarter 4 from Oct.-Dec. 31.

Cumulative Q4 = From Jan 01- Dec 31.

Project 001:

Quarter 1: The project is under budget. Ensure that change management (change order management) is well documented and entered into the system. Check the schedule; it is most likely delayed.

Senior managers may need to know if the scope of work has been reduced or if the project has started late. Senior executives can do this by checking the actual start date in the system. They may also need to find the change in financial situation. Are there any negative (Adverse) change orders, or are there savings? The problem may be internal since the management planned this project according to a linear method; work progress in winter is generally slow. The Project Manager must consider the Contractor's and Subcontractor's schedules, and the project may require forecast updates at this time.

Quarter 4: We have $2,000,000 for this project to spend in 2021; we did not use $400,000. Therefore, we may need to transfer $400,000 for 2022. Funding transfer can be done, in large companies, through a review of the fundings business case modification or Business Case Amendment "Creating a business case modification (B.C.)."

Project 002:

Quarter 1: In March 2021, the report shows that this project is over budget by $100,000.

In June 2021 (Q2), the report shows that the project exceeds the budget by 200,000 dollars; an investigation is needed to find out whether these additional charges are good indicators or not.

As a senior manager, review change orders in the system and look for new change orders to justify the cost increase. Also, look at the calendar. The contractor might have speeded up the work, which is a good indicator; however, now is the time to conduct all the necessary investigations. Don't assume the best and be more conservative until you are fully convinced that this project is doing well.

As a project manager, ask management to allocate more funds for 2021 and decrease the fund for 2022.

Project 003:

No flag to hoist. Review the change request logs and project plan if necessary. Make sure that no hidden costs arrive quarterly. Report progress to senior management as required by company protocols.

Project 004:

Not yet started. They are funding only for 2022.

SECTION 8
PROJECT QUALITY MANAGEMENT

Project Quality Management includes the processes and activities of the performing organization that determine quality policies, objectives, and responsibilities so that the project will satisfy the needs for which it was undertaken.

Project Quality Management processes include the following:

Plan Quality, Perform Quality Assurance, and Perform Quality Control.

When you plan the quality, ensure that there is a system for auditing (Quality Assurance) and monitoring (Quality Control).

CHAPTER 15 - PLAN QUALITY

The process of identifying quality requirements for the project and product, and documenting how the project will demonstrate compliance.

The quality department can implement a Quality Management System software that provides comprehensive data concerning Client satisfaction, the nonconformities encountered in developing the quality management system, and the various suppliers' performance. All of the data is analyzed to identify or track improvement areas applicable to create processes when required.

Develop Processes

Some companies establish, document, implement, review and update the Quality Management System and permanently improve its efficiency in conformity to the requirements of the actual International Standard. Examples of Areas of improvement:

Identify the processes necessary for the application of the Quality Management System throughout the company;
Determine the sequence and interaction of these processes;
Determine the criteria and methods necessary to ensure the effectiveness, the proper functioning, and the control of these processes;
Ensure the availability of the resources and information necessary for the proper functioning and supervision of these processes;
Supervise, measure, and analyze these processes;
Implement the actions necessary to obtain the results planned and the continued improvement of these processes.

Performance indicators for projects

Determine Objectives and Performance indicators for projects. The company can send project managers a form that looks like the example below to illustrate the vision for the company's performance for the current year.

SAMPLE 42. Quality Objectives & Performance Indicators

Quality objectives & performance indicators 2010	
Improve satisfaction rate of our Clients ***Client surveys:*** *Required annual average 2021 ≥* ***75%*** *Improve the* ***customer complaint*** *recording practices*	Average Last Years > 74%
Increase satisfaction rate of our partners (Vendors) ***Partners surveys :*** *Annual average 2021 ≥* ***70%***	>70%
Improve planning & management of our projects *Improve planned critical productions by* ***2%***	2%
Develop & recognize the sense of involvement within the firm *Retention of personnel ≥ 85%*	>83%
Optimize internal communications *Number of recorded Corrective Actions referring to communications < 5*	<6
Reduce the frequency & severity of accidents at work *Improve the annual overall performance Frequency < 5.00 Gravity < 65%*	<5 <65%
Be distinguished in the market by the excellence of its services ***Client-survey results > 90%***	>85%

Ensure customer satisfaction through the application of the following methods:

- Identify and record Customer requirements during contract review and processing of change orders;
- Measure customer satisfaction after each contract;
- Measure whether Customer requirements have been met by examining statistics of nonconformities; and
- Recording and processing of formal complaints from its customers through the application of corrective actions.

Project Management Quality Plan

The **cost of quality** will contribute to the project savings. Some companies include a third-party quality department to create and monitor this plan; other companies set up a quality service for this purpose. The quality plan can consist of all management and construction elements as benchmarks that project managers can follow as minimum quality requirements.

The primary benefits of meeting quality requirements include less rework, higher productivity, lower costs, and increased stakeholder satisfaction.
Companies that don't allocate funds for quality will suffer from the cost of poor quality.

There are no types of work excluded from the scope of application to the Quality Management System.

Companies create a Quality Manual, which may consist of the following: A description of the company; a quality policy of the company; a description of the organization; the general quality objectives; the necessary procedures required to implement a quality management system.

The Processes Manual may consist of the following: The list of processes applicable to the Company; the flowchart detailing each of the methods; the table of characteristics related to each of the operations; work instructions necessary for the implementation of the various processes; the registration forms required for each of the functions.

Figure 22. The project Balance

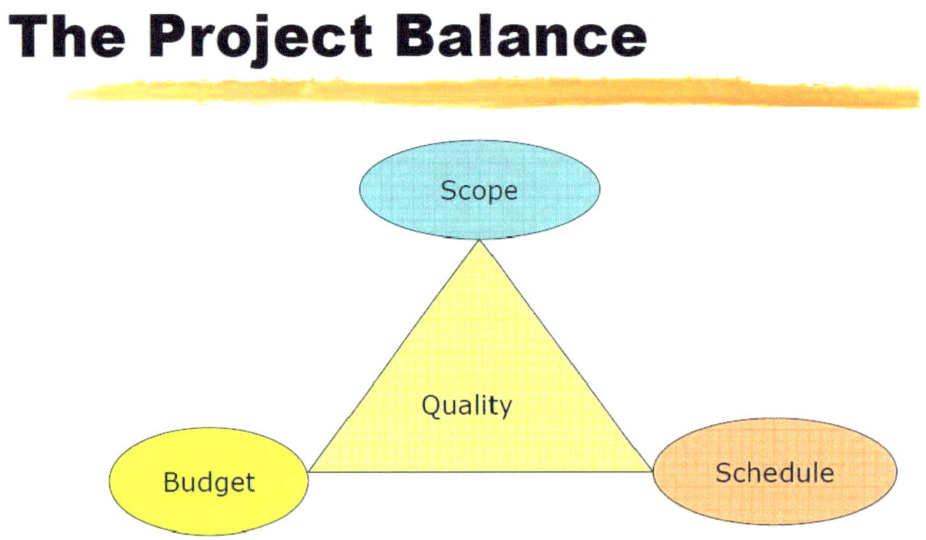

Project Management Quality Plan

Management Level can distribute this plan to all project managers at some intervals (such as hiring new employees). Quality plans can include tables as the sample explained in "Project Management Quality Plan Sample."

Quality Management System (QMS) department drafts the quality management plan for the following activities (among others not to mention here):

Work environment

Execution of projects, coordination meetings, planning the implementation of a project, project start-up meetings, H&S, Contract change orders, etc.

Tender Process

Tender selection, GO-NO GO process, preparing the bid, Addendum during the bid/tender process, reviewing the proposals, Following-up on bid results, Notice of Contract, Contract review, etc.

Design and development:

Planning of the design, internal design, external design, testing of the design, modification of the design, validation of the design, etc.

Cost Management

Creating a system for cost control sheets or systems, developing authorization flowcharts, analyzing post mortem reports, creating equipment management tools and verifications, developing vendor's performance reports, creating a process for managing non-conformities, etc.

SAMPLE 43. Project Management Quality Plan

Project Management Quality Plan						
1.0 PLANNING						
ACTIVITY	**DESCRIPTION**	**APPLICATION**	**FREQUENCY**	**RESPONSIBLE**	**REFERENCES**	**RECORD**
Schedule (Work breakdown structure WBS)	Indicate activity duration Sequence Applicable baseline	Weekly precision Produced two weeks before the beginning of works	Beginning of project	Project manager	Specifications	Excel or M.S. Project file
	Look ahead of 3 weeks 3 weeks schedule	Weekly precision	Daily updates	Project manager	Specifications	Excel or M.S. Project file
Budget	Budget breakdown and coding structure for the project	Construction director approval	Beginning of project	Project manager	Bid and contract	Excel file **Form(Hyperlink)**
	Budget presentation to accounting and procurement department	For Information	Beginning of the project and after approval	Project manager	Bid and contract	**Form(Hyperlink)**
Procurement	Equipment, material, and products list	Major products	Beginning of project	Project manager	**Procurement manual (Hyperlink)**	Equipment list **Form(Hyperlink)**
	Subcontracting list	Major services	Beginning of project	Project manager	Specifications	Subcontractors' list **Form(Hyperlink)**
Human Resources	To form a project management team	Experience and qualification related to the complexity of a project	Beginning of project	Project manager	Bid and contract & Specifications	Organization Chart **Form(Hyperlink)**
Equipment	Renting, Buying or Internal availability	Civil Works Building Works	Beginning of project	Project manager and equipment director	Bid and contract	Equipment list **Form(Hyperlink)**
Quality and security planning	*Project quality plan according to contract requirements*	To respect contract requirements according to the selected mode for the project	According to contract terms and conditions	Project manager and Quality manager	Bid and contract	According to contract terms and conditions
	Safety program	To respect contract requirements	According to contract terms and conditions	Project manager and H.R. director	Bid and contract Health & Safety Plans	Safety program **Form(Hyperlink)**

2.0 PROJECT START UP						
ACTIVITY	**DESCRIPTION**	**APPLICATION**	**FREQUENCY**	**RESPONSIBLE**	**REFERENCES**	**RECORD**
Insurance and bonding	Distribution of insurance and bonding	Confirmation to client	Beginning of project	Project manager	Bid and contract	Bonding and insurance forms of our insurance company **Form(Hyperlink)**
Notice Of Project	Notify the Ministry of Labour before carrying out the work	Post in the job site	Beginning of project	Project manager	Ministry of Labor	Opening Project **Form(Hyperlink)**Opening of Project Website **(Hyperlink)**
Start-up meeting	Preconstruction meeting with client and professionals	To allow parties to agree on different work procedures	Beginning of project	Project manager	Plans and Specifications	Precon. Meeting Minutes. **Form(Hyperlink)**
Progress Meetings	To allow parties to understand procedures, rules, and other necessary information for the project	For work coordination	During the project	Project manager & Superintendent	Plans, Specifications, Schedules, Change order logs	Worksite meeting minutes. **Form(Hyperlink)**

3.0 SUBCONTRACTOR MANAGEMENT						
ACTIVITY	**DESCRIPTION**	**APPLICATION**	**FREQUENCY**	**RESPONSIBLE**	**REFERENCES**	**RECORD**
Procurement	To verify material supplied by subcontractors	Coordination of material and significant types of equipment	Beginning of work and during a work period	Project manager	According to Plans and specifications	Bill of lading at work site
Coordination	Verify that work schedule is respected	To follow up work progress and Schedule (WBS)	During Execution	Project manager	Schedules	Biweekly Reports
Subcontractor Follow up	Inspect and verify to ensure work conformity	Conforming with the quality plan	During Execution	Project manager	Plans and specifications	Inspection report and follow up
Change Orders Management	Getting all required approvals	Follow internal workflow process	During Execution	Project manager	Plans and specifications (RFQ)	Change Order Log. **Form(Hyperlink)**
RFI's	Request For information send to the right person	Change orders could result from technical questions	During Execution	Project manager	Plans and specifications (RFQ)	RFI Log. **Form(Hyperlink)**
Payment request	Verify payment request of subcontractors	Ensure Consultant involvement	Monthly	Project manager	Progress billing	Payment Request **Form(Hyperlink)**

	according to work progress					
Shop-Drawings	Shop drawings are periodically updated by the Contractors and sub-contractors	Upload all approved S.D. to the system	Daily if necessary	Assistant Project Manager	Specifications	Shop Drawing Log **Form(Hyperlink)**
«As-Built» drawings	Ensure getting all the As-Builts Before Contractor completes the work	Upload all approved As builts to the system	At the end of each contract	Assistant Project Manager	Specifications	Contractors' drawings

4.0 SUBSTIANTIAL COMPLETION						
ACTIVITY	**DESCRIPTION**	**APPLICATION**	**FREQUENCY**	**RESPONSIBLE**	**REFERENCES**	**RECORD**
Deficiency list	Execute remaining minor works before the end of the project according to the client's list	Minor works non-executed-Final Walkthrough with the Owner	At the end of the project or during realization	Project manager	Specifications	List produced by the consultants
Document submissions	Transmit contractual documents	As-Builts, Warranties, Guarantees, Shop-drawings, Data Sheets, Manuals, Training, etc.	At Project closing	Project manager	Specifications	Transmission letter **Form(Hyperlink)**
Transfer to Owner	Return the project to the client	Deficiency list repairs acceptance, Owner receives all closeout documents	Key transfer or turnkey project transfer if it is the case	Project manager	Specifications	Transfer letter to client for ownership **Form(Hyperlink)**

5.0 PROJECT CLOSING						
ACTIVITY	**DESCRIPTION**	**APPLICATION**	**FREQUENCY**	**RESPONSIBLE**	**REFERENCES**	**RECORD**
Project Post Mortem	An internal meeting including construction, Equipment, and Procurement directors and project manager	Report of good and bad points of the projects- Lessons learned and nonconformities		Project Manager	Quality Plan Nonconformity Reports	Post Mortem report **Form(Hyperlink)**
Vendors Evaluation	Subcontractors, Consultants, and suppliers filling evaluation forms	Evaluate each vendor for future use	At the end of the service	Project Manager	Quality Plan	Vendor Evaluation **Form(Hyperlink)**
Client satisfaction evaluation	Meeting with client and Company Directors	To evaluate the project performance with the client	At Project closing	Project manager	Quality Plan	Client Satisfaction Evaluation **Form(Hyperlink)**
Archive	Send all the project documents to the archive	Plans, Specs, Tender, Estimation, ShopDrawings As builts, Warranties, etc...		Project manager	Quality Plan	
END OF ADMINISTRATION PROCESSES						

Technical Items are added to the tables if required, for example:

Table 28. Concrete Work Quality Management Plan

ACTIVITY	DESCRIPTION	FREQUENCY	RESPONSIBLE	REFERENCES	RECORD
Formwork	Make sure that the formwork conforms to requirements. Verify the quality of the forms before erection. Verify if the forms are well oiled, levelled, and well-assembled. Verify the cleanliness inside the forms.	During Execution	Project manager	Plans and specifications (RFQ)	Daily Report **Form(Hyperlink)**
Rebars, wire mesh, and anchors	Make sure that all Rebars, wire mesh, and anchors are conforming. Verify the rebars type, quality, and quantity against the shipping papers.	During Execution	Superintendent Foreman	Plans and specifications (RFQ)	Daily Report **Form(Hyperlink)**

QUALITYPLAN

SAMPLE 44. Quality Plan

Produced at the start of the project

1. Project Description:

Project no:	
Customer Representatives :	
Budget :	
Description of project:	
Project Manager:	
Project Director:	
Start- Finish:	

2. Organization Structure:

Figure 23. Organization Structure

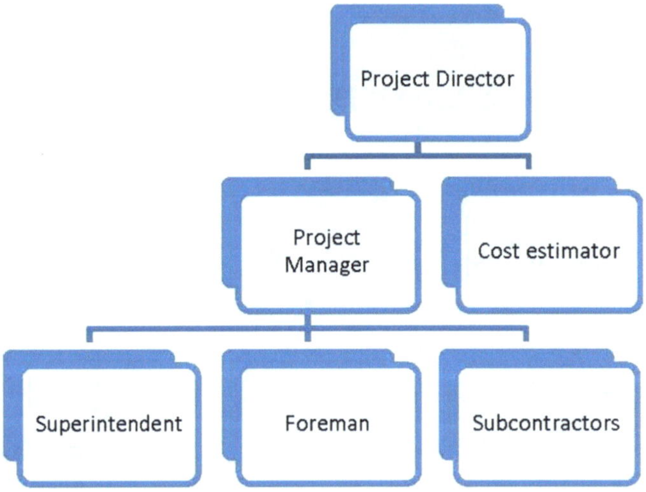

3. List of Subcontractors:

SAMPLE 45. List Of Sub-Contractors

Name of Subcontractor	Contact	Description of work	Amount of work

4. List of Specific Project Requirements:

SAMPLE 46. List of Specific Project Requirements

Requirements	Remarks	Checks and Controls
01 33 00		Specification Section
Documents and Samples to Submit	Submit documents and samples required to be verified by the Architect (using the form provided for this purpose)	Section 01 62 00
03 45 00		
Prefabricated Concrete Blocks	Submit the shop drawings required	section 01 33 00
Submit Samples	The sample of a full-size precast concrete element including the required details and display the color, quality, and finish prescribed, then deliver and set it up on-site, at the location indicated by the Designated Representative, to obtain the latter's evaluation before starting manufacturing the items required for the work.	Subcontractor Control
03300		
Concrete Mix	The manufacture of the concrete mixture: If the factory does not have a valid certificate of compliance, provide test data and certification issued by a qualified and independent inspection and test laboratory confirming that the concrete mix materials meet the requirements.	At least two (2) weeks before starting the concrete work, submit to the Engineer.

5. Control Sheets

SAMPLE 47. Quality Control Sheet

Sheet No.	Subject	Steps	Frequency	Responsibility
0102	SkyJack	Inspection	Monthly	Foreman
0105	PM Pickup	Inspection & Change oil	Each 3 months	Project Manager
0207	Progress Meetings	Invitations	Biweekly	Project Manager
0213	Cost Control Report	Compare Cost Vs Invoices	Monthly	Project Manager

SAMPLE 48. Document Control Planning

Document Control

Document control examples of quality management - to be adapted to each department: A document management system facilitates access to various forms and project records.

TYPE OF RECORDS/ENTRY	*DESCRIPTION*
DOCUMENT CONTROL	List of Documents
	Distribution Lists
	Modifications
	Approval Of Documents
VENDORS	List of Suppliers
	Evaluation of Performance
	Non-Conformities
	CONTRACTS: CCDC/PO
	As-Builts - ShopDrawings - Warrantees
IMPROVEMENTS	Corrective actions
	Preventive actions
NONCONFORMITIES	Nonconformity reports
	Log of nonconformities
TRAINING	Record of employee training
	Onboard Training
	Assigned training for each position – Automatic set up
H.R.	Employee Forms
	Competency profile by type of position
	Training records/entries
REVIEW COMMITTEE	Progress reports
	Portfolio projects schedules
	Post –Mortem reports
QUALITY AUDIT	Planning of the internal quality audits
	Audit reports
	Audit register
BIDS	Copy of bid estimates and method used by consultants
	Form of Tenders
PROCESS CHARTS	Procurement Charts
	Organization Charts
	Employee Roles and Responsibilities
	Creating Change Order Chart
	Authorization of Payments Charts

CHAPTER 16 - QUALITY ASSURANCE & CONTROL

Perform Quality Assurance

The process of auditing the quality requirements and the results from quality control measurements ensures that appropriate quality standards and operational definitions are implemented.

Quality control measurements are the results of quality control activities.

Auditing (Internal and External) is performed to optimize the company's performance. For example, they can audit and provide guidance on contract reviews, manage nonconformities, Client surveys, Client complaints or grievances, corrective and preventive actions, and training. Each year during Management's review, specific objectives are set as the methods to be used to measure the results. The results are evaluated throughout the year.

External Audit

Example: ISO 9001 Certification

The International Organization for Standardization develops specifications for products, services, systems, and procedures by which they can measure their level of excellence. A company cannot be considered genuinely standardized until it has earned its ISO Certification.

Becoming ISO 9001 certified means passing a physical ISO 9001:2015 certification audit by a registrar (a certifying agency).

What Are Some Reasons Why Companies Need ISO 9001 Certification?

- Many companies want ISO 9001 certification just to satisfy *one* customer requirement.
- Once you earn your ISO 9001 certification, you can advertise your quality certification and respond to requests for quotes (RFQ) from companies that make ISO 9001 certification a "must-have." ISO 9001 certification can open up new markets you were virtually unable to do business with before your certificate.
- Improve Company and Product Quality
- Describe, Understand, and Communicate Your Company Processes
- Develop a Professional Culture and Better Employee Morale
- Improve the Consistency of Your Operations
- Focus Management and Employees
- Improve Efficiency, Reduce Waste, and Save Money
- Achieve International Quality Recognition

ISO will Audit your Company yearly and update your certification if your company still meets the ISO's standards.

Internal Audit

An Internal Quality Department ensures that all processes are followed and meets regularly with the employees to recommend improvement or offer training.

Perform Quality Control

The Quality Plan described before in this book contains the measures to control the quality. The quality management plan describes how quality control will be performed within the project.

From the Quality Plan:

Point 4- Control Sheets

Sheet No.	Subject	Steps	Frequency	Responsibility
0102	SkyJack	Inspection	Monthly	Foreman

Point 5- List of Specific Project Requirements:

Requirements	Remarks	Checks and Controls

Forms, processes, and procedures are created inside companies to control quality performance.

Nonconformity Report

SAMPLE 49. Non-Conformity Report

NONCONFORMITY REPORT Company Logo	NO. Rev: Page: 1 of 3

Date of the Nonconformity :

Name of the Company :

Reason Client ☐ Sub-Contractor ☐ Professional ☐
N/A ☐

Client Name:

Subcontractor Name:
PO#:

Description of the problem:

Cause of the problem:

Proposed Corrective Actions:

Approved By :

Date:

Entered in the system ☐ Corrective Action required ☐ Corrected and Close Date:

Post Mortem

The Project Post-Mortem is an activity that should be carried out within a month of the project work ending. It captures details around how the project ended, as well as lessons learned. It should also be presented to the project sponsor and signed off to indicate formal project closure.

SAMPLE 50. Post Mortem

POST MORTEM
DATE: LOCATION:
Prepared By: Project No.: Present were: Distribution:

1. **CONTRACT**
2. **MANAGEMENT TEAM**
   Project Manager:
   Superintendent:
   Office Manager:
3. **SCHEDULE**
   Projected:
   Actual:
4. **WORK-RELATED ACCIDENTS**
5. **LOCAL IMPACT:**
6. **NON-CONFORMITIES AND CORRECTIVE ACTIONS (Insert Table)**
7. **LIST OF DEFICIENCIES, PROVISIONAL AND FINAL ACCEPTANCE**
8. **EVALUATION OF SUPPLIERS AND SUB-CONTRACTORS**

SUBCONTRACTORS	SPECIALTY	COMMENT	% Obtained. Passing Point 60%

9. **PROBLEMS ENCOUNTERED**
10. **FINANCIAL RESULTS**
    Expected profit: %
    Actual profit: %
11. **COMMENTS**

Documentation Management

SAMPLE 51. Documentation Process Chart

Company Name & Logo	Documentation	No.:
		Rev.: 00
		Page: 2 of 4

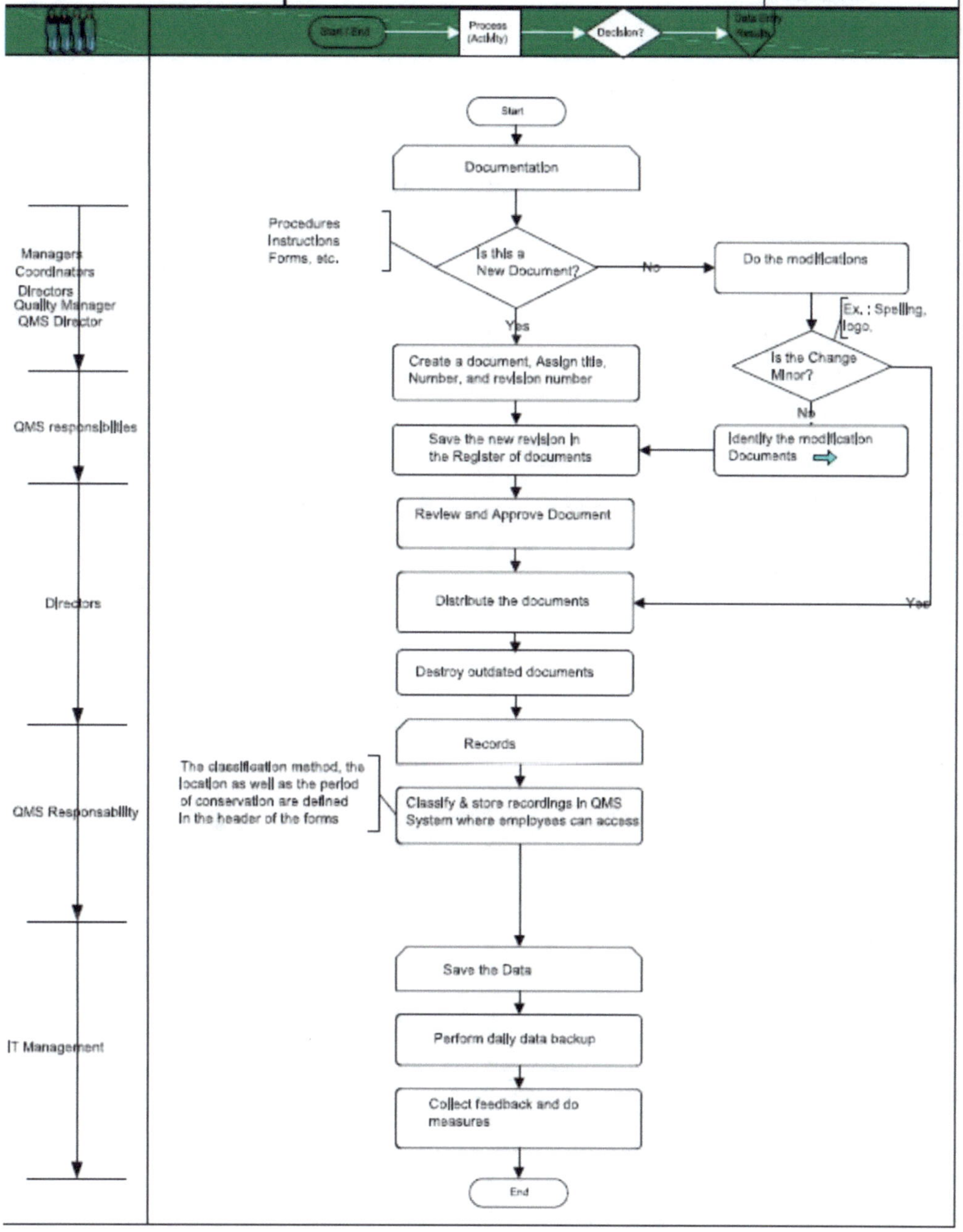

Material Acceptance Verification report

SAMPLE 52. Material Acceptance Verification report

Project Number: **Contract Number:**
P.O. #: Report # :

Material Received Description :

Supplier Name:
Transport Used: Transporter Name:

Verify Specifications	NC	C	N/A	Date of verification
Check that the delivery authorization is duly completed and approved.				
Verify that the delivery note includes factory acceptance and that this certificate confirms that the parts and materials supplied comply.				
Packing note: - Quantity received = that stipulated - Name of the equipment and its number indicated - Number and content of each box indicated - Specified total weight marked on the item - Dimensions indicated - Shipping method indicated - Specified storage type Missing pieces: Substitution of parts: Special handling:				
Check the blocking, packaging, and protection of the items.				
Check the condition of the items for damage before unloading				
Check whether unloading and handling follow the specified instructions.				
Check the items for damage after unloading (scratches, rust, deformation, etc.).				
Check whether the storage conforms to the specified instructions:				

Precaution to take: Storage location:				
Dimensional checks against drawings (one item per lot or according to the specifications).				
Remarks and results:				
Accepted By: NonConformity No.: Refused By:				
Legend: C=Conform NC=NonConform N/A: Not Applicable				
Inspector Name and Signature Date:				

SECTION 9
PROJECT HUMAN RESOURCE MANAGEMENT

CHAPTER 17 - HUMAN RESOURCE MANAGEMENT

Project Human Resource Management includes the processes that organize, manage, and lead the project team.

Develop Human Resource Plan

The process of identifying and documenting project roles, responsibilities, and required skills, reporting relationships.

SAMPLE 53. Request Project Resources

Request Project Resources			
No. Of Project:			
Project Funded by:			
Description of work:			
Address:			
Cost Estimator:			
Project Director:			
Value:			
Start Date:	End Date:		
POSITION	**QUALIFICATIONS**	**Supervisor**	**QUANTITY**
Project Manager	Background Civil Engineer- Writing Skills 5/6, Communication Skills 5/6, Excel, Microsoft Project, Cost Control, Supervision skills, Fast Learner	Manager/ Director	1
Superintendent	Reading Plans and Specs, Supervision skills, Ability to request materials (Civil and Building), Quantity Takeoff	Manager/ Project Manager	1
Foreman	Creating schedules for workers, oversee the quality of the site, Creating Daily Reports	Project Manager	2
Civil Engineer	Plan, direct and conduct investigations to establish and mark property lines, work with computers and electronic equipment to determine precise locations, advice on matters related to legal investigations.	Manager	1
Carpenter	Residential and Commercial Buildings. Preferable knowledge with Ontario building codes. Unionized.	Project Manager	8
Labor	Helpers for all activities		3
Operator	Skytrack, Backhoe, etc....		1
Etc.			

Acquire Project Team

After deciding on the quantity and job description, the hiring process according to the management quality plan occurs.

Some basic steps in the recruitment process:

Screening: Human resources evaluate CV and consult the operation team (Project Manager, Program Manager, Director, etc....)
Phone Interviews
First Interviews
Second Interviews
Assessment
Decision and job offer
Salary negotiation
Contract signature from both parties
Once employees start working, it's best to keep records of every important document relating to them. Keep copies of documents like employment agreements, timesheets, performance reviews, and descriptions of disciplinary actions.

These documents stand as your employee's protection and the business's protection in any event that a problem arises. Filing records is a best practice in Canadian H.R., and those records could be of help when it comes time for a promotion or even termination of your employee.

Develop Project Team

Improving the competencies, team interaction, and the overall team environment to enhance project performance.

On Boarding

New employee onboarding integrates a new employee with a company and its culture and gives a new hire the tools and information needed to become a team member. Onboarding is an integral part of helping employees understand their new position and job requirements.

Construction workers require training on safety procedures, proper equipment handling, project processes, and more. Having an appropriate onboarding process ensures that all aspects of the job are covered and should allow workers to communicate with their bosses and co-workers.

Ensure Employee Safety

Ideally, scheduled reviews should be included in every onboarding process at the 30-day, 60-day, 90-day, six-month, and 12-month mark, if applicable. These regular check-ins help ensure that new workers are getting the training they need and are enjoying their jobs. Of course, construction managers should make it clear that workers can approach them at any time with questions or concerns.

Increase Company Efficiency

Construction companies spend a lot of time and effort hiring new employees. From initial recruitment to on-the-job training, all aspects of the hiring process are the company's responsibility. When projects start quickly after winning a bid, there is minimal time to hire hundreds of workers. An automated tool allows recruits to complete any documentation and review company policies and procedures online before their first day on the job. Less time on paperwork means more time on the job, and a prior understanding of safety requirements could help reduce accidents. Losing employees due to accidents or injuries would mean that the entire investment in the business would go to zero.

Boost Business Reputation

Vital training programs can also, by extension, help reduce employee turnover rates. Think of it this way: if you've heard that Company A has a constant stream of workers leaving due to accidents or job dissatisfaction, would you want to work there? Or would you prefer to work for Company B, which has a high employee retention rate? Construction companies with a long-standing workforce are more attractive. After all, workers stay there for a reason.

Manage Project Team

RACI

Create Responsible, Accountable, Consult, and Inform (RACI) Charts or Tables when necessary.

- **Responsible:** a person who performs an activity or does the work.
- **Accountable:** a person who is ultimately accountable and has Yes/No/Veto.
- **Consulted:** a person that needs to give feedback and contributes to the activity.
- **Informed:** a person that needs to know of the decision or action.

Table 29. RACI (Responsible, Accountable, Consult, and Inform Chart)

RACI Chart	Person				
Activity	Ann (Project Manager)	Ben (Consultant) External Firm	Carlos (Superintendent)	Dina (Engineer)	Ed (Director)
Schedule	A	C	R	C	I
Workload Analysis	R	I	C	I	A
Update Budget	R	I	C	C	A
Hiring	A	I	C	I	R
Requisition of Site Materials	A	I	R	C	I
Payment Certificates	A	R	I	C	I
Invoice Payment	R	C	C	C	A
Allocate and Level Resources	A	I	R	C	I

Allocate and Level Resources

Resource allocation is assigning and scheduling available resources most effectively and as economically as possible. It is the management and delegation of resources throughout a project to ensure that it runs as smoothly and successfully as possible.

Resource leveling involves creating a balanced production schedule to minimize fluctuations in the number of resources used per period, such as a day. The project manager devises a plan that ensures continuous resources instead of sporadic increase and decrease in resources used. A balanced schedule typically serves as the most practical way of using resources.

The allocation of resources is pretty self-explanatory. If the project manager allocates stones for constructing a house, she must ensure that she obtains enough stones to complete the project. Regarding leveling, the project manager should ensure that it will be used regularly rather than sporadically rented and returned in case of equipment rental. If hiring carpenters, the project manager should maintain a set number of carpenters working a set number of hours over the project's life to ensure consistency. Carpenters may find it difficult to schedule more irregular hours into their Schedule, which means the business may need to hire more workers, leading to inconsistent results. During this time, the materials do not need to be leveled as they are purchased rather than rented or paid by the hour.

Figure 24. Allocate Resources

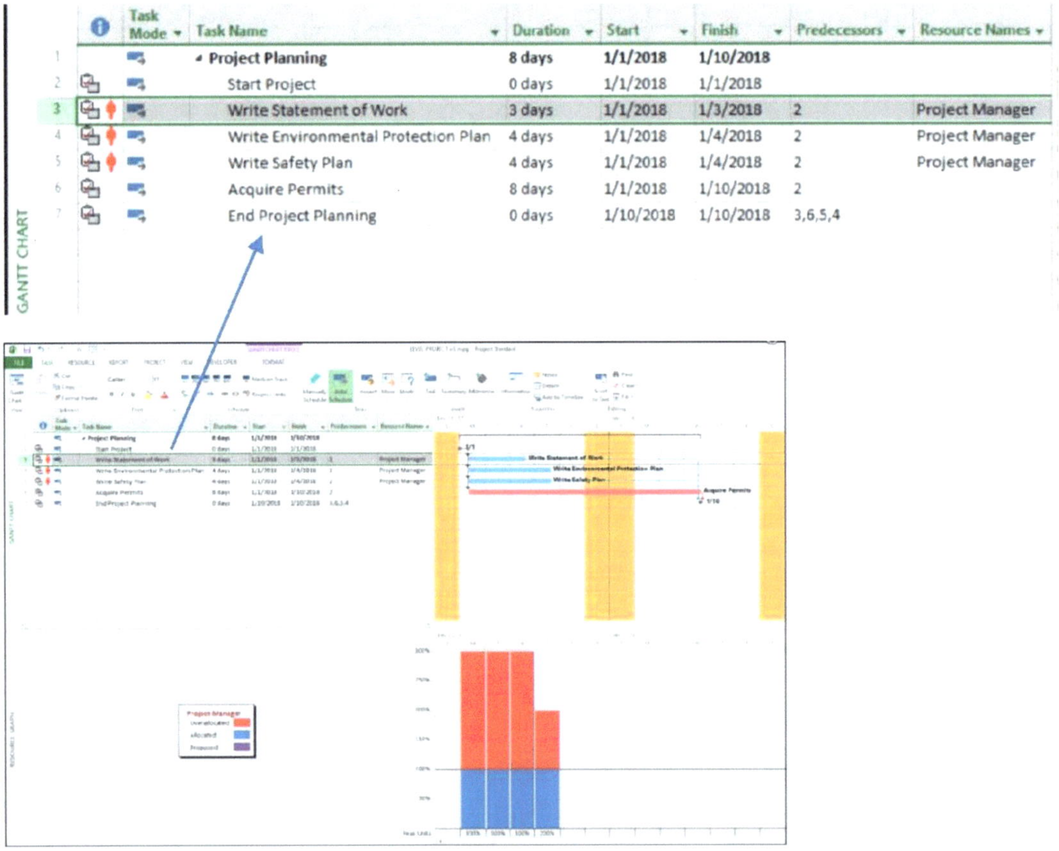

SAMPLE 54. Level Resources

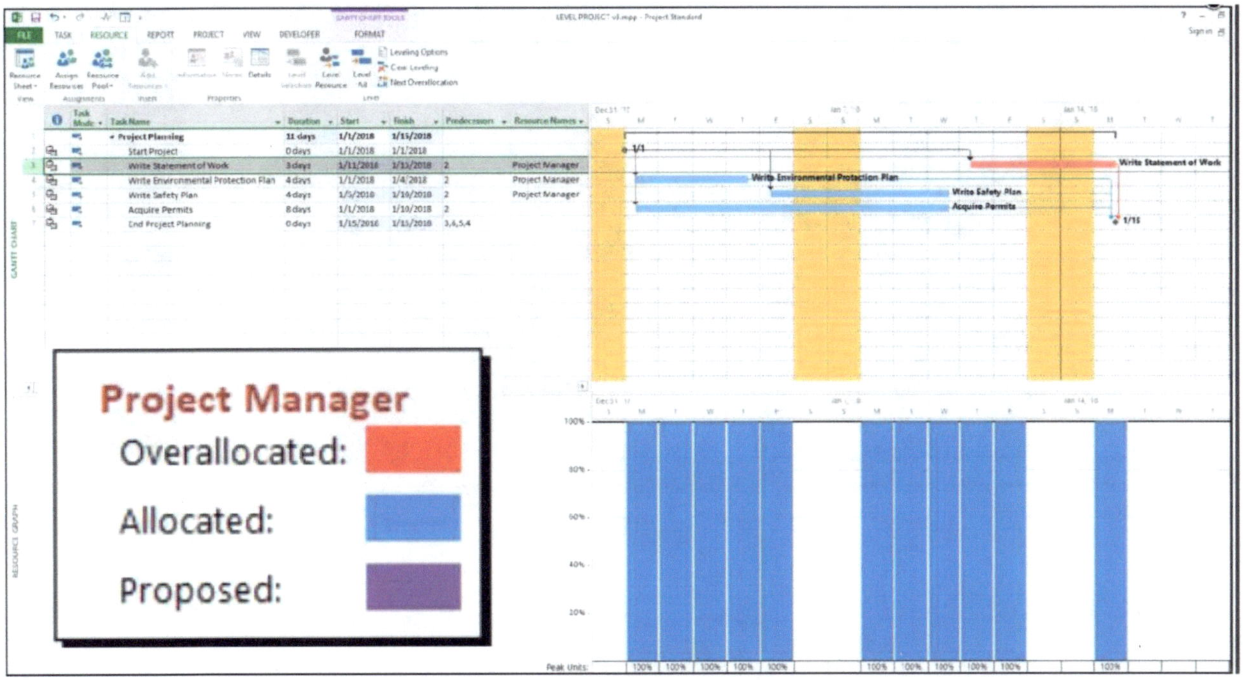

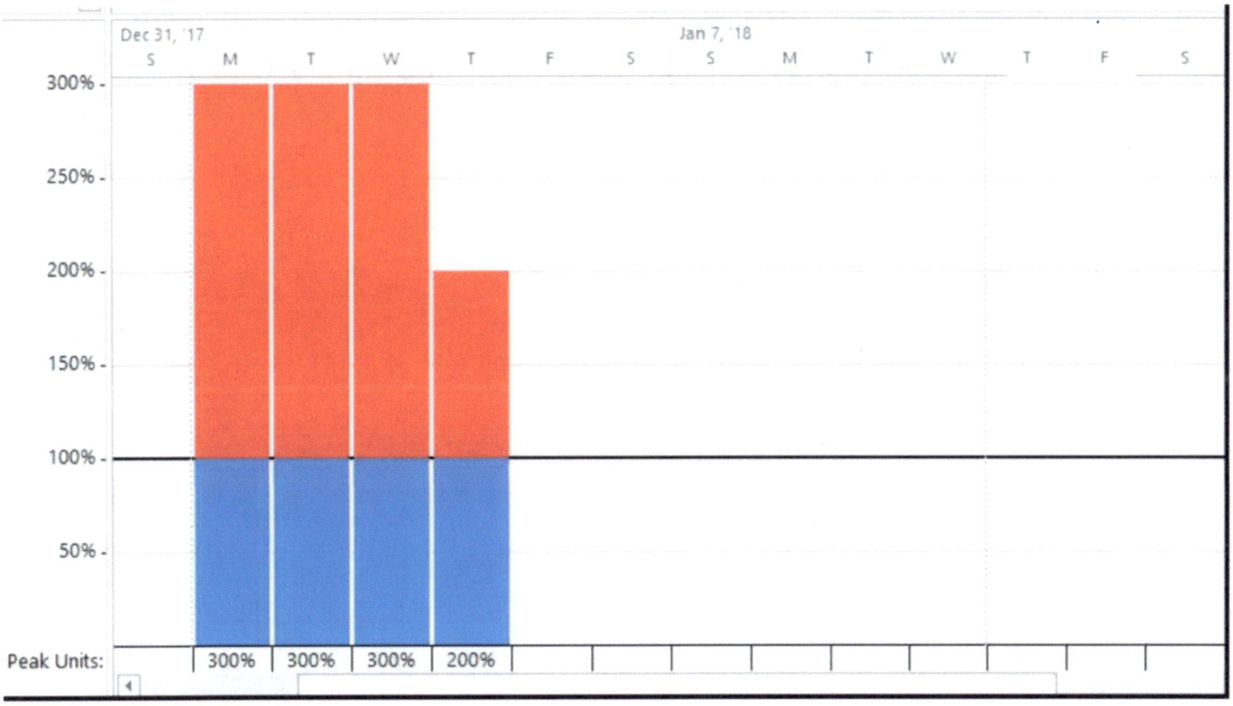

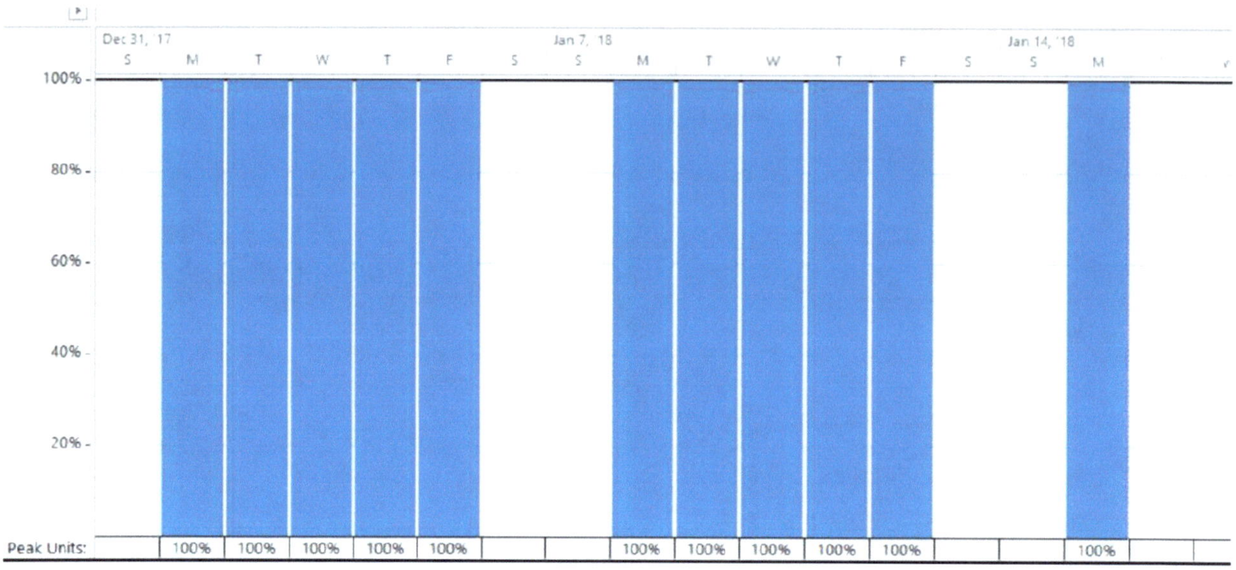
Dec 31, '17
Jan 7, '18
Jan 14, '18
S M T W T F S S M T W T F S S M
100%
80%
60%
40%
20%
Peak Units:
100% 100% 100% 100% 100%
100% 100% 100% 100% 100%
100%

Level Work Loads

A project manager or manager should distribute the project equitably to all direct reports by distributing the workloads equitably among subordinates.

Creating reports showing workloads and deadlines for all project managers is an important task to increase productivity and motivate the team equitably. Some managers have used software showing the cost breakdown of project managers' overall projects. At the same time, others prefer to display the loads manually on the team with a timeline such as bar charts. Microsoft Project can also perform this task. In the example below, we choose an efficient accounting method to capture an idea about the distribution of future projects within the team.

Table 30. Level Workloads, $Values & No. of Projects

Project Manager	Project Number	Budget including Co's	Budget Current Year -1	Budget Current Year	Budget Current Year +1	Budget Current Year +2
John	963851	$10,000,000	$2,000,000	$7,000,000	$1,000,000	
	963852	$3,000,000		$3,000,000		
	963853	$4,000,000	$500,000	$2,500,000	$500,000	$500,000
	741851	$3,000,000			$3,000,000	
	741852	$3,000,000			$500,000	$2500,000
John Total	**5**	**$23,000,000**	**$2,500,000**	**$12,500,000**	**$5,000,000**	**$3,000,000**
Alvic	963854	$8,000,000		$8,000,000		
	963855	$2,000,000		$2,000,000		
	963856	$2,000,000		$2,000,000		
	741853	$2,000,000		$2,000,000		
Alvic Total	**4**	**$15,000,000**		**$15,000,000**		
Mathieu	963856	$5,000,000		$500,000		
	963850	$500,000		$500,000		
	963847	$1,500,000		$500,000		
	741842	$2,000,000		$500,000		
	741843	$1,000,000		$500,000		
	815235	$4,000,000		$300,000		
Mathieu Total	**6**	**$14,000,000**		**$2,800,000**		

According to the table above, Mathieu has six ongoing projects. Although he has the most projects underway for the current year, the charges are only $2.8M. It is most likely decided that the manager will hand over the future project to him unless some of his projects require more attention due to the project's complexity, like a high-quality client that needs a full-time presence and a lot of paperwork.

SECTION 10
PROJECT COMMUNICATIONS MANAGEMENT

Project Managers spend most of their time communicating with team members and other project stakeholders, whether internal or external.

CHAPTER 18 - COMMUNICATION MANAGEMENT

Plan Communications

Developing an appropriate approach and plan for project communications based on stakeholder's information needs and requirements.

Managing communications is about keeping everyone in the know. The communications planning process involves defining what types of information you will provide, who will receive it, the format for communicating it, and when it will be published and distributed. It turns out that 90% of a project manager's work is spent on communication, so it's essential to make sure everyone gets the right message at the right time.

So how do you create a communication plan?

- Identify your stakeholders (to whom)
- Identify stakeholder expectations (why)
- Identify the communication necessary to meet the expectations of stakeholders and keep them informed (what)
- Identify the Schedule and/ or frequency of communication messages (when)
- Identify how the message will be communicated (the stakeholder's preferred method) (how)
- Identify who will communicate each message (who). Document items – templates, formats, or documents the project must use for communicating

Real-Life Examples

Plan meetings

After the project is awarded, call for a start-up meeting or pre-construction meeting. Plan the communication during this meeting, record the meeting minutes, and send them to all the involved personnel. Review pre-construction meeting example in Time Management Section.

You can add a table to the pre-construction meeting template to identify the communication methods.

Attendance: Joe xxx Sam xxx Catarina xxx etc.	Distribution: All attendees and John xxx Bill xxx Stephanie xxx Bernard xxx Golda xxx Nick xxx
Introduce Project Team including best telephone numbers to reach and emails	

Company Team Consultant 1 Team Consultant 2 Team Municipality Team Civil Engineer Team Contractor Team Etc.	
Communication Plan	
1. All site inquiries should be directed to the Company Superintendent with a copy to the Project Manager and Company Site staff. 2. All the technical problems of the Contractor will be sent to Consultant 1 for his direction, with a copy to the PM. 3. The Contractor must direct all resident issues to site staff and copy the PM. 4. All site personnel emergency site issues to be sent to the builder for immediate action. 5. Subsequently, site staff must send written notification to all parties for registration. 6. The Contractor sends all modification instructions to consultant 1, copy to Owner and PM. 7. The Contractor sends an inspection notice to the municipality, copy to the engineer, PM, and consultant 1 and 2. 8. The Contractor must send payment requests to the consultant no later than the 28th of each month, copy to engineer, and PM. 9. Etc.	

Getting a team together at the same time can be a challenge, primarily if they are spread across multiple time zones. Many types of communication do not require the parties to be present at the same time. Schedule your kickoff, progress, and milestone meetings accordingly.

Plan Sharing Folders

1. The Assistant Project Manager will probably upload all approved shop drawings to a shared folder accessible to the Owner, consultant, Contractor, and project team. (for example, FTP site, Dropbox.com, server, Sharepoint, etc.)
2. The Contractor will send all the as-built drawings in a shared folder and name the folder as, for example, ABD-*Contractor Name- Project Number- Date*. This will be accessible to the consultant for approval, PM for consultation, and client for archiving. The Contractor must send an email to all parties involved informing them that the as-built has been uploaded.
3. The manager should upload all plans with punch lists to a shared folder called PUNCHLISTS, accessible to the consultant and the project team, etc.

Manage Communications

Creating, collecting, distributing, storing, retrieving, and the ultimate disposition of the project.

Communications can be planned and managed in all aspects of a construction or design project. For example, the Quality department should distribute processes and forms discussed in quality management to the correct recipient.

A project manager can improve communication styles by enhancing the quality of their leadership.

Real-Life Examples

Create Project Status Reports

Daily reports

Daily reports, especially on a long-term project, are tedious. However, if there is a delay on your project, they can be your best friend. Daily Reports are a living story of what happens on a construction site. It can serve many purposes for a general contractor, but its primary benefit is to protect you. For example, if you need a construction lawyer to help you defend a delayed claim, having a daily report will make their efforts much more effective.

Components of a Daily Report

Weather conditions, site conditions, a summary of the day's activities including what was accomplished and any delays, on-site workers, on-site equipment including the state of equipment and whether owned or leased, materials received, quality of work, inspectors, and other on-site visitors, photos and videos, if applicable.

SAMPLE 55. Daily Report

DAILY REPORT		
Address:	Date: Weather:	Contract No.:

Internal Employees Activity and Timesheets			
Name	Total Hrs	Budget Code	Description of work
Alain XX	10	1039	Foreman
Bradley	9	07460	Exterior Sidings – Carpenter
David	7.5	07460	Exterior Sidings – Helper
Edward	9	07460	Exterior Sidings – Carpenter
Samuel	9	09900	Painting

Subcontractor Activity and Timesheets			
Name/Subcontractor	Total Hrs	Budget Code	Description of work
Travis/ABC	8	03100	Rebars for the slab on grade
Robin/ABC	8	03100	Rebars for the slab on grade
Richard/ ABC	6	03300	Pouring SonoTube
Noel	6.5	02200	The operator on an excavator
Joe- Engineering	5		Inspection

Report Summary of the day	**Significant problems, resolutions, or responsibility**
Structure Engineering Consultant Inspect the Rebar works	Joe + PM
Health and Safety Meeting from 7:30-8:00 am	Super+PM
Painting materials received and verification sheet filled up at 1:30 pm	AX Transport Foreman Super Justification Report # 123
Installing S.O.G steel rebars, Painting Rooms 101, 102, 105, 108 first coat, Grading the exterior, Exterior sidings	
Etc.	

Equipment			
Unity No.	Description	Hours	Comments
100532	Scissor Lift 40 Ft	6.5	Sidings
101325	Scissor Lift 26 Ft	0	Stand By
101456	Skytrack	4	Working with employees sidings

NONCONFORMITY			
Description	Number	C	N.C
Painting Materials justification report filled	9881	Yes	

Prepared By :

Approved By:

Distributed to:

Change Log

Creating different types of journals can improve communication between all parties. For example, a project manager can create a shop drawing journal, change order journal, RFI journals, milestone journals, etc.

A design manager, a program manager in a design and build company, can create logs for RFQs, RFPs, RFIs, approved projects, addenda, project costs, etc.

The example below shows a change order log from the contractor's perspective. It happens to include in the same record, all the site instructions and change notices of the consultant. The same type of log sheet can be used for shop drawing progress and others.

The Change Request Log should be distributed to the Consultant and Owner to the extent possible to ensure that any outstanding Change Orders will be processed following established procedures.

SAMPLE 56. Site Instruction (S.I.) Change notice (C.N.) & Change Order (C.O.) log

Site Instruction (S.I.) Change notice (C.N.) & Change Order (C.O.) log										
Project Name and Address:						Project No.: Client No.:				
Update: 01/01/2022		Prepared By:				Approved By:				
#	Work Description	Site Instruction No.	Change Notice No.	Quote No.	Quote Submitted	A=Approved V= Revision Required R: Rejected	Change order No.	Return Date	Amount ($)	Comments
1	Roof Access Hatch	SI#1	CN#2	Q2	2014.02.03	V		2014.02.13		The hatch specifications have been changed to reduce the price.
	Roof Access Hatch	SI#1	CN#2	Q2-R	2014.02.16	A	2	2014.02.20	$3,500	PO Received
2	Remove, Supply and install Door and Frame for accessing Expansion Tank	SI#2	CN#1	Q1	2014.01.20	A	1	2014.02.05	$3,000	PO Received
3	Additional Steel Structure	SI#3	CN#3	Q3	2014.03.15	R				Scope deleted
4	Relocation of Electrical Equipment	SI#4	CN#4	Q4	2014.03.15	V		2014.03.17		Price negotiated and lowered to take into account consultant comments.
	Relocation of Electrical Equipment	SI#4	CN#4	Q4-R	2014.03.20	A	3	2014.03.20	$1,500	**PO not Received**
							Total to date:		**$8,000**	

Note: Change orders that do not receive a P.O. adjustment cannot be invoiced until they are included in the original P.O. or in a new P.O. issued to cover the C.O. in dispute.

Report Performance.

Report Performance is the process of collecting and distributing performance information, including status reports, progress measurements, and forecasts. The performance reporting process involves collecting and analyzing baseline versus actual data to understand and communicate the project progress and performance, and forecast the project results.

Poor communication can negatively impact team morale. Managers unable to talk to their team can cause many issues. Projects fall behind Schedule when employees have no direction. Stressful deadlines get put in place to stick to the original plan, but this move results in significant burnout.

If an employee has a problem and requires leadership input, she may wait much longer than expected before bringing it to a manager. A minor issue rapidly snowballs into an avalanche during this time frame. If a manager is known for reacting poorly to criticism or negative news, the team ends up walking on eggshells around him.

Proper communication techniques are the most crucial tool to influence organizational culture positively. Managers must take steps to increase their team's comfort level.

Depending on the culture and vision of the company, how they implement quality management in their system, managers should use different techniques of presentation and communication with their teams.

Real-Life Examples

SAMPLE 57. Projects Performance Report

Project No.	From Cost Reports	From Schedule Reports & Completion %	From Quality Reports
20-01	On Budget	68%. On Schedule	Non-Conformity No.=0
20-02	- Above Budget by 5%. - Requested Budget Increase through a B.C.A.	-91%. Behind Schedule by 15%. -Reason: COVID-19.	-Nonconformity No.=9 -Corrective measures implemented. -End of project Evaluation (Post Mortem) will be prepared for lessons learned.
20-03	-Below Budget by 10% -Request Budget transfer to other projects. -Reason: scope reduced but no effect on our project value.	- 87%. Behind Schedule by 5%. -Reason: supplied materials delay.	- N.C. no. =3 - Corrective measures implemented. - Meeting with client after two weeks to discuss project performance.

SECTION 11
PROJECT RISK MANAGEMENT

CHAPTER 19 - RISK MANAGEMENT

Project Risk Management aims to increase the probability and impact of positive events and decrease the likelihood and impact of adverse events in the project.

Construction and Design-build is a risky business. Each project is unique and comes with its own set of challenges and opportunities. Identifying and managing project risks can be tricky but not impossible with careful planning and execution. When risk turns into reality, it can disrupt and derail a project, so construction risk management is essential. To avoid disaster, you need to be able to assess appropriately, control, and monitor risks once they've been identified.

Risks aren't always harmful. Identifying and managing risks effectively can lead to increased profits, establishing good relationships with clients that result in more projects, and expanding your business into new markets and sectors.

When risks come to fruition, they can have a severe impact on your project's costs, schedules, and performance, which will lead to delays and disputes down the road. The good news is that most of these risks can be managed and mitigated with proper planning and good project management.

Risks can be categorized into external, internal, technical, and project management risks.

Risk Management Process

1. Plan Risks
2. Identify Risks
3. Perform Risk Analysis
4. Plan Risk Responses
5. Monitor and Control Risks

Common Risks in the design phase

- Delay and difficulties in obtaining opinions and permits
- Conflict among design team members
- Incorrect investigations and reports
- Inexperienced workforce/ inadequate staff/ resource availability
- Incomplete Drawings and Poorly defined scope
- Design errors
- Wrong selection in materials
- Incompetent bidders
- Too many projects
- Historical site, endangered species, or wetlands present
- Etc.

Common risks construction projects

- Safety hazards that lead to work accidents and injuries
- Managing change orders
- Unknown site conditions
- Poorly written contracts
- Unexpected increases in material costs
- Labor shortages
- Damage or theft to equipment and tools
- Natural disasters- Force Majeure- Water Quality Issues
- Issues with subcontractors and suppliers
- Availability of building materials
- Poor project management
- Unexpected increase in material costs
- Changes in law
- Work Permissions
- Utilities
- Late Surveys, incomplete or wrong
- Environmental risks
- Etc.

Real-Life Example - Risk Management in Construction Projects

Table 31. Risk Register Design-Construction

Risk Register Design-Construction				Prepared By: Approved By: Presented To:		Date: Project Start Date: Project End Date:	Project Value: Design: $200,000 Construction: $10,000,000
Identified Risks	**Likeli-hood**	**Impact if the risk occurs**	**Severity: Based on Impact & Likelihood**	**Owner: Person who will manage the Risk**	**Mitigation Action**	**Contingent Action: Action to be taken If Risk happens**	**Resources:**
1 - Safety	High	High Cost: $20K Delay: 30 Days	High	Project Sponsor	1- Transfer to third party Consultant, 2 - Create a Constructor agreement to hold the G. contractor as the only one responsible for Site Safety, 3 - Safety Prevention Program to be approved by all parties, 4 - Daily meeting with the construction team and safety concerns discussed in each progress meeting.	1- Vendor management meeting with the constructor for immediate corrective action, 2- The Project Manager holds a site meeting with the safety consultant, GC, and the labor ministry to discuss corrective and preventive measures.	Template Prevention Program *(Form Hyperlink)*
2 - Change Orders	High	**Medi-um** Cost: $300K Delay: 45 Days	**Medium-High**	Project Manager	1- Complete the drawings and specs, 2- Get all the site investigation reports ready and send them to bidders, 3- Create Lumpsum Contracts, 4- Discourage change orders in the preconstruction meeting and progress meetings.	1- Get Consultant approval and recommendation for each CO, 2- Negotiate the price using the Datasheet attached as a reference for previous costs, 3- Getting three quotes 3- Identify the reason for a lesson learned: Site Conditions, Major Forces, design Omission, emergency, Safety, etc.	Company Previous approved Price Datasheet (Form Hyperlink)
3- Project Schedule not Defined	**Low**	**Mediu m** Cost: Delay:	**Medium**	**Project Manager**	**Hold scheduling workshops with project team to understand the plan and the likelihood of missed tasks are reduced.**	**Share the plan and go through upcoming tasks at each weekly project progress meeting.**	**Project Schedule Template (Form Hyperlink)**
4 - Cost Estimation Errors	**Medium**	High Cost: $25k Delay: 15 days	High	Project Manager-Design/ Build	Use two cost estimation methods, carefully track costs and forecast cost at completion, and make adjustments as necessary. Add in 10% contingency on Cost and Schedule.	Escalate to project sponsor and project board. Raise change requests for change to Budget – create Business Case Amendment.	Change Request and B.C.A. templates
5 - Project Purpose Not Well Defined	**Medium**	High Cost: To come Delay: 30 Days	High	Project Sponsor	Complete a business case if not already provided and ensure the purpose is well defined on Project Charter.	Escalate to the Project Board with an assessment of the Risk of runaway costs and time.	Business Case Questionnaire Template

6 - Work Permissions	**Medium**	High Cost: To come Delay: 20 Days	High	Project Sponsor	Complete a business case if not already provided and ensure the purpose is well defined on Project Charter.	Escalate to the Project Board with an assessment of the Risk of runaway costs and time.	External project Contact list (attached); Post Mortem Form (attached)
7 - Cost Overrun	**Low**	**Medi-um** Cost: $50k Delay: 14 days	**Medium**	Project Manager	- Provide monthly reports according to the company's accepted format, -Provide monthly Earned Value analysis model, -Update monthly forecast and flag any expected delay or cost overrun, - Provide a complete communication plan at the start of the project.	- Negotiate the future contract, -Define the reasons each month and take immediate corrective actions, -Conduct more progress meetings to ensure better communication - Use contingency to cover overruns - Send an amendment to the business case - Record problems in the post mortem form as a lesson learned.	Monthly Report Template (attached) Post Mortem Form (attached)

SECTION 12
CASE STUDIES

CHAPTER 20 - CASE STUDIES

CASE STUDY# 1 RFQ IN PRIVATE SECTOR

RFQ Example - RFQ Consultant In Private Sector

As a client project manager, you need to prepare for engineering consulting services. Write a general quote request (RFQ) that will show consultants what your business expects from these services. What kind of detailed Quotation can the Client receive? And how can the consultant turn on his quote to a contract?

Answer:

Subject: Request for Quotation RFQ

Project Summary

The Phase 3 servicing design was submitted to the Town of Wastage Beach for approval in August 2012. The project has been approved for construction. ABC Homes wishes to proceed to the building as soon as possible in 2022, working through the winter to complete base asphalt in 2023.

The site is currently being used to access the Lamont Creek bridge construction project, where sections have been partially graded; however, the majority of earthworks still need to be completed. You have advised that the earthworks operations should include both Phase 3 and Phase 4, located at the northwest section of the development.

Tender preparation and contract award will be handled by ABC Homes directly, and therefore no allowances have been carried for this task.

General Project Scope

The proposed scope of Work for the remaining services is provided in the following sections.

1. Contract Administration to Base Asphalt
2. Contract Administration after Base Asphalt (to assumption)
3. Plot Plan Approvals / Lot Grading Certification

1.0 | Contract Administration to Base Asphalt

1. Part-time inspection during site preparation and site grading activity.
2. Periodic inspections of erosion sediment control measures (ESC) and issue status reports required satisfying NVCA and the Town of Wasaga Beach.
3. Monitor contractor activity to determine compliance with terms and conditions of permits and approvals.
4. Continuous inspection services during servicing and road construction to the base asphalt as required by the Town of Wasaga Beach supported by periodic visits to the

site by senior personnel during the construction period to ensure that Work is carried out in general accordance with the plans and specifications (layout to be provided by the Contractor).

5. Project coordination to review and assist with contractor verification (spot check elevations, field measures for payment, and inspection with Town staff), attend bi-weekly project meetings, review construction schedules and prepare minutes.
6. Coordinate materials engineering services to ensure appropriate testing and sampling.
7. The Client shall engage the testing company directly.
8. Process contractor's payment requests and issue Payment Certificates to the Client.
9. Review and verify all contractor claims, including all justifiable extras to the Contract.
10. Receive, assess, and respond to reasonable complaints emergencies related to the contract works during servicing and road construction.
11. Provide and maintain adequate records related to the Contract.
12. Consider and approve reasonable requests for alternatives in methods and material proposed by the Contractor, issue change orders as required, and report to the Client.
13. Carry out inspections and coordinate rectifications as required by the Town, or any other approval authority, for issuance of Preliminary Acceptance and assist in acquiring building permits.
14. Apply for and assist in attaining reductions of Servicing Securities in a timely manner.
15. Attend utility coordination meetings and document site surface inspections before and after utility installations.
16. Prepare and submit as-constructed drawings per Town requirements.

2.0 | Contract Administration after Base Asphalt (to assumption)

1. Inspection services as required by the Town during the secondary roadwork's construction period (top stage curb, sidewalk, top asphalt) to ensure that Work is carried out according to the plans and specifications (layout to be provided by the Contractor).
2. Project coordination to review and assist with contractor verification (spot check elevations, field measures for payment, and inspection with municipal staff), attend project meetings, review construction schedules and prepare minutes.
3. Coordinate materials engineering services to ensure appropriate testing and sampling. The Client shall engage the testing company directly.
4. Process contractor's payment requests and issue Payment Certificates to the Client.
5. Review and verify all contractor claims, including all reasonable extras to the Contract.

6. Receive, assess, and respond to reasonable complaints in emergencies related to the contract works during secondary road construction.
7. Coordinate all necessary inspections with all required approval authorities.
8. Coordinate with the staff of all approval agencies and the sub-consultants to assist with a timely assumption of the subdivision. Assumption means Municipal acceptance of built services and release of all applicable securities.
9. Apply for and assist in attaining reductions of remaining securities.

3.0 | Lot Grading Review and Approval

3.1 | Plot Plan Review

1. Review and certification of the plot plans submitted by the Client's architect for conformity with the approved Lot Grading Plans and Town standards.

3.1 | Plot Plan Review

1. Carry out pre-sod grading inspection and provide comments on a batch or block basis
2. Carry out post-sod (final) grading inspection with Town staff on a batch or block basis
3. Provide deficiency list to Builder or issue Lot Grading Certification (i.e., certify to Town that grading is in "general conformance with approved plans").

After sending the RFQ, you will receive Quotes. (Remember to send a set of plans related to the quote work area if available).

Example of a Consultant Quote

The offer received **can be the same RFQ with modified sections if needed**, the values $, and the addition of other elements. See below to $ value quotation and the exclusions.

4.0 | Professional Fees

SAMPLE 58. Consultant Quote Private Sector

The fees estimated for this proposal are based on assumptions with respect to project requirements and our estimate of time required to carry out the work. To a large extent this is dependent on the rate and quality of work carried out by the contractor(s).

	Item	Total	Fee Basis
	Contract Administration		
1.0	Contract Administration and Inspection to Base Asphalt	$140,000	Fixed Fee
2.0	Contract Administration and Inspection after Base Asphalt to Assumption	$40,000	Fixed Fee
3.0	**Lot Grading Review and Approval**		
3.1	Plot Plan Review and Certification (80 lots – 14 TH Blocks)	$11,880	$110/Lot $220/TH Block
3.2	Pre-Sod Inspection (80 lots – 14 TH Blocks)	$11,880	$110/Lot $220/TH Block
3.3	Lot Grading Certification (80 lots – 14 TH Blocks)	$11,880	$110/Lot $220/TH Block

Invoicing will be in accordance with our standard terms and conditions (per attached). Invoicing will occur upon month end based on progress, and is payable by the Client within 30 days.

5.0 | Exclusions and Qualifications

The work program and fees outlined in this proposal are based on the following assumptions:

- Fees are exclusive of HST.
- Disbursements and mileage are not included and invoiced at cost (mileage will be billed from the consultant's office to the job or meeting site).
- Earthworks inspection includes part-time inspection over ten weeks.
- Servicing contract administration has been assumed to occur in a single phase of Work requiring full-time inspection services over 20 weeks.
- If these schedules are exceeded, fees will be adjusted to reflect the actual construction duration on a prorated basis.
- All survey layouts will be provided by the Contractor.
- We have allowed one week of part-time service for deficiency rectification and one week of part-time service for preliminary acceptance and permit release.
- Information required to complete as-built drawings to be provided by the others (Contractor, OLS).
- Completion of top asphalt and maintenance start is assumed to occur within two years of base asphalt, with the final assumption within two years following.
- Above ground as-constructed information (if required) to be provided by the Client O.L.S.
- Plot plan approvals and grading inspections for less than five units would be billed hourly.
- All minor works that are outside the scope listed above would be charged on an hourly basis.
- Tasks and budgets will be submitted for review before initiating the Work. For any substantial change to the Scope of Work, a new scope would be defined, and a fee provided for your approval before commencement of the Work.

6.0 | Closure

Our standard Terms and Conditions of Service are attached. If you agree with the proposal as outlined, please sign the Authorization form and return it to our office. Please call us if you have any questions.

We trust all of the above is satisfactory and thank you for considering DEF & Associates Limited for this Work.

Yours truly,

Usually, the Consultant will add a page to turn this quote to a contract as an Authorization to proceed page:

SAMPLE 59. Authorization To Proceed- Private Sector

Authorization to Proceed
Date: October 31st, 2017
Client: Name, ABC Homes
Submitted By: Name, CET.
Project: Wasaga Phase 3
Town of Wasaga Beach
Project No.: 3000

I, , being an employee of ____________________,

hereby authorize EFG & Associates Limited (the Consultant) firm to arrange for or perform the Work described in the Proposal Letter dated October 31st, 2017.

I understand that the payment is based on Fixed Fees as outlined in Section 4.0 of this Proposal.

By affixing my signature, I understand that the attached Standard Conditions of Service govern the Scope of Work contained in the Proposal Letter (noted above and attached).

xxxxxxxxxxxxxxxxxxxxxxxxxxxxxxxxx
Signature

xxxxxxxxxxxxxxxxxxxxxxx
Date

xxxxxxxxxxxxxxxxxxxxxxxxxxxxxxxxxxxxxxxx
Position/Title

I have the authority to bind the Corporation.

This ATP must be signed and returned to DEF & Associates Limited within 30 days from the date above to guarantee the rates and pricing provided in the attached proposal.

(Review Consultant RFP in Private Sector in Chapter 2- Tendering Phase)

CASE STUDY# 2 - PUSHING A CONSULTANT

SAMPLE 60. Pushing a Consultant

Real-life Example Pushing a Consultant

Storm Water Management (SWM) Pond.

We hired an engineering company to do an SWM pond topographic and bathymetric survey. After the pond clean-up exercise, the Consultant would determine (in AutoCAD) the actual volume of silt removed for payment to the Contractor, based on the topographic survey of the pond's bottom submitted by the Contractor.

To explain in more detail the previous paragraph. We hired a contractor to clean up the sediment (silt) that had accumulated over 10 years. We also hired a surveyor to get the as-built (the actual levels of the pond). As you may know, the as-built, in this case, is a point system that shows the elevations at different contour lines.

Below are the contents of the approved Quotation.

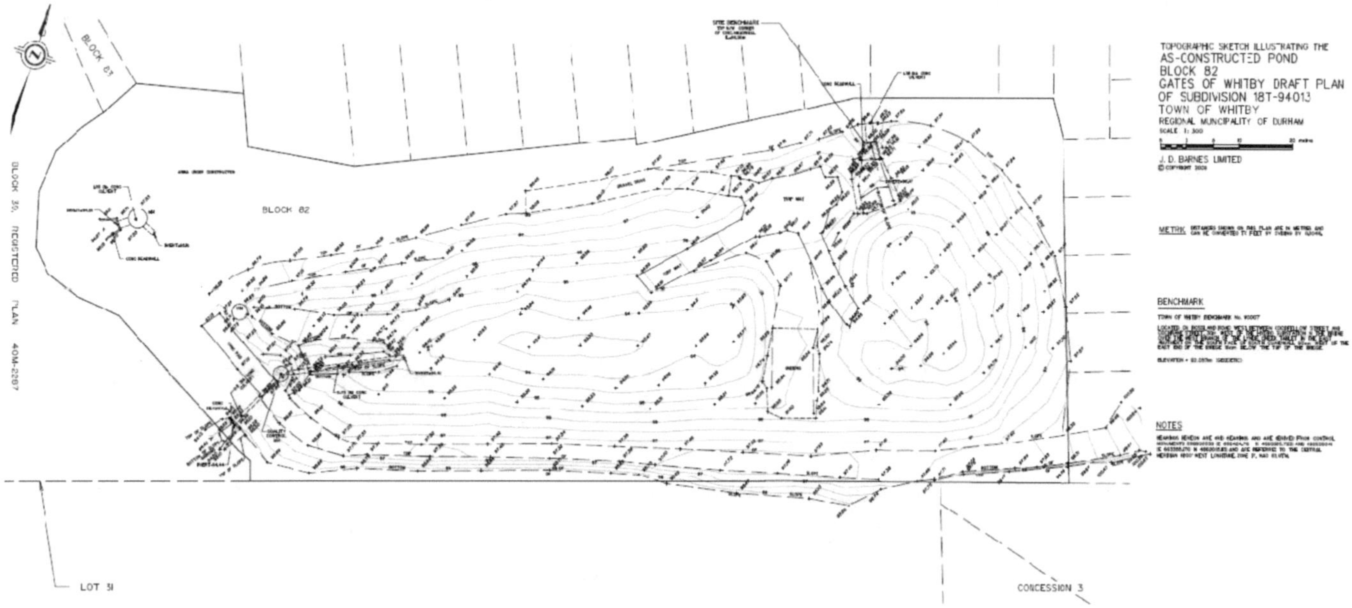

SAMPLE 61. Consultant Quotation SWM POND

CONSULTANT LOGO AND COMPLETE ADDRESS

QUOTE# **235**

SUBMITTED TO: ABC HOME BUILDER DATE: JAN 15,2021

Re: SWM Pond Topographic and Bathymetric Survey Quote
Whitby Subdivision 5, Whitby, Ontario

We are pleased to provide an estimate of our topographic and bathymetric services of the Whitby Subdivision 5 Pond in Whitby, Ontario. We understand you wish to ascertain the depth of silt material required to be removed from this pond.

Included in this fee are the following tasks:

- One-day bathymetric survey of the pond to the permanent pool elevation and necessary tie-in topographic data collection (including mobilizing and clean-up, disbursements, and benchmark data collection to confirm the proper function of our survey equipment).
- Inlet/outlet invert and headwall elevations and inverts within the outlet headwall structures will be collected.
- Data download, QA/QC, and cut-fill analysis conducted within AutoCAD to determine the proposed volume of silt to be removed.
- After the pond cleaning exercise, we will determine (within AutoCAD) the actual volume of silt removed for contractor payment purposes, based on the Contractor's submitted topographic survey of the pond bottom.
- Barring any extreme weather conditions, we will complete this project as soon as the ice has melted for the season (estimate date for completion; April 21, 2021)

Our Fee to undertake the tasks listed above is SEVEN THOUSAND FIVE HUNDRED DOLLARS ($7,500.00), including all disbursements but does not include taxes. Should you agree with this proposal, please sign and return our one-page terms and conditions.

The old survey as-built, the bathymetric survey, and the new topographic survey are now with the engineer. One month has passed since the Contractor completed the Work; however, we have received no response from the engineer. The Contractor had to invoice the Work with an estimated quantity on his side (how many trucks he had to empty). Our agreement with the Contractor stated that the Client would make the payments according to the engineer's reports. Several attempts were made with the engineer to take the actual quantity. The Consultant responded that the task was complicated and that more internal resources had to re-verify
the data.

The Client Project Manager was taking a course with Seneca College in Toronto called Civil 3D. At that time, he knew how to compare two surfaces and get the actual cut and fill using this software. He called for a meeting, sat down with the technical engineer, and showed him how to do this exercise independently. He was surprised that the PM had this specialized experience, and the following week the PM got the required data.

What were the strengths of the previous real example?

A. The agreement with the Contractor indicated that the Consultant would confirm the quantities of materials cut;

B. An independent consultant completed all surveys on time;

C. All AutoCAD survey files have been provided to the customer, and

D. A project manager has implemented a pushing technique. In this case, show the knowledge for this area. There are many other pushing techniques, such as visiting the Consultant's office and observing how the Work is done. Never give up until you get the result you want.

Once the consultant sent the required data, he also sent a progressive invoice for the parts of the Work completed to date.

Figure 25. Consultant Invoice by hours spent

Phase : 100 – DESIGN REVISION

INVOICE 2134
Through August 2017

Obtain previous SWM report, As Builts (from archives)
Review Town's concerns regarding As Builts and inconsistencies
Review As Built drawings, make list and obtain missing As Built information for As Builts
Update As Built pond bottom vs. design pond bottom and quantify cut required to achieve required volume
Assemble and forward exisiting report, As Builts, 2010 Topo Survey and summarize findings
Update stage-storage curve based on As Built volumes and elevations
Research CLOCA regulatory limits re: future pond work

Rate Schedule Labour

Class / Employee Name	*Hours*	*Rate*	*Amount*
Name of employee 1 and his position	37.00	114.00	4,218.00
Name of employee 2 and his position	2.00	123.00	246.00
Name of employee 3 and his position	5.00	163.00	815.00
Name of employee 4 and his position	0.50	163.00	81.50
Labour			***5,360.50***

Total Phase : 100 – DESIGN REVISION	**Labour :**	**5,360.50**
	Disbursements :	**0.00**
Total Project: 2820907 -- GATES OF WHITBY PHASE III		**$5,360.50**

CASE STUDY# 3 - RFP TO HIRE A CONSULTANT IN THE PUBLIC SECTOR

SAMPLE 62. RFP Consultant Public Sector

Scope of Project document

[Project name - see below]

Date]

[Insert table of contents if required] See following Example.

1. Project name

This should accurately describe the project, with some detail, for example "Design services for architectural and structural remedial works for a mid-rise seven-story residential building."

2. About the Client: Example about the City of Toronto

Example: Toronto is Canada's largest city and a world leader in business, finance, technology, entertainment, and culture. Its large population of immigrants worldwide has also made Toronto one of the most multicultural cities in the world.

3. Project scope statement

The scope statement should summarize the project or product objectives. Objectives should be measurable and achievable within the time allotted.

4. Introduction/Background to project

Information here might include the client's original request and any refinements to reach the agreed understanding of what the project will entail. For example: Explain **why** the project is being undertaken and the business benefits that will be gained.

5. Deliverables

'Deliverables' refers to the outcome or parts of the product that lead to the project's successful completion. The Deliverables section is the longest part. The table of content will appear **as Appendix A or B or C etc.** - see an example of a table of content in the following example.
Example:

Phase 1 - Design Development (Including Investigation)

A. Investigation (Describe the services needed in detail)
B. Reporting
C. Recommendation
D. Design Development
   - Site Plan
   - Architectural Plans
   - Structural Plans
   - Plan and Section Details
   - Items shall be considered in the design stage. Such as Details needed. Suppliers to be used, minimum design thresholds, etc.

Phase 2 - Construction documents: Describe what is needed.

Phase 3 - Tender Phase: Quotation and Tender Review, Addenda, Contract Award, Communications.

Phase 4 - Construction and Contract Administration

A. **Project administration, monitoring, and reporting**: For example:
   a. Frequency of any project meetings
   b. Reporting, such as progress reports or other monitoring, including:
      - Approximate % work completed vs. schedule
      - Outstanding issues
      - Change order logs
      - Outstanding shop-drawings
      - Etc.
B. Send the client recommendations regarding change orders and compare values to market price.

Phase 5: Closeout Documents
Explain what the client requests the Consultant to provide at the end of the project.

Examples:

- Substantial Completion
- Coordinate the Final Walkthrough meeting
- Confirm that there are no outstanding and no deficiencies of works
- Obtain all guarantees and warranties
- Approve As-Built drawings
- Send a final set of approved
- Shop drawings
- Etc.

6. **Constraints**

Constraints refer to any limits, deadlines, delivery dates, building occupied measures, etc., which will govern the approach you're going to take to complete the project.

7. **Key people/Key stakeholders**

You could list the prominent people involved and their responsibilities on this project - internal and external, as appropriate.

- Project lead or project manager
  [Name, contact details]
  Responsible for ...
- Client - or named contact in the area of the business the project is being carried out for
  [Name, contact details]
  Responsible for ...
- Project support or project administration
  [Name, contact details]
  Responsible for ...

8. **Out of scope**

Describe what the project will not cover. For example, training in using a new system or providing ongoing user support is unlikely to be covered by a project.

(Review Consultant RFP in Private Sector- Chapter 2 Tendering Phase)

CASE STUDY# 4 - Tender Documents – Construction Management

A- Invitation to Tender

SAMPLE 63. Invitation To Tender- Construction Management

> **Expression of Interest**
> = Invitation To Tender
>
> **CM Service:** Indicate the type of Contract to

School Project
Roman Catholic Toronto School Board

Expression of Interest
Construction Management Service

Roman Catholic Torontian School Board intends to tender the project implementation using the **Construction Management method**. The project is subject to the approval of the Ministry of Education MOE.

> MOE may require specific Vendors to quote

To be considered, you are requested to submit Proposal Documents which are available on our website. The Proposal Documents consist of CCDC 11 together with a list of supplementary questions. The board's primary objective is to construct a single-storey school of about 1080 sqm, having a construction budget of $1,300,000, and complete to permit occupancy by October 4, 2023. Following an evaluation of the submissions, a shortlist of candidates will be selected and invited to submit a detailed offer of Construction Management Services.

The determination of a shortlist of applicants will be determined depending on the answers provided by the proponents. Rated criteria for evaluation purposes can be found on our website for a consultation.

Submissions identified with the project title shall be accepted at the Board Offices no later than 3:00 p.m. December 16th, 2022, and shall be addressed :

John Smith
Roman Catholic Toronto School Board
Pacific Road
Whitby, Ontario

> **This invitation describes the project size, value, and start dates.**

The sample above is an invitation to tender in t~~he form of an "An Expression of Interest"~~ for a construction management contract management.

The Invitation to Tender indicates that a construction management contract, a CCDC 11 (Pre-qualified statement, also known as a CCA 11), and supplementary conditions are expected to be addressed.

(Review Invitation to Tender & Contractor RFQ in Chapter 2 Tendering Phase.)

B- Vendor Evaluation and Contract Award.

Contractors:

1. Read RFQ documents, plans, specifications, general requirements, etc.
2. Sent the RFI's in accordance with the deadline for questions mentioned in the RFQ Time Table- (Review Table of Contents RFQ Timetable in Chapter 2- Tendering Phase.& Bid Management in Chapter 9 – Cost Estimation)
3. Made the necessary cost estimate and created the original Budget for this job (Review Activity Cost estimate in Chapter 9- Cost Estimation & Chapter 10- Determine Budget)
4. Filled up CCDC 11 and responded to all supplementary questions (Review Use of Estimate & BID Form in Chapter 9- Cost Estimation "Breakdown of Bid price & Bid Form)
5. The Cost Estimator discussed the price with the manager, added administration and profit, and sent all the documents requested by the client's website. **(Review Pricing Form in Chapter 3-Contract)**

Consultant:

1. Inquiries (RFI's) are handled in a timely manner. (Review Bid Management in Chapter 9 – Cost Estimation.)
2. Received all the prices and sent them to the client without opening the quotes.
3. Prepare the Building Permit Package with all construction documents.
4. Will send the building permit package with the final construction drawings to the client and assigned Contractor.

Client:

1. The client (public agency) leads the evaluation process by establishing a committee of evaluators and compares the submitted documents (not including the prices). **(Review Rated Criteria in Chapter 2 Tendering phase)**
2. The client excludes contractors who did not answer all questions and failed the review process (those who get lower scores).
3. The consultant or client informs contractors who do not meet minimum standards.
4. The customer opens the Bid form, which includes the prices, and compares the quotes received with the cost estimate.
5. If the lowest Quotation received is between - 10% and +10% of the cost estimate (depending on each Company's procurement plan), the client will send a letter of intent to award the Contract. (Review Award The Contract in Chapter 9 - Cost Estimation)
6. Suppose the deviation from the lowest estimate is more significant than ± 10% of the estimate. In that case, (According to each Company's procurement plan), the client will likely call for a vendor meeting and discuss the Scope of Work with the best bidder.

CASE STUDY# 5- RFP TO HIRE A CONTRACTOR IN THE PUBLIC SECTOR

SAMPLE 64. Extract from RFP Public Sector

Below is an extract from what you may find in an RFP document – Similar example can be consulted for RFQ. REAL RFP can reach hundreds of pages.

PART 1 – INTRODUCTION AND EXECUTIVE SUMMARY

1.1 Invitation to Respondents

This Request for Proposals (the "RFP") is an invitation by the ....Company Name ......to prospective respondents (each a "Respondent") to submit Quotations ("Quotations") for the provision of ..... Title of the Project....& Complete Address ..... For ....Company Name ......and ..Locations...., as further described in Appendix A – for the pricing established in Appendix C. The Proponent selected under this RFQ process will be informed electronically via ..e-mail/ Bidingo/ Bonfire/ Merx/ Bids&Tenders/ Bidscanada/ Procore/ ConstructConnect ....or other.

1.2 About the ..Company...

The ....Company Name ......is .....a detailed description of the company profile..... Additional information is available at the website ....

1.3 Executive Summary

a) Summary of RFP Requirements

This RFQ intends to select one (1) Respondent with extensive experience that will satisfy the following requirements:

a. A minimum of ten **<u>(10) years</u>** of experience providing ..... explain the service similar to the requirements outlined in this RFP........
b. Preparation of construction working drawings, fixture layout plans, reflected ceiling plans, and as-built drawings; renderings; and various project services including, without limitation, building permit application submissions, site verification/measurements, and tender specifications/scope of work assembly, as per the ....Company name .... communicated standards, specifications, and expectations.
c. Provide the deliverables following predetermined schedules mutually agreed upon by the successful Respondent and the ....Company name ...., for any project assigned according to this RFP.
d. Ensure that all drawings/Specifications and services are checked for accuracy before issuance to the ....Company name ....,.
e. Other services as outlined in this RFP.

b) Type of Contract

The ....Company name ....,. Intends to enter into a Contract, substantially upon the terms and conditions in Appendix C – "Terms and Conditions," with only one (1) legal entity. Respondents should note that the **....Company name ....**,. will also have an option to terminate the Contract for convenience upon thirty (30) days prior written notice to the successful Respondent.

1.4 RFQ Timetable

RFQ TIMETABLE	
RFQ NO.	23-011
RFQ Title	Building New 12 detached houses for seniors
Deadline for Questions	
Submission Deadline	
Rectification Period	
Estimated Commencement of Contract	

1.5 Company Contact and Proponent Questions

For this RFP process, the "...**Company name** ..Contact" is ...., Procurement Specialist, xxxx.xxxx@company.com

Respondents should promptly examine all of the documents comprising the RFP and should:

a) report any errors, omissions, or ambiguities; and
b) direct questions or seek additional information

in writing by e-mail to the ....Company name ....,. Contact on or before the Deadline for Questions. Respondents are advised to seek clarification from the **....Company name ....**,. Contact on any matter considered to be unclear. The **....Company name ....**,. is not responsible for any misunderstanding by a Respondent concerning the RFP.

All questions submitted by Respondents by e-mail to the **....Company name ....**,. Contact shall be deemed to be received once the e-mail enters into the **....Company name ....**,. Contact's e-mail inbox. No such communications are to be directed to anyone other than the **....Company name ....**,. Contact. While the ....Company name ....will make commercially reasonable efforts to answer any Respondent questions; it is under no obligation to provide additional information. In the interests of clarity and brevity, the **....Company name ....**, may also combine similar or related questions.

PART 2 – SUBMISSIONS INSTRUCTIONS

2.1 Proposal Submission Information

2.1.1 Timing for Submissions

Timetable for Quotation submissions are indicated above in the RFQ Timetable

2.1.2 Proposal Structure

Respondents should structure their Proposals per the instructions in Appendix xx – "Evaluation and Negotiation Process." Where information is requested in Appendix xx, any response made in a Proposal should reference the appropriate section numbers of the RFP where that request was made. Respondents who do not reference and title their proposal with each corresponding section number and title of the sections outlined in Appendix B may, at the ...Company name.... sole discretion, have the overall points awarded to them in the evaluation stage reduced by up to an overall total of five (5%) percent.

2.1.3 Mandatory Submission Requirements

2.3 Amending and Withdrawing Proposals

A Proposal may not be amended after the Submission Deadline by a Respondent except as expressly set out in terms of the RFP; however, at any time throughout the RFP process, a Respondent may withdraw a submitted Proposal if the Respondent no longer wishes to participate in the RFP process.

PART 3 – TERMS AND CONDITIONS OF THE RFQ PROCESS

3.1 Nature of Procurement Process

No Contract A and No Claims

The procurement process is not intended to create and shall not create a formal, legally binding process and shall instead be governed by the law applicable to direct commercial negotiations. For greater certainty and without limitation: (i) the RFP shall not give rise to any Contract A-based tendering law duties or any other legal obligations arising out of any process contract or collateral contract; and (ii) neither the Respondent nor ...the **Company name**.....shall have the right to make any claims (in Contract, tort, or otherwise) against the other concerning the award of a Contract.

No Contract until Execution of Written Agreement

No legal relationship or obligation regarding the procurement of any good or service shall be created between the Respondent and the **...Company name....** by the RFP process until the successful negotiation and execution of a written contract to acquire such goods and/ or services.

Pricing Information

While the pricing information provided in Proposals will be non-binding before executing a written contract, such information will be assessed while evaluating the Proposals and the Respondents' ranking.

3.2 Inappropriate Conduct and Conflict of Interest

The ...Company name.... may prohibit a Respondent from participating in a procurement process based on past performance or based on inappropriate conduct in a prior ...Company name .....procurement method.

3.3 Prohibited Communications and Confidential Information

The Respondent shall not engage in any Conflict of Interest communications and should note the Conflict of Interest declaration form.

3.4 References and Past Performance

The ...Company name.... evaluation may include information provided by the Respondent's references, if applicable. It may also consider the Respondent's past performance on previous contracts with the ....Company name.... or other institutions.

3.5 Evaluation Process

Stage I: Mandatory Requirements

During Stage I, The ...Company name will review each proposal to determine whether it complies with the Mandatory Requirements.

Stage II: Pricing

During Stage II, the price evaluation will only be undertaken after the assessment of Mandatory Requirements, and any rated requirements have been completed. Upon completion of Stage II, the lowest priced (Excluding HST) Proponent for each location as established under the evaluation for the project will be selected to agree to provide the Deliverables.

3.6 No Guarantee of Volume of Work or Exclusivity of Contract

The ...Company name.... and its advisers make no representation, warranty, or guarantee as to the accuracy of the information contained in the RFP or issued by way of addenda. Any quantities shown or data collected in the RFP or provided by a form of addenda are estimates only and are for the sole purpose of indicating to Respondents the available amount of the Work.

CASE STUDY# 6 - COST & TIME CONTROL THROUGH PROJECT LIFE

A governmental Client Award the Contract to a middle-size Contractor- Project value $15M. Briefly state some (not all) necessary steps as a project manager you will need to deal with. Use five steps method:

either: DEFINE, PLAN, ORGANIZE, CONTROL, AND CLOSE

or: INITIATING, PLANNING, EXECUTING, MONITORING & CONTROLLING, AND CLOSING

Review Chapter 1

CONTRACTOR

(1) & (2) Define & Plan

1. The Company issues the project charter authorizing the project manager and describing the Project values, deadlines, authorization of purchase, etc. (Review Project Charter in Integration Management).
2. The PM opens the project with the necessary governmental and safety departments and sends all the required notices.
3. The Company, with the PM assistant, prepares the Project's Quality Plan.
4. The Cost Estimator meets with the project manager, if different, to explain the project in detail, transfer the last drawings, specs, and other documents. Finally, discuss the project's problems and essential milestones.
5. The PM or Quality Department (Q.D.) prepares communication, stakeholder plan, risk plan, and develops a human resource plan.
6. The PM sends ASAP the Kick-off or Pre-construction meeting invitations to all project teams and stakeholders.
7. If it includes technical specifications (specs) from the Quality Plan, the PM extracts all critical milestones and integrates them into a detailed schedule. For example, Inspections, Important deadlines, etc.
8. The PM creates detailed project stakeholder's contacts and roles information.
9. The PM prepares/reviews and sends the safety plans.
10. The PM studies the budget and flags any underestimated activity from the early start.
11. The PM Develops a human resource plan, risk plan.

(3) & (4) Organize and Control

12. PM conducts the Pre-con meeting, ensures all parties are well introduced and connected.
13. The PM Updates the Schedule, searches for any possible fast-tracking activities to reduce the project's duration, connects with the subcontractors to ensure or enhance deadlines.
14. The PM may need to negotiate the subcontractors' estimated prices to enhance profits. The contract administrator or project manager will help in executing the contracts or PO's.
15. The PM acquires, develops, and manages the project team.
16. The PM conducts frequent progress meetings.
17. The PM manages risks and creates corrective actions and preventive measures where necessary.
18. The PM updates the communication plans.
19. The PM reviews shop drawings submissions.
20. The PM manages change orders.
21. The PM updates quality plans, schedules, budgets as necessary.
22. The PM prepares progress payments and gets the consultant's approvals.
23. The PM uses different methods to control the budget and schedule, including but not limited to crashing, fast-tracking, resource leveling, workload leveling, etc.
24. The PM approves invoices and sends them to the next workflow person.
25. The PM uses various tools to report progress and highlight issues.

(5) Close

26. The PM calls for a final walkthrough with the client and works with all the trades to correct deficiencies.
27. The PM collects the end-of-contract documents and sends them to the consultant and client.
28. The PM evaluates each subcontractor and employee as required in the project plan.
29. The PM writes a post mortem of the project for archiving lessons learned.

CONSULTANT

(1) & (2) Initiating & Planning

1. The Company issues the project charter authorizing the project manager and describing the Project values, deadlines, authorization of purchase, etc. (Review Project Charter in Integration Management).
2. The Company, with the PM assistant, prepares the Project's Quality Plan.
3. PM ensures that the last revisions of construction drawings and specs are in possession of the Contractor.

(3) & (4) Executing, Monitoring & Controlling

4. The PM provides administration of the Contract as described in the Contract Documents.
5. The PM visits the Place of the Work at intervals appropriate to construction progress to become familiar with the Work's progress and quality, and determine if the Work is proceeding in general conformity with the Contract Documents.
6. If the Owner and the Consultant agree, the PM provides at the Place of the Work, one or more project representatives to carry out the Consultant's responsibilities.
7. The PM promptly informs the Owner, of the date of receipt of the Contractor's applications for payment.
8. The PM reviews and takes appropriate action upon Shop Drawings, samples, and other Contractor's submittals, per the Contract Documents. PM updates or requests updating the different logs (Shop-drawings, Cos, Site Instructions, etc.)
9. The PM prepares Change Orders and issues Change Directives.
10. The PM reviews invoices received by the GC, ensures that justification documents and proper invoices are attached and issues certificates of payments recommending payments.
11. The PM attends the progress meetings and probably conducts meeting minutes.

(5) Closing

12. The PM attends the final walkthrough and issues a list of deficiency.
13. The PM receives and reviews written warranties and related documents required by the Contract and provided by the Contractor and forwards such warranties and documents to the Owner for the Owner's acceptance.
14. The PM ensures that deficiencies are corrected and receives written confirmation from the Contractor.
15. The PM sends all other closeout documents such as closing permits, final governmental acceptances, and assumptions.

16. The PM recommends closeout actions to the client, such as retrieving securities from the governmental bodies, back-charging the GC for unsolved deficiencies, etc.
17. The PM evaluates the Contractor as required in the project plan.
18. The PM writes an internal post mortem of the project for archiving lessons learned.

Client

(1) & (2) Initiating & Planning

1. The Company issues the project charter authorizing the project manager and describing the Project values, deadlines, authorization of purchase, etc. (Review Project Charter in Integration Management).
2. The Company, with the PM assistant, prepares the Project's Quality Plan.
3. PM ensures that the last revisions of construction drawings and specs are in possession of the Contractor.
4. PM ensures that all notices are sent.
5. PM ensures that the safety liabilities and risks are dealt with.

(3) & (4) Executing, Monitoring & Controlling

6. PM states clearly their expectation in the kick-off meeting.
7. PM attends progress meetings.
8. PM reviews recommended change modifications and approves them.
9. PM ensures that the Contractor is aware of any significant coming scope of Work or schedule.
10. PM ensures that fundings are available and forecasts cash-ins cash-outs reports to estimate spending through the year.
11. PM Monitors and controls the project costs and schedule and recommends corrective actions, and estimates associated costs.
12. PM creates reports showing major milestones progress and variances.
13. PM recommends corrective actions and estimates associated costs.
14. PM ensures that all quality records are received and well documented.
15. PM updates project budgets and contingencies.

(5) Closing

16. The PM attends the final walkthrough, discusses the list of deficiencies, and reviews timelines.
17. The PM evaluates the Contractor and consultants as required in the project plan.
18. The PM writes an internal post mortem of the project to document lessons learned.

CASE STUDY# 7 - WBS OWNER

You (Mike) work for a home builder in the planning and development department. Your team (direct reports) consists of a PM civil engineer (Adam), a PM architect (Joe), and a PM planner (Antony)

Questions:

- Create a work breakdown structure which shows some of the activity you will be dealing with.
- Assign responsibilities.
- As a project manager, view the main documentation files you have created for this project.
- Create a schedule and a cost report through MS Project to demonstrate costs and schedules.

Answers:

WBS

SAMPLE 65. WBS Owner

WBS Example Owner

1. Recruitment of consultants for the design and supply of a technical assistant, including project management and on-site consulting
   - 1.1 Civil Engineering firm covering Civil, Environmental, and Public Infrastructure
   - 1.2 Landscape architectural
   - 1.3 Electrical & Mechanical Engineering Firm
   - 1.4 Structural Engineering firm covering house design
   - 1.5 Architectural firm covering house design

2. Civil Design
   - 2.1 First draft approval sent to the City (Milestone)
   - 2.2 Second and Final Draft Plan approved by the City (Milestone)
   - 2.3 Pond design

3. Civil Construction Management
   - 3.1 Prepare Tender Documents (RFP)
   - 3.2 Invitation to Tender (Milestone)
   - 3.3 Award Contract for a General Contractor (Milestone)
   - 3.4 Construction
     - 3.4.1 Excavating and Backfills
     - 3.4.2 Subdivision Servicing Contract
     - 3.4.3 Street Lights
     - 3.4.4 Pond Construction
     - 3.4.5 Bell

3.4.6 Rogers
3.4.7 Surveying
3.4.8 Subdivision assumption from the City (MileStone)

4. Building Civil Services
   4.1 Payment of Development Charges
   4.2 Surveying
   4.3 House Construction for 15 houses
   4.4 Occupation Permit (Milestone)

A. Assign responsibilities: (Review RACI in Chapter 17). Mike calls for a meeting to discuss the RACI chart with the project team.

RACI Chart	Project Managers				
Activity	Mike (Senior Manager)	Adam (Civil engineer)	Joe (Architect)	Antony (Planner)	Owner
Schedule	R	C	C	C	I
Workload Analysis	R	I	I	I	I
Update Budget	R	C	C	C	A
Hiring	R	I	I	I	A
1.1	A	R	I	C	A
1.2	A	R	I	C	A
1.3	A	R	I	C	A
1.4	A	R	I	C	A
1.5	A	I	R	C	A
2.1	A	C	I	R	A
2.2	A	C	I	R	A
2.3	A	R	I	C	A
3.1	A	R	I	C	I
3.2	A	R	I	C	I
3.3	R	C	I	C	C
3.4.1 to 3.4.7	A	R	I	I	I
3.4.8	A	R	I	C	I
4	A	C	R	C	C

B. As a project manager, show primary documentation folders that you created for this project.

Answer:

C. Create a schedule and cost report through MS Project to show costs and schedules.

If the system in the company does not provide detailed assistance for such an exercise, recommend using excel, MS project, primavera, or other presentation software to show the activities, costs, durations, responsibilities, milestones, etc.

Below is an example of MS project documents with a rough estimate of each activity's project duration and costs.

Figure 26.Schedule by MS Project

Hyperlinks can be added to MS Project to display PDF documents such as contract, invoice or to link to a case.

		WBS	Task Name	% Complete	ede				Names				
0			PROJECT 12345	0%		$76,600,000.00	$0.00	No			206 days	Mon 21-08-02	Mon 22-05-16
1		1	CONSULTANT RECRUITMENTS	0%		$150,000.00	$0.00	No			20 days	Mon 21-08-02	Fri 21-08-27
2		1.1	engineering	0%		$55,000.00	$0.00	No	ABC ENG.	ADAM	20 days	Mon 21-08-02	Fri 21-08-27
3		1.2	Architect	0%		$30,000.00	$0.00	No	CDE	ADAM	20 days	Mon 21-08-02	Fri 21-08-27
4		1.3	Landscape Architect	0%		$25,000.00	$0.00	No	EFG	ADAM	20 days	Mon 21-08-02	Fri 21-08-27
5		1.4	Electrical and Mechanical	0%		$20,000.00	$0.00	No	GHI	ADAM	20 days	Mon 21-08-02	Fri 21-08-27
6		1.5	Structural	0%		$20,000.00	$0.00	No	JKL	JUE	20 days	Mon 21-08-02	Fri 21-08-27
7		2	CIVIL DESIGN	0%		$0.00	$0.00	No			30 days	Mon 21-08-30	Fri 21-10-08
8		2.1	First draft approval sent to the City	0%	2FS+20 s,4FS+20 s,5FS+20 days	$0.00	$0.00	Yes	ABC ENG.	ANTONY	0 days	Fri 21-09-24	Fri 21-09-24
9		2.2	Second and Final Draft Plan approved by the City	0%	8FS+10 days	$0.00	$0.00	Yes	ABC ENG.	ANTONY	0 days	Fri 21-10-08	Fri 21-10-08
10		2.3	Pond Design	0%	2	$0.00	$0.00	No	ABC ENG.	ADAM	20 days	Mon 21-08-30	Fri 21-09-24
11		3	CIVIL CONSTRUCTION MANAGEMENT	0%		$1,450,000.00	$0.00	No			35 days	Mon 21-08-30	Fri 21-10-15
12		3.1	Prepare Tender Documents (RFP)	0%	2	$0.00	$0.00	No	ABC ENG.	ADAM	15 days	Mon 21-08-30	Fri 21-09-17
13		3.2	Invitation to Tender	0%	12	$0.00	$0.00	No	ABC ENG.	ADAM	4 days	Mon 21-09-20	Thu 21-09-23
14		3.3	Award Contract for a General Contractor	0%	13	$0.00	$0.00	No	ABC ENG.	ADAM	3 days	Fri 21-09-24	Tue 21-09-28
15		3.4	Construction	0%		$1,450,000.00	$0.00	No			13 days	Wed 21-09-29	Fri 21-10-15
16		3.4.1	Excavating and Backfills	0%	14	$85,000.00	$0.00	No	ABC ENG.	ADAM	5 days	Wed 21-09-29	Tue 21-10-05
17		3.4.2	Subdivision Servicing Contract	0%	14	$1,200,000.00	$0.00	No	ABC ENG.	ADAM	6 days	Wed 21-09-29	Wed 21-10-06
18		3.4.3	Street Lights	0%	17	$40,000.00	$0.00	No	ABC ENG.	ADAM	7 days	Thu 21-10-07	Fri 21-10-15
19		3.4.4	Pond Construction	0%	14	$120,000.00	$0.00	No	ABC ENG.	ADAM	10 days	Wed 21-09-29	Tue 21-10-12
20		3.4.5	Bell	0%	16	$0.00	$0.00	No	ABC ENG.	ADAM	4 days	Wed 21-10-06	Mon 21-10-11
21		3.4.6	Rogers	0%	16	$0.00	$0.00	No	ABC ENG.	ADAM	4 days	Wed 21-10-06	Mon 21-10-11
22		3.4.7	Surveying	0%	21	$5,000.00	$0.00	No	ABC ENG.	ADAM	1 day	Tue 21-10-12	Tue 21-10-12
23		3.4.8	Subdivision assumption from the City	0%	22	$0.00	$0.00	Yes	ABC ENG.	ANTONY	1 day	Wed 21-10-13	Wed 21-10-13
24		4	Building Civil Services	0%		$75,000,000.00	$0.00	No			153 days	Thu 21-10-14	Mon 22-05-16
25		4.1	Payment of Development Charges	0%	23	$0.00	$0.00	Yes		JOE	1 day	Thu 21-10-14	Thu 21-10-14
26		4.2	Surveying	0%	25	$0.00	$0.00	No	CDE	JOE	1 day	Fri 21-10-15	Fri 21-10-15
27		4.3	House Construction for 15 houses	0%	26	$75,000,000.00	$0.00	No	CDE	JOE	150 days	Mon 21-10-18	Fri 22-05-13
28		4.4	Occupation Permit	0%	27	$0.00	$0.00	Yes	CDE	JOE	1 day	Mon 22-05-16	Mon 22-05-16

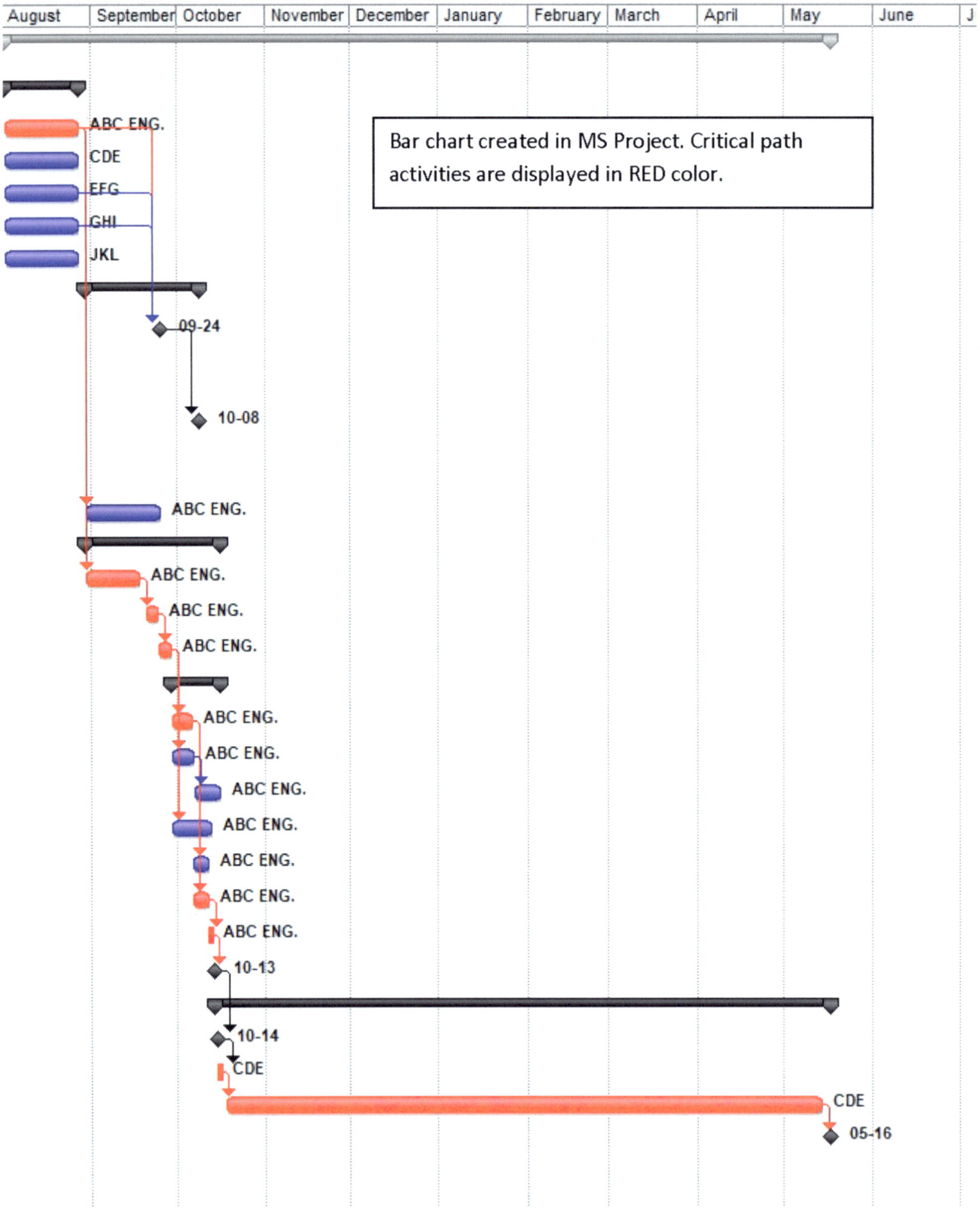

Bar chart created in MS Project. Critical path activities are displayed in RED color.

APPENDIX

TERMS USED IN CONTRACT DOCUMENTS

Inspired By CCDC Documents

Addendum or **Addenda**. Any document or documents issued by The Company prior to the Submission Deadline that changes the terms of the RFQ or contains additional information related to the RFQ.

Agreement. Any written contract entered into by a Proponent and The Company (or any purchase order issued by The Company to a Proponent) connected with the Deliverables will be deemed to include the terms and conditions of the RFQ.

Change Directive. A Change Directive is a written instruction prepared by the Consultant and signed by the Owner directing the Contractor to proceed with a change in the Work within the general scope of the Contract Documents prior to the Owner and the Contractor agreeing upon adjustments in the Contract Price and the Contract Time.

Change Order. A Change Order is a written amendment to the contract prepared by the Consultant and signed by the Owner and the Contractor stating their agreement upon.

- a change in the Work;
- the method of adjustment or the amount of the adjustment in the Contract Price, if any; and
- the extent of the adjustment in the Contract Time, if any.

Construction Equipment. Construction Equipment includes all machinery and equipment, either operated or not operated, must prepare, fabricate, convey, erect, or otherwise perform the Work but is not incorporated into the Work.

Consultant. The Consultant is the person or entity engaged by the Owner and identified as such in the agreement. The Consultant is the Architect, the Engineer or entity licensed to practice in the province or territory of the Place of the Work. The term Consultant includes the Consultant or the Consultant's authorized representative.

Contract Documents. The Contract Documents consist of those documents listed in Article of the Agreement - CONTRACT DOCUMENTS and amendments agreed upon between the parties.

Contract. The contract is the undertaking by the parties to perform their respective duties, responsibilities and obligations as prescribed in the Contract Documents and represents the entire agreement between the parties.

Contractor. The Contractor is the person or entity identified as such in the agreement. The term Contractor. The Contractor or the Contractor's authorized representative as designated to the Owner in writing.

Day. A business or working day other than a Saturday, Sunday, statutory holiday, or statutory vacation day is observed by the industry relating to the RFQ.

Deadline for Issuing Addenda. The deadline following which The Company will issue Addenda in connection with the RFQ. It is specified in the RFQ Timetable.

Deadline for Questions. The final deadline by which Proponents must ask any questions they may have regarding the RFQ. The Deadline for Questions is specified in the RFQ Timetable.

Deliverables. All services to be provided by the selected Proponent, as described in the RFQ.

Drawings. The Drawings are the graphic and pictorial portions of the Contract Documents, wherever located and whenever issued, showing the Work's design, location, and dimensions, generally including plans, elevations, sections, details, and diagrams.

HST. Harmonized Sales Tax

Owner. The person or entity identified as such in the agreement. The Owner or the Owner's authorized agent or representative as designated to the Contractor in writing but does not include the Consultant.

Place of the Work. The Place of the Work is the designated site or location of the Work identified in the Contract Documents.

Product. Product or Products. Material, machinery, equipment, and fixtures forming the Work but do not include Construction Equipment.

Project. The total construction contemplated of which the Work may be the whole or a part.

Proponent. A legal entity (whether an individual, corporation, partnership, or other legal entity) interested in delivering a Proposal to The Company in response to the RFQ with a view to entering into an Agreement with The Company with respect to the Deliverables. If two or more legal entities wish to submit a Proposal jointly, one member of the couple or group must be identified as the Proponent.

Provide. Provide means to supply and install.

Quotation or **Proposal**. The final submission package to be delivered by Proponents to The Company responds to the RFQ, consisting of all required Submission Forms and related documents as described in the RFQ.

Rectification Notice. A written notice delivered by The Company to a Proponent requesting that it clarify and/or rectify any aspect of its Proposal. Failure to rectify a Proposal according to the Rectification Notice within the Rectification Period will result in disqualification.

Rectification Period. The period during which a Proponent may rectify its Proposal. The Rectification Period shall run from the date and time that The Company issues a Rectification Notice to that Proponent, until the date and time stipulated in the Rectification Notice.

RFQ Timetable. The table is set out and provides information on important dates, including the Submission Deadline.

RFQ. The Request for Quotations package in its entirety, including any schedules, exhibits, appendices, and Addenda that may be issued by The Company in connection therewith.

Shop Drawings. Shop Drawings are drawings, diagrams, illustrations, schedules, performance charts, brochures, Product data, and other data which the Contractor provides to illustrate details of portions of the Work.

Specifications. The Specifications are that portion of the Contract Documents, wherever located and whenever issued, consisting of the written requirements and standards for Products, systems, workmanship, quality, and the services necessary for the performance of the Work.

Subcontractor. A Subcontractor is a person or entity having a direct contract with the Contractor to perform a part or parts of the Work at the Place of the Work.

Submission Deadline. The final deadline for Proposal submissions, specified in the RFQ Timetable.

Submission Form. A form further described in the RFQ, which must be completed and submitted as part of every Proposal.

Substantial Performance of the Work. Substantial Performance of the Work is as defined in the lien legislation applicable to the Place of the Work. Substantial Performance of the Work shall have been reached when the Work is ready for use or is being used for the purpose intended and certified by the Consultant.

Supplemental Instruction. An instruction, not involving adjustment in the Contract Price or Contract Time, in the form of Specifications, Drawings, schedules, samples, models, or written instructions, consistent with the intent of the Contract Documents. It is to be issued by the Consultant to supplement the Contract Documents as required for the performance of the Work.

Supplier. A person or entity having a direct contract with the Contractor to supply Products.

Value-Added Taxes. Such sum shall be levied upon the Contract Price by the Federal or Provincial or Territorial Government and computed as a percentage of the Contract Price.

Work. The Work is the total construction and related services required by the Contract Documents.

Working Day. A day other than a Saturday, Sunday, statutory holiday, or statutory vacation day that is observed by the construction industry in the area of the Place of the Work.

GLOSSARY

Actual Cost (AC). Total Costs incurred in accomplishing work performed during a given time period for a scheduled activity or WBS component. See earned value management.

Actual Cost of Work Performed (ACWP). See actual Cost (AC).

Actual Duration. The time in calendar units between the actual start date and the scheduled activity's actual or planned end date.

An Expression of Interest. (Sometimes referred to as 'request to participate'). It is a submission made by a prospective tenderer in response to an advert (or contract notice) for the supply of goods or services.

Authority. The right to apply project resources, expend funds, make decisions, or give approvals.

Award Contract. The Client agrees with the successful bidder and awards the contract.

Back-charge. The back charge is for an expense actually, necessarily, and reasonably incurred by the party claiming it; the general Contractor incurs the Cost because of the subcontractor's default to which the charge relates; and before incurring the price, the general Contractor gives notice to the subcontractor of default and provides a reasonable opportunity to cure it.

Baseline. An approved plan for a project. It is compared to actual performance to determine the variances.

Bonds

Performance Bonds. The performance bond protects the Owner from the Contractor's failure to complete the contract per the contract documents. The Contractor chooses a third-party financial institution that stands behind the Contractor to limit the penal amount of the bond.

Payment Bonds. Labor and Material Bonds protect those who have supplied material and labor to a project. The bond protects owners from liens or other claims made against the property on non-public projects after completing the Work.

Budget at completion (BAC). The sum of all the budgets established for the work to be performed on a project or a WBS component or scheduled activity. The total planned value for the project.

Budget. The approved estimate for the project or any WBS component or any scheduled activity.

Budgeted Cost of Work Performed (BCWP). See earned value (EV).

Budgeted Cost of Work Scheduled (BCWS). See planned value (PV).

Buffer. Project buffer is the extra time you add to a task so that even if it gets delayed, it won't affect the overall project schedule.

Business Case modification. When the project exceeds its baseline budget (for example, when increasing the scope of work), the client in public bodies will have to add additional funds to the original budget by filling up a modification request to increase the funding already asked for in the original business case. The same applies when decreasing the budget. See also Business Case.

Business Case. Also called in this book Business Case Original (BCO). In the very early stages of a project, a preliminary business case should be prepared. The business case is the document used to determine whether authority should be given for the preferred option to progress to the next stage (e.g., Design, Construction, etc.). The rationale behind the initiation of a new building project. It may consist solely of a reasoned argument. It may contain supporting information, financial appraisals, or other background information. It should also highlight initial considerations for the Project Outcomes.

In summary, it is a combination of objective and subjective considerations. Preparing a business case may require input from independent client advisers (such as management accountants, business development advisers, facilities managers, managers, etc.). A business case may include Confirmation that the project is compatible with the client's stated vision, mission, and objectives, Confirmation that feasibility studies have been completed, the appropriate options have been explored and a preferred option identified, Budgets, Schedule, Cash flow projection, projected profit, etc. The business case should be written in clear, concise language that is easy to understand and may include diagrams and illustrations where appropriate.

Buyer. The acquirer of products, services, or results for an organization.

Change Order. "Change order" is just the industry term for an amendment to a construction contract that changes the contractor's scope of work. Most change orders modify the work required by contract documents (which, in turn, usually increases the contract price) or adjust the amount of time the contractor has to complete the work or both. For there to be a valid change order, the Owner and contractor must agree on all terms.

Claim. A request by a seller against the buyer, or vice versa, for consideration, compensation, or payment under the terms of a legally binding contract, such as for a disputed change.

Close-out Documents. Items that need to be completed, submitted, turned over, etc., to meet all detailed requirements of the bid package—examples. Warranties, Guaranties, As-builts, Complete set of shop drawings, manuals, training, etc.

Closing date. Also known as the deadline for submission. This is the date and time that a tender submission needs to be delivered and received. Tenders submitted after the date might not be considered in the competition—construction Phase.

Contingency Allowance. See Contingency.

Contingency Reserve. The amount of funds, budget, or time needed above the estimate that reduces the risk of overruns of project objectives to a level acceptable to the organization.

Contingency. There is always uncertainty about the actual content of all items in the estimate, how work will be performed, what work conditions will be like when the project is executed, etc. These uncertainties are risks to the project. Some refer to these risks as "known-unknowns" because the estimator is aware of them, and based on past experience, can even estimate their probable costs. The estimated costs of the known unknowns are referred to by cost estimators as cost contingency.

Control Costs. The process of monitoring the project's status to update the project budget and managing changes to the cost baseline.

Control Schedule. The process of monitoring the project's status to update project progress and managing changes to the schedule baseline.

Corrective Action. Documented direction for executing the project work to bring expected future performance of the project work in line with the project management plan.

Cost Performance Index (CPI). A measure of cost efficiency on a project. It is the ratio of earned value (EV) to actual Costs (AC). CPI= EV/ AC

Cost to Come. See Estimate to Complete (ETC).

Cost Variance (CV). A measure of cost performance on a project. It is the difference between earned value (EV) and actual cost (AC). CV= EV minus AC.

Cost-Plus-Fixed Fee Contract. A type of cost-reimbursable contract where the buyer reimburses the seller's allowable costs plus a fixed profit (fee).

Cost-Plus-incentive-Fee Contract. A type of cost-reimbursable contract where the buyer reimburses the seller's allowable costs. The seller earns its profit if it meets defined performance criteria.

Crashing. Decreasing the total scheduled duration by compressing the schedule for the least additional costs. Typical approaches to crashing require increasing the assignment of resources on activities planned. See also Fast Tracking.

Create WBS (Work Breakdown Structure). The process of subdividing project deliverables and project work into smaller, more manageable components.

Criteria. Standards, rules, or tests on which a judgment or decision can be based or by which a product, service, result, or process can be evaluated.

Critical Activity. Any Scheduled activity on a critical path in a project schedule.

Critical Path. Generally, the sequence of scheduled activities determines the duration of the project. It is the longest path through the project.

Defect. An imperfection or Deficiency in a project component where that component does not meet its requirements or specifications must be either repaired or replaced.

Deliverable. Any unique and verifiable product, result, or capability to perform a service must be produced to complete a process, phase, or project. All project deliverables can be completed independently or stacked with numerous smaller deliverables within one more significant deliverable. Some project deliverables may rely on previous project deliverables, which means that those cannot be completed until the prior ones are finished.
A deliverable could be a report, a document, a permit, or any other building block of an overall project.

Design Stage. In very general terms, design is the realization of an idea, or the resolution of requirements, through means of communication such as drawings, plans, specifications, and models.

Design-build. (or design/build and abbreviated D–B or D/B accordingly) is a project delivery system used in the construction industry. It is a method to deliver a project in which the design and construction services are contracted by a single entity known as the design-builder or design-build contractor. It can be subdivided into the architect-led design-build (ALDB, sometimes known as designer-led design-build) and contractor-led design-build.

Determine Budget. The process of aggregating the estimated costs of individual activities or work packages to establish an authorized baseline.

Develop Human Resource Plan. The process of identifying and documenting project roles, responsibilities, and required skills, reporting relationships, and creating a staffing management plan.

Develop Project Charter. The process of developing a document that formally authorizes a project or a phase and documenting initial requirements that satisfy the stakeholders' needs and expectations.

Develop Project Management Plan. The process of documenting the actions necessary to define, prepare, integrate, and coordinate all subsidiary plans.

Earned Value (EV). The value of work performed is expressed in terms of the approved budget assigned to that work for a scheduled activity or WBS component, also referred to as the budgeted cost of work performed (BCWP).

Earned Value Management (EVM). A management methodology for integrating scope, schedule, and resources. Managers use this method to measure project performance and progress. Performance is measured by determining the budgeted Cost of work performed (i.e., earned value) and comparing it to the actual cost of work performed (AC).

Estimate at Completion (EAC). The expected total Cost when the defined scope of work will be completed. It is often referred to as the latest revised estimate.

Estimate to Complete (ETC). The Expected Cost is needed to complete all the remaining work. See Cost to come.

Estimate. A quantitative assessment of the likely amount or outcome. It should always include some indication of accuracy (e.g., ± x percent).

Fast Tracking (Technique). A specific project schedule compression technique changes network logic to overlap phases that would typically be done in sequences, such as the design phase and construction phase, or to perform scheduled activities in parallel. See also Crashing.

Float. Also called slack. Total Float. The total amount of time that a scheduled activity may be delayed from its early start date without delaying the project finish date.

Forecast. An estimate or prediction of conditions and events in the project's future based on information and knowledge available at the forecast time. The data is based on the project's past performance and expected future performance and includes information that could impact the project in the future, such as to estimate at completion and estimate to complete.

Free Float. The amount of time that a scheduled activity can be delayed without delaying the early start date of any immediately following scheduled activities.

Gantt Chart. A graphic display of the schedule. Typically, bar chart presentation on the right side and a table containing activity descriptions, durations, etc., on the left side.

Lag. Delay in the successor activity. For example, in a finish-to-start dependency with a ten-day lag, the successor activity cannot start until ten days after the predecessor activity has finished. See also Lead.

Lead. An acceleration of the successor activity. For example, in a finish-to-start dependency with a ten-day Lead, the successor activity can start ten days before the predecessor activity has finished. A negative Lead is equivalent to a positive Lag. See also Lag.

Lessons Learned. The learning gained from the process of performing the project.

Leveling. See resource-leveling.

Life Cycle. See project life cycle.

Log. A document used to record and describe or denote selected items identified during the execution of a process or activity is usually used with a modifier, such as Deficiencies Log, Shop-drawing Log, Change Order Log, etc.

Logical Relationship. A dependency between two scheduled activities or between an activity and a milestone. The four possible types of logical relationships are Finish-to-Start, Finish-to-Finish, Start-to-Start, and Start-to-Finish.

Material. The aggregate of things used by an organization, such as equipment, apparatus, tools, machinery, gear, material, and supplies.

Milestone. A significant point or event in the project.

Organization Chart. A document that graphically depicts the team members and their interrelationships for a specific project.

Percent Complete. An estimate, expressed as a percent, of the amount of work completed.

Perform Quality Assurance. The process of auditing the quality requirements and the results from the quality control measurements to ensure appropriate quality standards and operational definitions are used.

Perform Quality Control. The process of monitoring and recording results of executing the quality activities to assess performance and recommend necessary changes.

Plan Communications. The process of determining project stakeholder information needs and defining a communication approach.

Plan Procurements. The process of documenting project purchasing decisions, specifying the approach, and identifying potential sellers.

Plan Quality. The process of identifying quality requirements and/ or standards for the project and product, and documenting how the project will demonstrate compliance.

Plan Risk Management. The process of defining how to conduct risk management activities for a project.

Plan Risk Responses. Developing options and actions to enhance opportunities and reduce threats to project objectives.

Planned Value (PV). The authorized budget for the schedule works to be accomplished, also referred to as the budgeted cost of work scheduled (BCWS).

PMBOK Guide: PMBOK stands for Project Management Body of Knowledge, and it is the entire collection of processes, best practices, terminologies, and guidelines that are accepted as standard within the project management industry.

Portfolio. A collection of projects or programs which may not necessarily be interdependent or directly related.

Preconstruction meeting. Also called Kick-off meeting. The primary purpose of a project kick-off meeting is to establish communication methods between the client and the agency, and finalize project timelines. As client-side project managers, this is one of the most important meetings that you can have. This is the chance for you to set clear expectations with everyone in the project team to ensure the successful delivery of your project.

Predecessor Activity. The scheduled activity determines when the logical successor activity can begin or end.

Prevention Action. A documented direction to perform an activity can reduce the probability of negative consequences associated with project risks.

Private sector. It is the section of the national economy run by private individuals and businesses, usually as an enterprise for profit. It is distinguished from the 'public sector' run and controlled by the state and from the 'voluntary sector' run by charities and non-profit organizations.

Procurement documents. The documents utilized in bid and proposal activities include the buyer's invitation to tender, RFI, RFQ, RFP, etc. And the seller's responses.

Project Charter. A document issued by the project initiator or sponsor formally authorizes a project and allows the project manager to apply organizational resources to project activities.

Project Lead. Or project leader, is a professional who leads people and makes sure a project is carried through. The project leader engages the team, motivating them, taking care of their needs, and maintaining a friendly and productive work environment. A project leader can be a project manager. Still, the project manager is not a project lead.

Project Life Cycle. A collection of generally sequential project phases whose names and numbers are determined by the control needs of the organization or organizations involved in the project.

Project Manager (PM). The person assigned by the performing organization to achieve the project objectives.

Project Schedule. The planned dates for performing scheduled activities and the planned dates for meeting scheduled milestones.

Project Scope. The work must be performed to deliver a product, service, or result with the specified features and functions.

Proper Invoice. A 'proper invoice' has a specific definition in the Act, which outlines precisely what an invoice must contain in the construction industry. A proper invoice is a written bill or another request for payment for services or materials regarding an improvement under a contract. Ensure that the contractor can meet the "proper invoice" requirements. Although some basic mandatory requirements for a "proper invoice" are included in the Construction Act, owners are allowed to include additional requirements, for example, WSIB clearance certificates, statutory declarations, updated work schedules, project reports, testing and commissioning reports, and possibly even claim waivers related to work billed in the previous payment period.

Public sector. It consists of governments and all publicly controlled or publicly funded agencies, enterprises, and other entities that deliver public programs, goods, or services.

Purchase Order. A purchase order (PO) is a commercial document and the first official offer issued by a buyer to a seller indicating types, quantities, and agreed prices for products or services. It is used to control the purchasing of products and services from external suppliers. Purchase orders can be an essential part of enterprise resource planning system orders.

Report Performance. The process of collecting and distributing performance information, including status reports, progress measurements, and forecasts.

Request for Information (RFI). An RFI is primarily used to gather information to help decide on what steps to take next. RFIs are, therefore, seldom the final stage and are instead often used in combination with a request for proposal (RFP), request for tender (RFT), and request for quotation (RFQ).

Request for Proposal (RFP). A request for proposal (RFP) is a document that solicits a submission, often made through a bidding process, by an agency or company interested in procurement of a commodity, service, or valuable asset to potential suppliers to submit business proposals. It is introduced early in the procurement cycle, either at the preliminary study or procurement stage. An RFP is used where the request requires technical expertise, specialized capability, or where the requested product or service does not yet exist. The proposal may require research and development to create whatever is being requested.

Request for Quotation (RFQ). A request for quotation (RFQ) is a business process in which a company or public entity requests a quote from a supplier to purchase specific products or services. RFQ is generally the same thing as Call for bids and invitation for bids. RFQs often include the specifications of the items/services to ensure all the suppliers are bidding on the same item/service. The more detailed the specifications, the more accurate the quote will be and comparable to the other suppliers. Another reason for sending out an RFQ is that the specifications could be used as legally binding documentation for the suppliers.

Requisition. A purchase order request or purchase requisition is sent internally within a company to obtain purchased goods and services. The request is a document that tells the purchasing department or manager precisely what items and services are requested, the quantity, source, and associated costs. A Purchase Requisition Form (PRF) is filled out before purchasing goods as a form of tangible authorization. Purchase request forms are often used in smaller businesses that do not have a computer-based system. However, many computer (included web-based solution) systems are available on the market to facilitate the capture of purchase request information. Purchase order requests can also be passed to the purchasing department via a management information system.

Requisition. Externally. A document issued by a buyer to a seller indicating types, quantities, and services required and requesting a cost item for each. Internally. A document issued by personnel (e.g., a PM) to the company's buyer to request the purchase of products or services.

Resource Leveling. A technique in which start and finish dates are adjusted based on resource limitation balances, the demand for resources with the available supply. Leveling could result in a later project finish date if the tasks affected are on the critical path.

Resource. Skilled human resources, equipment, services, supplies, commodities, materials, budgets, or funds.

Risk Acceptance. A risk response planning technique indicates that the project team has decided not to change the project management plan to deal with a risk or identify any other suitable response strategy.

Risk Transfer. A risk response technique that shifts the impact of a threat to a third party (e.g., transferring the safety risk to the constructor and a safety consultant).

Risk. An uncertain event or conditions that, if it occurs, positively or negatively affect the project's objectives.

Schedule Performance Index (SPI). A measure of schedule efficiency on a project. It is the ratio of earned value (EV) to planned value (PV). SPI=EV/PV.

Schedule Variance (SV). A measure of schedule performance on a project. SV=EV-PV.

Scope of Work. The SOW typically includes detailed requirements and pricing, with standard regulatory and governance terms and conditions. It is often a necessary accompaniment to a master service agreement or request for proposal (RFP). The scope of work is a section within the statement of work.

Site Plan. A site plan or a plot plan is a drawing used by architects, landscape architects, urban planners, and engineers which shows existing and proposed conditions for a given area, typically a parcel of land which is to be modified. The site plan typically shows buildings, roads, sidewalks, paths/trails, parking, drainage facilities, sanitary sewer lines, water lines, lighting, landscaping, and garden elements.

Slack. Also called float. See float.

Specifications. A set of documented requirements to satisfy a material, design, product, or service. There are different technical or engineering specifications (specs), and the term is used differently in different technological contexts. They often refer to particular documents and/or particular information within them. Specifications in North America form part of the contract documents that accompany and govern the construction of building and infrastructure projects. Specifications describe the quality and performance of building materials using code citations and published standards.

Sponsor. The person or group that provides the financial resources for the project.

Stakeholder. Person or organization (e.g., customer, sponsor, performing organization, or the public) actively involved in the project or whose interests may be positively or negatively affected by execution or completion of the project.

Statement of Work (SOW). A narrative description of products, services, or results to be supplied.

Statement of Work. The Statement of Work, or SOW, lays out the foundation of the work necessary for a particular project. The SOW makes the Client and vendor aware of the responsibilities the project will entail. For instance, the SOW will tell the vendor what they will be responsible for, how to accomplish it, what materials need to be used, and the time frame for each task. It defines project-specific activities, deliverables, and timelines for a vendor providing services to the Client.

Statutory Declaration. Statutory declarations are commonly used to allow a person to declare something to be true for satisfying some legal requirement or regulation when no other evidence is available. They are thus similar to affidavits, which, however, are made on oath. Statutory Declaration of Progress Payment Distribution by Contractor is a sworn statement for use by the Contractor as a condition of receiving payment for either the second and subsequent applications for progress payment or the release of holdback funds. The Canadian Construction Documents Committee (CCDC) has produced Statutory Declaration forms CCDC 9A (prime contractor) and CCDC 9B (subcontractor). These may be downloaded free of charge from the CCDC website. Your completed statutory declaration must be signed in front of a Commissioner for Taking Affidavits, a Notary Public, or a Justice of the Peace.

Successor Activity. The scheduled activity that follows a predecessor activity, as determined by their logical relationship.

Tender Documents. The tender documents contain the bill of quantities (BOQ), specifications of the works to be carried out, time frame for completing the job, conditions of the contract, and plans and drawings. These documents are provided to the contractor on the payment of specific fees.

Threshold. A Threshold Amount is the maximum dollar amount allowed per transaction. If a transaction exceeds your defined limit, the transaction is declined.

Vendor. A vendor can sell their products and services to small and large businesses, while vendors primarily work with institutions and individuals who need some projects. Additionally, vendors provide long-term services, while contractors work on short-time projects, which might be renewed after some time. In the book, the vendor term is used to describing a supplier or a contractor.

Work Breakdown Structure (WBS). A deliverable-oriented hierarchical decomposition of the work to be executed by the project team to accomplish the project objectives and create the required deliverables. "A work breakdown structure defines all the things a project needs to accomplish, organized into multiple levels, and displayed graphically." Everything you need to accomplish in the project is shown in a single, easy-to-understand chart. The purpose of this chart is to break down complex activities into smaller, more management constituents.

Work Order. A work order WO is usually a task or a job for a customer scheduled or assigned to someone. Such an order may be from a customer request or created internally within the organization. Work orders may also be made as follow-ups to Inspections or Audits. A work order may be for products or services. A work order may include one or more of the following. Instructions, cost estimates, Forms, date and time to execute the work order, information about the location and entities to perform the work order, and the person to whom the work order is assigned. A work order is a document that provides all the information about a maintenance task and outlines a process for completing that task.

Workload: Workload management is assigning tasks to keep the team working while monitoring their progress throughout the project. It provides a framework of what tasks need to be done and who on the team is supposed to be working on those tasks.
Workload management Examples: (1) Look for team members who are over-allocated. That means that they have been given more work than they can do in the time available. (2) Look for employees who don't have enough work to do. Keep your team motivated by ensuring they have meaningful tasks to fill the day. (3) After identifying over and under-allocated staff, adjust the team workloads.

WSIB. Workplace Safety & Insurance Board WSIB, a term used in Ontario, Canada, provides support and insurance for workers injured on the job. Each workplace has insurance to assist workers if they get hurt while on the job. Each province in North America may have a different name. For example, Quebec (CNESST), Manitoba (WCB), etc. WSIB in Ontario is a mandatory part of any invoice submission for construction work as a clearance certificate. The WSIB issues a clearance certificate (hereafter clearance) to relieve a principal of liability for payment obligations to the WSIB that a contractor or sub-contractor may incur concerning a contract entered into between the principal and the contractor or sub-contractor during the validity period of the clearance. By issuing this clearance, the WSIB waives its right to hold a principal liable for unpaid premiums and other amounts the contractor owes the WSIB for the certificate's validity period. A clearance is valid for up to 90 calendar days, depending on its issued and renewable date.

ACRONYMS

AC. Actual Cost

BAC. Budget at Completion

BC. Business Case

BCO. Business Case Original = Business Case

BCWP. Budgeted Cost of work performed

CM. Construction Management; Construction Manager

CPI. Cost Performance Index

CV. Cost Variance

DB. Design-Build; Design Builder

EAC. Estimate at Completion

ETC. Estimate to Complete

EV. Earned Value

GC or G.C. General Contractor

N/A. Not Applicable

NC: Non-Conformity

PM or P.M. Project Manager.

PO or P.O. Purchase Order

PV. Planned Value

Q. Quarter

RACI. Responsible, Accountable, Consult, and Inform

SOW. Statement of Work

SPI. Schedule Performance Index

SV. Schedule Variance

WBS. Work Breakdown Structure

WSIB. Workplace Safety & Insurance Board

REFERENCES

- CCDC.Org.
- CON 5104 Construction Contracts and Documents Course. Algonquin College
- Frederick E. Gould, MANAGING THE CONSTRUCTION PROCESS, Prentice-Hall, New Jersey, page 68
- https.//www.simplilearn.com/project-integration-management-tutorial
- https://procurementoffice.com/wp-content/uploads/Owning-Up-to-Your-Major-Construction-Projects.pdf - Understanding Integrated Project Delivery BY Paul Emanuelli
- https://projectzendo.com/rfi-rfp-sow-msa-contract-whats-the-difference/
- https://thedigitalprojectmanager.com/project-charter/
- https://www.pmi.org/learning/library/stakeholder-management-task-project-success-7736
- https://www.project-management-prepcast.com/pmbok-knowledge-areas-and-pmi-process-groups
- https://www.projectsmart.co.uk/earned-value-management-explained.php
- https://www.smartsheet.com/rfq-process
- https://www.workfront.com/project-management/knowledge-areas
- Inspiration from companies worked for: Cree Construction and Development Company (CCDC); Baycliffe Homes and Toronto Community Housing (TCHC)
- Occupational Health and Safety Act
- Projectmanager.com
- Richard Clough and Glenn Sears, CONSTRUCTION PROJECT MANAGEMENT, 3rd Edition, Wiley and Sons Inc, 1991, pages 5
- Richard Clough and Glenn Sears, CONSTRUCTION PROJECT MANAGEMENT, 3rd Edition, Wiley and Sons Inc, 1991, pages 5-6
- S.W. Nunnally, CONSTRUCTION METHODS AND MANAGEMENT, 3RD Edition, Prentice-Hall, page 417
- vital-learning.com

INDEX

D

E

F

G

I

L

M

S

T

U

V

W

REAL-LIFE EXAMPLES INDEX

Real-Life Examples

Made in the USA
Monee, IL
05 November 2026

67810983R00144